Robert McMurdy

Sketch of Joseph Benson Foraker, 1883

Robert McMurdy

Sketch of Joseph Benson Foraker, 1883

ISBN/EAN: 9783337733216

Printed in Europe, USA, Canada, Australia, Japan

Cover: Foto ©ninafisch / pixelio.de

More available books at **www.hansebooks.com**

SKETCH
—of—
Joseph Benson Foraker,

—:1883:—

WITH AN APPENDIX,

—:1885:—

JOSEPH BENSON FORAKER.

[This hastily prepared sketch is made by a sincere friend of intellectual, moral and patriotic worth, and without consultation with any politician whatever. It aims to discern the real, essential man, through the accidents of soldier, student, lawyer, officer, and judge. By reaching the veritable manhood of JOSEPH BENSON FORAKER as exhibited in his past and the living present we can be quite confident of his future.

Trifling inaccuracies may be found as the writer has had no access to the Judge is his distant campaign.]

Press of U. B Publishing House, Dayton, O.

JOSEPH BENSON FORAKER.

MEN AND PRINCIPLES.

It is said with reference to the duty of citizens at the polls, "Principles and not men;" and, again, that only the character of candidates for office is to be considered. Is not the true maxim, "Men, and also principles?"

We have in Judge Foraker, both the noble, pure and patriotic man, and sound and well-tried principles. Nothing from his birth has been suggested that needs defense or apology. Hon. B. Butterworth says of him:

"He is a man without a flaw in intellect or morals. I would trust him with my dearest interests. If I lay on my death-bed and J. B. Foraker took my hand and said, 'I will look after your little ones,' I should be entirely satisfied. I know him to be afraid of but one thing—to do wrong."

Foraker's opponent, Judge Hoadley, admits the very temperate and pure mode of life of the Republican candidate for Governor. He says "J. B. Foraker ain't the man who would ever say a thing which he was conscious was untrue," even in politics.

Judge Foraker, at fourteen years of age, while on the farm, became a communicant of the church, and so continues. His piety is not ostentatious, but quiet and modest. He courts not business nor promotion by his religious association, nor by any connection with any society whatever.

FORAKER'S NOMINATION.

Judge Foraker's nomination was not of the ordinary political sort. It was without the usual political conferences. It was without effort upon his part. He did not seek it. He did not even desire it. The *Enquirer* said of Foraker, "He is not an office-seeker." The candidacy for Governor came to him from the people, from his neighbors, from his clients, from the private soldiers. It was free, hearty, enthusiastic, whole-souled. When it was generally determined that the candidate for Governor must be sought in southern Ohio, men of cool reflection and judgment, men of business and of morals, men of patriotic record, and men of patriotic impulse at various points, turned with spontaniety to Judge Foraker.

When the gubernatorial candidacy was seriously pressed upon Foraker, he thought of the regular duties of his office, of his fond wife and dear children, and of his domestic and social happiness, although all was plain and ordinary in his $3,000 house on the airy hills. Ever ready to serve his country, he thought the sacrifice great. He had made little more than a living in his honest practice, and in his honest administration of office. He could see before him only self-denial and continued scantiness of income. He coveted not mere honor. In his full heart he said to his friends:

"If Mr. ——— will make the race, you can draw on me for $1,000 for the campaign fund, but I refuse to contribute the smallest amount for my own candidacy." But the people said, our candidate you must be.

They had known Judge Foraker in the humbler, and they could trust him in the higher sphere of duty. He came before the people of Ohio as did Lincoln of Illinois, and as did Grant in his army promotion. As Lincoln was not the choice of politicians, nor Grant that of the generals, so Foraker's meritorious properties were first appreciated and recognized by the people. He was the choice of the people of his section, and is that of the whole State for governor, and his character as developing in the canvas, is giving him a reputation among the people of the country at large.

Views of political preferment beyond the position of governor were presented to encourage consent. He frankly said that he had no ulterior ambition; that he preferred home and his profession, and his regular income; that he could give but two years to his State and party; that if thought necessary, he consented to this arduous service as he would renewedly enter upon the defense of his country, against domestic or foreign foe.

There was a general feeling over the State for a new man. The people wanted purity of character, and freedom for political combination.

After consent was given to be a candidate, he said, "I shall do nothing to create a boom for myself at the convention. I shall set no wires. The convention must settle the question."

The prayer at the opening of the convention was answered, that the "men nominated should be men of integrity and honor, of purity and of blameless life; men who will do justly, who love mercy, and walk humbly before God."

Hon. Mr. Watson said in convention:

"More than twenty years ago, when Republicanism was the only power that was guiding this nation in the darkness of the civil war, a boy sixteen years of age entered the army as a private soldier. He sought neither fame nor glory. His only love was love for his country. His highest and holiest ambition was to fight in the ranks and for the flag. A year later, for special bravery on the battle-field, he was made a captain—the youngest captain in all that mighty host that battled for the stars. He was with that magnificent army—the grandest that ever stepped to martial music—whose achievements thrilled the nation with joy and the world with wonder as it marched to the sea and restored the flag to eternal supremacy in the land of its banishment."

His nomination was made by acclamation, followed by a scene of wild enthusiasm. Delegates rose in their places, and jumping on their chairs waved their hats and handkerchiefs frantically. The spirit of the movement animated all. Shout after shout, hurrah after hurrah went up, and the noise was beyond description. Even the sedate assembly of gentlemen on the stage forgot their dignity and reserve and joined in the tumultuous applause. The great sound was heard in the street, and thus the fact of Foraker's nomination was known to the outside world.

Among the good things in the Judge's speech of acceptance before the convention is this:

"The twenty-five years of Republican rule have been twenty-five years of triumph—triumph in war, triumph in peace, triumph at home, and triumph abroad, —until the whole globe has come to be circled with a living current of respect and esteem for the American flag and the American name that is absolutely without a parallel in the case of any other nation on the face of the earth." [Applause.]

The reporters at the convention said that Judge Foraker's speeches, extempore as they were, were exceptionally free from grammatical or constructional errors. There is no pretence of eloquence, but his speeches are ringing in well chosen, crisp language.

After the nomination prominent Democrats in southern Ohio testified to the Judge's worth

Hon. Thos. Paxton declared him to be "an honor to the bar, an excellent citizen, a worthy gentleman."

Judge Wilson said: "Foraker is no fossil, and represents the progressive elements of his party. Judge Foraker's nomination is the very best that the Republican party could have made. He is a man of ability, of fine character, and as courteous a public officer as ever officiated. He deserves all the warm friends he has made in his official career."

Hon. Mr. Follett said, "Foraker is a strong and a good man."

Hon. Mr. Jordan considered Judge Foraker "a man of eminent ability, and socially very popular."

Representative Butterworth said, "No one doubts the character of Foraker. His record as a soldier, citizen, and lawyer is brilliant. Every part of his record from the cradle has been searched, and there is not a flaw in it. A party, that has had in its heart to nominate such a man, who represents such a pure and exalted morality, deserves to be victorious."

Hon. Mr. Townsend said at Athens that "Foraker is a high-minded citizen, with qualifications of the highest order—patriotism, sincerity, and honesty. His appearance wins. He is prudent, thoughtful, and a man who does not blunder. In his speeches he is judicial, with depth and dignity. Foraker can not be the tool of any man. His dignity protects him from such insinuations. He is too great a man to be subordinate long anywhere."

Hon. Thos. M'Dougall said at Magnetic Springs of Judge Foraker:

"For many years my warm personal friend, my associate at the bar, and my neighbor, I can speak of him from personal knowledge. People say of him he has no record, What do they mean? True, he has not the record of a political acrobat. * * * * He did not seek, did not need to seek, his nomination. There are no heart-burnings, no factional fights attached to his record. * * * * Ben. Foraker has nothing to explain, no apologies to make, no telegrams to send. * * * * Ben. Foraker—his only record is that of a loyal and affectionate son, a brave and brilliant soldier, an honorable, able, and conscientious judge, an honest, manly, and patriotic citizen, and a loving and devoted husband and father.

"'And thus he bears without abuse
The grand old name of gentleman.'

"Eminently qualified and completely equipped, the office sought him by acclamation, with honor and credit, and he has more than fulfilled in his conduct of the campaign, the high expectations of those of us who knew him best and had formed of him. the opinion that

"'From men like these Ohio's greatness springs
That makes her loved at home, revered abroad;
Princes and lords are but the breath of kings—
An honest man is the noblest work of God.'

"In him you have one whose heart is true to law, to liberty, to right, who has the brain to plan and the courage to execute the purposes of such a heart. When, some years ago, the convention of which I was a member nominated him, then comparatively unknown in our city, for Judge of the Superior Court of our city, people said he had no record, and asked. 'Who is he?' They soon found out who he was. I knew him then; I know him now. When nominated for governor the same cry arose, 'He has no record.' 'Who is he?' They are finding out who he is."

Senator Sherman in his address at Cincinnati said that he never saw Judge Foraker till he met him at the state convention, and he was immediately pleased with his bearing, with his manner, his speech, and his conduct; he was gentle, kind, intelligent; but firm and strong. The conversation he had with him before his nomination impressed upon him that he was a man worthy to carry the Republican banner; he has made no mistake in his canvass, but has borne the Republican banner on from victory to victory.

WHAT THE TIMES DEMAND.

"God give us men a time like this demands,
  Great hearts, strong minds, true faith, and willing hands;
    Men whom the lust of office does not kill,
  Men whom the spoils of office can not not buy,
    Men who possess an opinion and a will,
  Men who have honor, who will not lie."

FORAKER'S BIRTH AND EARLY HOME.

Like Lincoln and Grant, our candidate for governor was born July 5, 1846, among the hills and in the country, and like Lincoln and Harrison, in a log cabin; born the second son and fifth child, one mile north of Rainsboro, and ten miles due-east of Hillsboro, Highland County, Ohio, on the Chillicothe and Milford turnpike. The Judge's father frequently has said that Saturday, the fourth, there was a militia muster at Rainsboro, in connection with the anniversary, and that on account of the Mexican war which commenced that year, and was then in progress, there was an unusual excitement about it, and he was especially anxious to attend. On account of the Judge's expected arrival, he stayed at home and cradled wheat all day.

The Judge is one of eleven children, six boys and five girls; two of whom, one boy and one girl, died in infancy. The remaining nine, grown to manhood, are still living, except Burch, his oldest brother, who won position, honor, and respect, and died at the age of thirty-four.

His sisters living, are Sarah Elizabeth, wife of Milton McKee-

THE OLD MILL. (See page 13.)

THE FORAKER LOG CABIN.

han; Louisa Jane, widow of Samuel Amen; Maggie Reece, wife of Wm. C. Newell, son of the old miller, and all resident at Hillsboro. His brothers are James Ross, a law partner of the Judge, and Charles Elliott, and Creighton, at home.

In the wild and picturesque valley of Rocky Fork, in Highland County, Ohio, was Foraker's paternal home for ten years, in the log cabin near Rainsboro, and nine miles from Greenfield.

Scenery, hills, the country, climate, and honest and sturdy neighbors had somewhat to do with puerile development; but parental character and care vastly more.

Into the Rocky Fork Valley of Paint Creek, David Reese came in 1802, from Virginia, on account of his detestation of slavery, and as a pioneer in what was then a wilderness. He cleared his farm and had not completed his task when, in 1812, he entered the army and served on the northern frontier. He represented Highland County in the State legislature—an honest and respected citizen. One of his daughters, the Judge's mother, married Henry S. Foraker, the father of the Judge, whose family had also settled in Highland County, moving from Delaware because of their distaste of slavery. Into their possession came the old farm and saw and grist-mill, where Joseph Benson spent most of his early days.

SAW-MILL AND SCHOOL.

In this old saw-mill was often the church-gathering on Sunday for the pioneer families, the preacher putting his Bible and hymn book on the top of an up-ended puncheon, and the congregation seated on improvised benches. This was the early church of the Forakers and Rees.

THE OLD SCHOOL HOUSE.

The school-house was a poor cabin, deserted by its original tenant for a better location. The ventilation was abundant, and the scholars picked out the clay of the chinking until every cranny was open to the wind. The teachers could sit near the fire-place, the pupils write with their faces toward the window, but in conning their lessons straddling the benches without a back, the girls on one side and the boys on the other of the room.

The reign of the rod was not disputed by the teacher, who taught but few branches in winter, and wrought in summer. The tramp of the pupils for miles through the untrodden snow, with the cold dinner, was of itself discipline enough.

Such was the pioneer school of the Foraker s, at Rocky Fork.

A correspondent of the *Commercial Gazette* in a late visit to Highland gives us information as to Foraker s parents. Upon his inquiry as to Ben's father, the store-keeper of the hamlet at Rainsboro, replied :

"Well, he's in the back of the store now, trading some butter."

Looking in the direction indicated, an elderly man, dressed as a farmer, with sunburn face and hands, was seen. His broad-brimmed straw hat, which was darkened and formless from long exposure to all kinds of weather, was pushed back from his forehead, and his thin, snowy locks were in full view. He is, every inch of him, a hale, hearty old man, whose appearance tells of a head stored with good, sound common sense, and he belongs to that class whom one delights to refer to as the 'bone and sinew.' His distinguished son resembles him very much, the father's high brow, and nose with the firm, open nostrils, being duplicated in the son. He had just come in from the farm, bringing with him six great rolls of yellow, sweet-smelling butter, which Mrs. Foraker had churned but a few hours before, and which he was exchanging for groceries.

"What do you want it in ?" the store-keeper was heard to ask.

"My wife told me to get it in sugar, to put up her blackberries and things."

While the sugar was being put up, the correspondent introduced himself to Mr. Foraker, who straightway insisted that he should accompany him home, and, as it was near dinner time, an extra plate would be put upon the table.

"There's always enough, and it's good, hearty country fare," he urged ; "but I'm sorry you came all the way from Cincinnati, and I didn't know beforehand, for we can't make an extra spread for you now. You see, one of our neighbors is threshing, and we lent our hired girl to help them, and so Mrs. Foraker is all alone ; but our friends are always welcome."

THE FORAKER FARM.

The Foraker farm, which consists of 170 acres of good upland, is on the Hillsboro pike, from which the plain, comfortable house, painted white, with reddish-brown shutters, is plainly visible. The immense barn is between the house and the road, and the first thing one sees on reaching the place is a towering heap of wheat straw, which has just been threshed, and which is piled so high as to fairly eclipse the barn. In front of the house are aged trees, in whose grateful shade unnumbered chickens and curious young turkeys lazily take their noon-time rest, scarcely moving as the newspaper visitor makes his way up the walk. On the porch are Mr. Foraker and his son, Charles, a younger brother of the Judge's, who is determined to be a farmer, who greet the traveler hospitably, and all these engage in a political discussion, while the lady of the house can be heard bustling about inside getting dinner.

THE ARMY.

"Mr. Foraker," asked your correspondent, "didn't you object to the Judge entering the army?"

"I did, but the boy was set upon it, so I let him go. You see his elder brother, Burch, was in a law office in Hillsboro, and when he enlisted, Ben thought he must go and fill his place. By and by he caught the fever, too, and said he was going to be a soldier. I told him that he was not mature enough; that he could not endure the long marches with the heavy burdens he would be obliged to carry; that he would become sick, go to the hospital and perhaps die. I thought it was good sensible advice to tell a boy of seventeen that he could not do a man's work. But my refusal weighed upon his mind and so I had to let him go. In his first letter home, from Virginia, I think it was, he jubilantly wrote that while he was carrying a load for a pony and was feeling well as ever, men of two hundred pounds were dropping by the road side."

"Did you think that the Judge was going to be nominated?"

"I felt it in my bones, and when the day arrived I didn't need any telegram to tell me what had happened. Before the Convention I received a letter from Ben saying that if he was nominated, Hoadley would be worthy any man's steel, and that it would be no disgrace to be beaten by such a man, while to be victorious would be honor indeed."

"Were you at the Convention?"

"No, it was right in the middle of harvesting, and I could not be spared."

FATHER AND SON.

"I suppose you are proud of your boy?"

"Proud of him? proud of Ben? Why, I'm his father, and I'm prouder of him since the campaign opened than ever. I knew that Ben was pretty solid, but whether he could compete with Hoadly on the stump was a matter of doubt. Now, of course, I'm partial, for I'm his father, but when it comes to facts I know that Ben's always on hand.

"Have you seen him since he was nominated?"

"He wrote me just after the Convention that he wanted to come here and rest for a day or two, and then he wrote again that he was kept so busy that he din't know if he would ever come, but I saw him when he made his Fourth of July speech at Leesburg. For a long time I tried to get him alone, and finally we succeeded in slipping out into the bushes, and I stole a half hour's chat with him."

"And what did you talk about?"

"I told him that I had read every word of his speeches, and that so far he had made no mistakes, and to be very careful. I told him to keep out of anything low or mean, to be conscientious, but he don't need any such advice from me. He's got more sense as regards politics and behaving himself than I ever will have, but he listens like a good son to everything I say."

"Tell me, Mr. Foraker, are you going to take an active part in the campaign?"

"All his old friends in Highland County are going to vote for him without being asked, but I am a judge of election, and feel that to be perfectly square I should be above electioneering."

"How did the Judge happen to choose the law?"

"I guess it was natural in him. When he was getting his education I was asked what I was going to make of him. I always had an ambition to educate my children. I always felt the need of a good education myself, and I prepared my boys so that when the time came they could themselves decide upon what they wanted to do. Ben first wanted to be a soldier, but after a bit he decided to be a lawyer. When he went to Cincinnati I told him that he couldn't live there, that it was full of lawyers and that he would starve, but he said 'if you want to do business you must go where it is done,' and so he went. He only knew one man there when he went, but he got along all the same."

MOTHER AND SON.

And then the proud old father told the story of his "boy's" triumphs and successes, of his goodness and kindness, and his eyes lighted with pleasure as he spoke. While he was still chatting Mrs. Foraker came to the door and announced that dinner was ready. She is an active old lady, a typical farmer's wife, with sharp, kindly twinkling eyes, and hands that are ever busy, and in seeing her, one understands from whence comes the Judge's indomitable courage and unceasing work. And oh how proud she is of her son! Her face fairly beams with joy at the mere mention of his name, and when his brilliant career is spoken of she smiles in an excess of happiness. She said that she had been "putting up" blackberries all morning and that the visitor would have to excuse the ordinary farmer's fare, and looked dubious when your correspondent told her that an honest home meal was fit for a king. And now that the dinner is a thing of the past he can bear witness that Mrs. Foraker is as excellent a cook as her son is a political speaker. Of course the conversation at the table was almost entirely concerning "Ben."

THE COFFEE-SACK BREECHES.

"Mrs. Foraker," said the writer, "nearly everybody in Ohio wants to know the truth about those coffee-sack breeches. Now tell me, did you ever make him such a pair, or is it only a campaign fabrication?"

"Oh, no," the lady replied with a laugh, "it is the solemn truth, and what is more he wore them out. You see it was in the fall when Ben was about ten years old, and the men folks were all busy building a dam, and in the house the girl and myself had all we could do preparing for them, as there were a lot of extra hands. Ben was under the necessity to have another pair of pants or he couldn't go to school. Everybody was too busy to go to town to buy any cloth, and for a time I didn't know what to do. All at once I thought of an inside coffee sack that was in the house, and so I made the breeches out of it. When I showed them to the boy, he look disappointed and said: 'I don't want to wear them, the boys will make fun of me.' 'Never mind,' said I, 'if you make a smart man people will never ask what kind of pants you wore when a boy."

"Yes," broke in Mr. Foraker, "that's the truth of it, and it wasn't from extreme poverty as some of the papers said. My wife is a saving kind of woman—a fortune to any man—and that coffee sack just happened to be handy." [Foraker's coffee-sack breeches are not yet worn out. They will stick to him like Grant's hides, Old Abe's axe, and Washington's little hatchet. Such a man will win in Ohio and the country all the time.]

"There never was a better boy to his mother than Ben," continued Mrs. Foraker, "and he helped round the house as good as any girl. I taught all my boys to wash, iron, milk, cook, spin, and Ben used to have to pick the geese."

THE CORN.

"Ben," supplemented the father, "was one of the kind of boys that thought that if any of the rest of his companions was able to do anything he could do it too. One day his elder brother, Burch, put up thirty-three shocks of corn, for which I paid him one dollar, and Ben felt that he ought to earn some money as well. I told him that he was too small to do such hard work, for the corn was strong and high, but he said he was going to try. That day I went to the fair, and when I came back I found that he had put up his thirty-three shocks. He was not tall enough to tie them, and so he had got his little sister to stand on a chair and do it, while he held the stalks in place. It was a powerful day's work for a boy, and I don't see how he ever did it."

Running about one of the pastures on the farm is an old, dun-colored pony, which was owned as a colt and broken in by the now Judge. There is a story told that when he was still a "beardless youth," he fell in love with a Mt. Carmel girl, and so as to be near her he refused to go to the Rainsboro Sunday-school, but rode his pony to the one which was attended by the object of his affection. But, alas! for the poor boy. When he went off to fight his country's battles, she forgot him and married another fellow. The pony was ridden after Morgan, at the time of his celebrated Ohio raid, by Mr. Foraker, and at present the little son of the Judge, when he is visiting at the farm, rides the ancient nag to the Post-office for the semi-weekly mail, and, by-the-way, the farm was bought and presented to his parents by their ever-thoughtful son.

THE SECRET.

In the foregoing, we have the secret largely of Judge Foraker's character and success. It should be added that these parents are pious Methodists, with their morning and evening worship, with their regard for the sacredness of Sunday and of religious institutions, with their temperate habits and honest ways, and with their observance of the maxim not to "make haste to be rich." They had moved from a state cursed with slavery to begin life on free soil. They read little, but read thoroughly. They study the Bible and good books. They are most familiar with the Methodist commentary on the Bible—that of Joseph Benson. Hence the Judge was baptised Joseph Benson. Josephus and Bunyan's Pilgrim's Progress are family text-books. The books were few, but they were well read. *Multum, non Multa.*

The boy, Foraker, was noted from earliest years for energy, perseverance, truth, and honesty. He was a hard-wrought boy, ploughing with a span of horses when ten years old. He took no pleasure in depressing his companions; and while frequently aid-ing them in tasks and lessons, he excelled by his own innate strength. He led naturally. He was the chosen chief for victory in sports and games. In one of his feats of daring this barefooted and berry-stained boy, with pockets bulging with green apples, fell into the mill-race, and was rescued by Samuel Newell, for a long time miller on Rocky Fork, who so admired his wise pluck in struggling for life that that the rescuer said that boy would be governor some day, and, who, again, a few years after, when he had a discussion with a Democratic relative, picked up his favorite boy and said, "We'll beat you some day for governor with this farmer boy."

THE SPARGURS AT RAINSBORO.

September 15, 1883, the Spargurs of Ohio gathered on the farm of Jno. Bedkey, in view of the site of the Foraker log cabin. "Uncle Joe" Spargur was chairman. Rev. Cunningham, of Hillsboro, offered prayer. Rev. Somner, of Virginia, gave a Bible talk. Mrs. Bedkey's Spargur re-union song was sung, to an air, the product of the music-loving Milton W. Spargur. After dinner Hon. H. L. Dickey's speech was on "Character"—its importance illustrated in the families of Rainsboro before him. Mr. A. D. Wiggins followed. Judge Foraker was then introduced, by "Uncle Joe" Spargur, as *Ben Foraker Spargur*, when the assembled six thousand made the forests ring with shouts of recognition and of their fondness for their neighbor, their soldier boy. No introduction was necessary, as the Judge was at his boyhood home, and among the friends and companions of his youthful days, where he had romped, and among the "boys in blue," with whom in riper years, but a boy still, he marched to meet unblushing treason in battle array.

THE BREECHES AT HILLSBORO.

September 19 is said to have been the greatest day in the history of Highland. From far and near came Highland's hosts to pay tribute to her honored son. The streets were crowded, and it was almost impossible to get around. A moderate limit places the number at six thousand, which has only been exceeded once before—during the Brough-Vallandigham campaign. Judge Foraker arrived on the noon train from South Salem, where he addressed a great audience, September 18, in the campus of the academy. Here the Judge attended school after the war, and was personally known. The boys greeted him as Ben, both Republicans and Democrats, and Ben recalled the names of Beech and Amos and hundreds of his old school and army friends. At Hillsboro the Currier Band of Cincinnati escorted the Judge to the Kramer House. Here he was waited upon by the entire conference of the African Methodist Church, with their bishop. Visitors were introduced by Col. Glen of the 89th, his old commander. From Paint Township (the Judge's) came a long procession, headed by a dun pony, which the Judge rode when a boy, and followed by wagons containing thirty-eight boys with coffee-sack breeches, and a number of girls, dressed in red, white, and blue. One of the wagons bore the motto, "Paint Township will Whitewash Hoadly." Flags were shown on all the principal buildings, and across Main Street hung an immense banner bearing the words, "Old Highland welcomes her honored son, Ben Foraker, the next Governor of Ohio." Banners bore numerous mottoes, among them, "'This boy will be our Governor yet'—Samuel Newell;" "Paint Township will whitewash Hoadly;" on the wagon bearing the boys in coffee-sack breeches, "We will be voters by and by."

The Beardless Achilles of the War.

J. B. FORAKER, CO. A, 89TH REGT., O. V. I.

Born on the day succeeding the Fourth of July, Ben was an extraordinarily patriotic lad. This miller farmer boy of Rocky Fork enlisted as a private, July 14, 1862, in Company A, of the

89th Ohio Infantry, the first man mustered into his regiment, and the last man mustered out.

His chief and perhaps his only act of positive disobedience and wilful resistance against parental authority was when he made a bundle of his scanty wardrobe and started off for the recruiting rendezvous, depositing his baggage in a corner of the car of a freight-train, determined to go to the defense of his country as a religious duty. When his departure was discovered, it was agreed to leave the matter to his brother, Burch, and he decided that the boy should go, as he thought he had a mission of patriotism.

Captain Glenn (afterward colonel) in raising his company, at Hillsboro, promised the position of first or orderly sergeant to the soldier securing the greatest number of recruits; and that of second sergeant to the private bringing in the next largest number. Ben went rapidly over Clermont, Ross, and Highland counties, and was soon in possession of the promised place. A boy of but sixteen years of age, he said that he knew nothing of military affairs and generously and gracefully yielded the place to the private next to him in efficient recruiting, he taking the second sergeantcy, August 26th, 1862. This was in the second year of the war, Ben being only fifteen at the breaking out of the rebellion. His brother, the lamented Captain Burch Foraker, had preceded him in the service of his country. Reluctantly did his fond parents consent to part with another son.

The 89th, without having been in military retreat and discipline, was hastened into a service at once active and severe. Ben was in its exhausting marches, its camp privations, and its losses by battle and disease. He was made second lieutenant January 24th, 1863; and then, first lieutenant, February 1st, 1864. Late in the summer of 1863 he was sent to Ohio to recruit for the regiment. He was on this duty when the famous battle of Chickamauga took place—that battle of which the author of "Ohio in the War" said:

"Falling back on Chattanooga, our army went into intrenchments. Monday morning at nine o'clock, Surgeon Crew, the only commissioned officer in the fight left, all being killed, wounded, or taken prisoners, of the Eighty-ninth, sick with jaundice, and just able to ride on horseback, found himself half a mile in front of our line of battle with forty wounded, twenty sick and seventy-five well men,—all that was left of the Eighty-ninth."

"Captain Jolly, who had been at home recruiting, arrived at Chattanooga the day after the battle, with the sick who had recovered. He was promoted to Major, and took command. The Eighty-ninth soon mustered two hundred men. For six weeks it lay in the marble quarry at Chattanooga with shell bursting over its camp from Lookout Mountain, subsisting on half rations, scantily clothed, and braving the rigors of winter. It witnessed Hooker's charge up the steeps of Lookout Mountain, and joined in the shout of victory as the enemy gave way and fled. The next day, when the charge was made on Mission Ridge, Major Jolly, at the head of his little band of two hundred men, led them to victory in the front of the attacking column."

Foraker, then but seventeen years old, reached Chattanooga the night before the charge of Mission Ridge. Receiving no orders, he entered his regiment as it was going into battle, instantly took command of his company, led it to the charge, and was chivalrously the first man of his regiment over the enemy's works. He served in the field with the Third Division of the Fourteenth Army Corps, Army of the Cumberland. He was with the Eighty-ninth at Dalton, Georgia; in Rocky Face charge, February 25th; in the campaign against Atlanta, and in the battles of Buzzard's Roost, Resaca, Burnt Hickory, Peach Tree Creek, Hoover's Gap, Lookout Mountain, Mission Ridge, Ringold, Kenesaw Mountain, Eutoy Creek, Averysboro, and Bentonville.

After the fall of Atlanta he was placed on duty with the Signal Corps. In Sherman's March to the Sea, November, 1864, he was on the Staff of Major General Slocum, commanding the army of Georgia. He remained with Slocum in the campaigns to the Sea and through the Carolinas. He was mustered out June 13, 1865, while serving as Aid-de-Camp on Slocum's staff.

The U. S. Fleet lay off the mouth of the Savannah river, eighteen miles below the city, without knowledge that Sherman had reached Savannah. The river was as full of torpedos as the banks were of rebels. Foraker was selected to let the loyal people of the country know through the fleet that Sherman had finished his campaign. Foraker secured a row-boat and the services of two faithful negroes as rowers, and in the night, with one orderly, began his perilous adventure. The boat ran aground several times in the darkness and barely escaped capsizing, took to the fleet the first news of Savannah's capture, as he will in October, send the message all over our patriotic country, that another battle for freedom has been fought and won.

HOW THE NEWS REACHED THE PRESIDENT.

There are thousands of citizens of Ohio who can recall with great distinctness the days and weeks of agonizing suspense during Sherman's march from Atlanta to the sea, in November and December, 1864. How the great heart of the North fairly stood still, in anxiety to hear reliable tidings of his progress, and the condition of his army! What battles had been fought; what brave soldiers were slain or wounded? These were questions that were in every mind. No news came except through rebel sources, and there were stories of disaster to our army, put forth, as we afterwards knew to fire the flagging zeal of the Southern people, but they served to increase the anxiety of Ohio people who had thousands of husbands, sons and brothers in that army.

FORT M'ALLISTER

Was taken by assault, but Savannah still held out and offered a strong obstacle to our march. Finally, however, that city was taken, but there was no means of direct communication with the North to transmit the news, Foraker reached the fleet, carrying Sherman's famous dispatch to the President, which our readers read on the morning of December 26, 1864, and which electrified the nation, as follows:

SAVANNAH, GA.

To His Excellency President Lincoln:

I beg to present to you as a Christmas gift the city of Savannah, with one hundred and fifty heavy guns and a plenty of ammunition, and also about twenty-five thousand bales of cotton.

W. T. SHERMAN, Major General.

The safe conduct of that dispatch was a daring feat, requiring the highest degree of courage and judgment. People will readily remember the incident and the dispatch, but the modest young bearer of it has been known to but few persons until late years, though he is to be better known in the future.

His superior officer in Military Division, Mississippi, said in his report: "* * * Lieut H. W. Howgate and J. B. Foraker succeeded in getting a part of the rebels' signal corps.

Captain James M. McClintock, with his detachment with the right wing, acting in accordance with general instructions given by me to all the signal officers of the army of Georgia, to use every possible effort to communicate with the fleet on our coming near the coast, on the 12th inst. he took with him Lieut. Sampson and several men, and went to Dr. Cheeve's rice mill, on the Great Ogeeche, within three miles of Fort McAllister to try, if possible, to communicate with the fleet if any portion of it came up the river. During the night they tried to draw the fire of the Fort if possible, and during the night threw up rockets to attract the attention of any vessel that might chance to be in hearing or in sight, but without success. During the day and night a section of artillery (twenty pound Parrots) under command of Capt. Degrasse came down and fired at the Fort. During the day and during the night of the 12th instant, until midnight, a gun was fired every ten minutes, and at the same time a rocket was sent up by the officers, but without any success.

On the 13th instant communication was opened with Lieuts. Sherfey and Adams, who accompanied the Second Division Fifteenth Army Corps, under orders to take the Fort. General Sherman, who was at the Rice Mill Station, sent his orders by signal to Gen. Hazen, to make the assault on the Fort.

IN SIGHT.

At 3 P. M. a vessel came up the river in sight. They now called the vessel, and after some time a signal flag was hoisted. I ordered them to put themselves in communication with the officer on board; but instead of answering the call, he began to call them; they answered his call, and at once opened communication with the fleet. The officer on board the vessel asked "Who is there?" In reply, General Sherman sent the following message, "General Sherman's Army is now here all well. Savannah and Fort McAllister closely invested." A number of messages passed over the line, when at 5 P. M., Fort McAllister was carried by assault.

General Sherman now sent the following message to the vessel:

"Fort McAllister just taken by assault; come to the fort immediately." Communication was opened from the station at the Rice Mill immediately after taking the Fort.

On the 14th inst., Lieuts. Dunlap and J. B. Kelley relieved Capt. J. McClintock and Lieut. Sampson, at the Rice Mill Station. On the 16th inst. I received orders from General Sherman to establish a line from Fort McAllister to his headquarters, some ten (10) miles distant. On this line Lieuts. Sherfey, Shellabarger, and Worley did duty. Some work was done on this line.

On the 21st inst. the enemy evacuated the city, and I at once went into the city to superintend the opening of communication with Fort Pulaski, and also to communicate with the fleet, or Major General Foster. * * *

LIEUT. J. B. FORAKER

Was ordered to proceed down the river and open communication with Fort Pulaski, if any signal officer was there. But finding it impossible to go far enough, owing to the marshy nature of the ground, he returned to Fort Jackson, procured a small boat, and pressing two negroes for oarsmen, he, with his flagman (second class private Thomas E. Matteson), started for Fort Pulaski, some nine miles distant, which point he reached some time after dark. He communicated soon after with Maj. General Foster, in person, some two miles off. He was the first to give him the news of our troops occupying the city of Savannah. On the following day he returned with General Foster to the city. The line from Headquarters Military Division of Mississippi to Fort McAllister was broken up and one established from the latter place to Rose Dew Battery.

In conclusion, too much cannot be said of the conduct, efforts and energy displayed by the officers of the corps in trying to establish communication with the fleet. * * * Also Lieut. J. B. Foraker, acting signal officer, in carrying out his orders, in a small boat over unknown waters, almost at the peril of his life.

Of the other officers and men, to whom no fine opportunities were presented to distinguish themselves, all have willingly, faithfully, and well performed their duty. I am Colonel, very respectfully,

Your ob't serv't, SAM. BACHTELL,

Capt. and Sig. Officer, U. S. A.

Lieut. Col. WM. J. L. NICODEMUS, Act. Chief Sig. Officer, U. S. A.

I certify the above is a true copy of my official report of services performed by my command, for the month of December, 1864.

SAM. BACHTELL, Late Chief Sig. Officer, Mil. Div. Miss.,

and Brevet Lieut. Colonel."

The confidence reposed in this soldier-youth was manifested upon various occasions.

When Sherman had deflected his columns, and with confidence of no further interruption, sought to open communication with Schofield, Johnson, with his usual skill, had fortified his position of defense. When Sherman's left wing was marching with the belief of freedom from any attack, it came directly upon Johnson's skirmishers. The Union troops were driven in with some loss. Who was the trusted messenger sent by Slocum to Sherman to tell him that he (Slocum) was confronted by Johnson's whole army, and thus save the patriotic army and the campaign? Our Highland County soldier, who observed Slocum's injunction, "Be careful, but don't spare horse-flesh! He thus bearing the order for Hazen's division of the Fifteen Corps, and returning with it, reached the battle-field at three o'clock in the morning. It was by no political influence, or by the pleading of influential friends that Foraker was breveted captain, but for such services:

"Efficient services during the recent campaigns in Georgia and South Carolina, to date from March 19, 1865," as reads General Order No. 97, of the War Department.

The people of Ohio felt that patriotism needed a revival, and they turned to the honest, faithful, and patriotic soldier as their candidate, who enlisted at the age of sixteen, and had earned his position of honest respect when the country was almost in the agony of dissolution, and when men were falling in battle like leaves before the frost.

A well-known private soldier writes:

"For sixteen years and more at all our soldiers' meetings and re-unions, we of the rank and file, while conceding to the officers a fair share of the civil offices, have kept demanding for the private soldiers some reasonable portion of the elective offices in our State and Nation.

To be candid, for myself I hardly ever expected to see the day when I would have the privilege of voting for a real live private for Governor of Ohio. But now, in obedience to this demand of at least one hundred thousand voters in Ohio, one of the rank and file of the Union Volunteer Army has at last been nominated for that great office. Foraker must serve the good purpose of showing those who sneer at us that a man may have been a private soldier and yet may be a great statesman besides.

Other titles Judge Foraker has of good right—judge, jurist, scholar, and all that—to recommend him to the respect and confidence of the people of Ohio; but his prominent recommendation among soldiers is the fact, and the fact it is, that he once wore the humble blouse and did the duty of a gallant private in the Union army. He was not one of those gilt-edged privates of whom we have so often read, who was only nominally for a day a private—with a full understanding that on the morrow the politicians would have a commission sent to him; but he was at the front on the march, in battle, with his musket, knapsack and old canteen, just like the rest of the boys. He is our comrade by the strongest of ties. We must not let the politicians say to us hereafter, 'Here, now, you fellows have been asking us to nominate a private, and when we did so, you defeated Private Foraker.' Let every soldier in Ohio vote for Foraker."

The private soldiers of Ohio knew Foraker's soldier-worth and demanded and secured this private as candidate for governor of Ohio. As the officers in the person of Grant and of many others have been honored, so in Foraker is the whole rank and file of the army.

PATRIOTIC DETERMINATION.

Capt. James Duffy, the well-known Roman Catholic and Irish Democrat of Pickaway County, says that he will vote for Foraker. His language is:

"I think it my duty to God, my country, and myself. When we needed men to go to the front, Foraker, boy as he was, shouldered his musket and marched away. I was with him fighting for our country. He can be trusted in war and in peace. He risked his young life for us, while other candidates were feathering their own nest. As a soldier and a citizen, I shall vote for Foraker."

Captain Cable says, "While Foraker is a very popular candidate with the Ohio voters generally, he is especially so among the veterans, who are proud of their candidate and the boy soldier."

BEN FORAKER'S BREECHES—BY PRIVATE BILL JONES.

"Ben needed a new pair of pants when he was a boy, and Mrs. Foraker was too poor to buy the goods for them, and had nothing in the world to make them out of but an old coffee sack. Ben looked a little ashamed when he first put them on, but his mother said, "Never mind, my boy; if you grow up to be a good and useful man nobody will ever ask what kind of breeches you wore.'"—*Commercial Gazette's* Highland County Correspondence.

  Old lady, you're just a leetle off
   In your britches pint of view—
  The kind of britches a fellow wore
   Made a difference in sixty-two!

  There was the chaps that wore them gray,
   With gray-backs in every hem,
  And ragged and dirty—*but they was brave;*
   We shot, but respected them.

  And there was them that sneaked at home
   And called us "Lincoln dogs"
  And "hired cut-throats" and all such stuff—
   Them fellers wore *butternut* togs.

  I guess, old lady, about this time
   You've stumbled onto my cue,
  And it is scarcely necessary to speak
   About the "boys in blue."

  Yes, I was out in the Eighty-ninth,
   And fought the whole war through
  With your boy Ben, and *I* can swear
   Ben Foraker's britches was blue.

  For I saw him go up Mission Ridge—
   Ahead of the regiment, too,—
  And jump the works and straddle a gun,
   So I had an excellent view

  And we marched together to the sea
   And up through the Carolinas,
  And Ben was with us *ev-e-ry time*
   Amongst the swamps and pines.

>   Just call on the boys of the Eighty-ninth
>   And ask them a question or two,
>   And you will find that your boy Ben
>   Was, *britches and heart, true blue!*
>
>   And when us fellers walk up to the polls
>   To vote for a Governor,
>   We're agoing to ask *"when we was out
>   What kind of britches he wore!"*-

A FEW EXTRACTS FROM FORAKER'S DIARY.

We have been privileged to inspect the diary of this patriotic young and private soldier. We have space for but a few extracts

June 5, 1863. . As tired a boy as you can ever find. .

June 6, 1863. . Very sick all day. Longed for home. Marched nine miles. After a rest, ordered to march again. Sicker than ever. . .

June 7. . . Marched to Murfreesboro—twenty miles; worse on the way and gave out. Rode to Col. Glenn's house—nine miles. . .

June 10. . Burch [his brother] came. Never so glad to see any one. . .

June 11. . Burch and myself went all over the battle-field. I saw enough to sicken my heart. War is a curse and our conflict a sad necessity. . .

June 16. Ten months to day since I left "Old Hillsboro." . . .

June 17. Night, and in charge of 155 men on the outpost—picketing. .

Lynchburg, Ohio, Oct. 8. 1863. Here trying to recruit for our regiment. Dull business. Hope I shall not be compelled to remain here long. The old 89th has been in the great battle of Chickamauga. I feel sadly disappointed in not being there. . . .

Oct. 13. . Much fun last night—burning "tar barrels" and hurrahing for Johnny Brough and the Union. . . . .

Oct. 14. Highland County has gone for the Union by a very decided majority. . . . . .

Oct. 15. An immense torch-light procession for the great Union victory in Highland County and Ohio. Brough's majority reported at seventy thousand. The supporters of Vallandingham look ashamed. . . .

Oct. 25. Low spirited—want to go to the regiment. . . . .

Nov. 10. Start for the regiment to-morrow. . . . .

Chattanooga, Dec. 4, 1863. Reached the regiment just in time to go into a fight. Don't like fighting well enough to make a profession of it. War is cruel, and when this conflict is over I shall retire from public life. . .

New Year's-day. Cold as Greenland, . Nothing to eat, scarcely any wood to burn, and enough work for ten men. . .

Jan. 4. 1864. Would like to be in Hillsboro to-day to go to church. Many a poor soldier to-day hovers over his smoky fire, while the cold, heartless winds come tearing through his thin tent, almost freezing him to death, and yet you hear no word of complaint. They are the bravest men that ever composed an army; and while my suffering is equal to their's, I feel proud of my condition—a clear conscience that I am doing my duty; and this affords me more comfort than all the enjoyments of home. I feel a pride rising in my bosom in realizing that I am a member of the old 14th Corps of the Army of the Cumberland. . . . . .

Feb. 5, 1864. . . Getting along well; but would get along better if I were not on duty almost every day; but what matters this? I am serving my country, and this is consolation enough. . .

March 14. 1864. Would like to be at home, going to school and preparing myself for future duty; but my country calls and I remain. . .

From some memoranda of burials of soldiers the writer judges that our soldier lad read the burial service occasionally over a dead comrade, beginning, "Man that is born of a woman," etc.

TWO OF THE BOYS.

Mr. Doughty, of Company F, Eighty-ninth O. V. I. (Foraker's old regiment), an invalid at the Soldiers' Home, said to a correspondent of the *Commercial-Gazette,* "That he knew Judge Foraker from the time of his enlistment to the close of the war. My company was next to his in the ranks and in camp, and I had opportunities for close acquaintance."

"How was he regarded by the boys?"

"Nobody was more popular. He was so generous and unassuming that he was universally liked. When he was promoted he put on no airs. Neither did our Colonel Glenn, of Chillicothe. Yet it was unusual for men promoted from the ranks to behave so. 'Ben,' as we always called him, engaged in our sports, and was as much of a boy with us as ever, though he could be dignified when it was necessary and proper. I verily believe that there is not a man of the old Eighty-ninth but will vote for Foraker, no matter what may be his party."

"You look young. What was your age when you enlisted?"

"I was only nineteen, just three years the senior of Judge Foraker, and had a fellow-feeling with him as a young man."

"Have you long been an invalid?"

"Yes, my health early failed in the Kanawha Valley, where many were taken down with camp-fever. Since then I have scarcely been well."

"Does your regiment have re-unions?"

"Yes, it is to have one at Amelia, on the Cincinnati Eastern, the twentieth of this month. Judge Foraker will be there, I have no doubt, and I intend going if I possibly can. It is a great honor to the Eighty-ninth to have a nominee for Governor, and the boys will show their appreciation, by helping their old comrade all they can."

Your correspondent then found another comrade of Foraker—Al. Bieber, of Company H, Eighty-ninth O. V. I. Bieber is employed at Ritty's restaurant, (Dayton), and was glad to express his opinion of "Ben." He said that Ben never lost his popularity on account of promotion or anything else. "He was the same in manners from first to last," said Bieber. "A good many of those fellows when they got shoulder-straps on, wouldn't associate with the poor devils who hadn't the intelligence, or the influence, or the opportunity to get promoted. We couldn't all be officers, and Ben seemed to understand that, and think just as much of us anyhow."

"What's your politics?"

"I am a Republican, but if I were a Democrat, I would vote for Ben. He's my man, and I don't see why he isn't going to be elected. It looks to me as though nothing could stop him now. He has the start of the other man, and will be likely to keep it. It's just like him. When he was Orderly Sergeant he always had his reports and other papers ready before any one else."

THE TRUE SON AND A TRUE SOLDIER.

Extracts from correspondence of the young private with his parents.

In his letter from West Point, Va. Oct. 16, 1862., after describing the country and the situation of the army, he expresses his affection for "Company I," of his regiment, he being on detached service. He refers to the sad necessity of using churches at times for army quarters.

1862.

August 17, 1862. Camp Dennison: "* * We visited the hospitals. We saw hard sights, some with their arms cut to pieces, some with their legs shattered by balls and mangled. * * There are 100 secession prisoners here captured at Pittsburg. They all confess a determination not to join the army of the Confederacy again. * * Instead of the ring of the church bell, I hear the drums and the fife. * * Sunday is not known here."

September 20, 1862. Camp Shaler, Ky.: * * "I spent no money foolishly. * * We had Friday a nice flag presented by George Coleman, of Cincinnati.

Above Clifton, Va., Nov. 3, 1862. Father Dear. * * Two weeks ago we left Point Pleasant without tents or transportation, except that of the back. We marched fifteen miles the first day. We were compelled to use the rails of a hot rebel farmer, it was so cold. We built large fires and slept around them, but not very warm. * * We marched every day until Friday. This night, dark as it was, we perilously marched over hills and hollows, and stumps and rocks. It was cold and dark, and we were not permitted to talk above a whisper. * * We reached the enemy's camp to find it deserted. * * We have had one-third rations for two weeks. * * Hard business. * * The nearer they come to killing me, it seems, the better I like it.

Nov. 9, 1862. *Cotton Hill, Va.* * * Out all night and snowing all the time. Very cold this morning. * * In a snap we cut limbs of brush and propped them up for shelter for fifteen or twenty, building large fires in front. These the boys call boars' nests, bearing a strong resemblance to a hog bed. * * Battles have been fought all around It is the place where our forces tried to capture Floyd.

Nov. 18, 1862. *From Camp Fredrick, Va.* Dear parents. * * You have no idea how much good it does me to hear from home and Burch at the same time. * * Uncle Sam owes me $51, and when paid I will send it home. I want something to show when I get home, for God knows that if anybody earns his money it is the private soldier. You write that you have hard times feeding sixty hogs and gathering the corn, but your work done, you have a house and a good fire for warmth with a table filled with plenty, a bed to sleep in. I get up from the ground at 5:30 A. M., call the roll, get a cup of coffee and a hard cracker, sling my knapsack and accoutrements, and start upon the mountain march of twenty-five miles, and then throw myself on the ground (wet or dry), with a thin blanket for cover. * * Poor Jack Foraker is about gone up with the rheumatism * * I sometimes think it is no use to fight any longer when such men as —— ——, (a noted northern rebel) is allowed to live in Hillsboro.

1863.

January 22, *1863, Camp Rosecrans, Va.* How did Burch (his brother) get along in the recent great battle? I learn he was on Gen. Rosecran's staff, and was riding over the field when the bullets flew thickest. He always was a lucky fellow at home. I saw five shots fired from up on the hill above our camp in a minute. The long roll was beat, and then you ought to have seen your Ben. . . . .

January 30, 1863, Steamer Express. I send you $60, to use the best you can; if your Ben never gets to his earthly home do what you please with it. Company A is without a captain, but Ben Foraker will never ask for a place. I have done my duty always, and have done nothing in the army I would not have done at home. I know I have friends and, what is above all, a clear conscience. . . .

Nashville, Tenn., Feb. 8, 1863. I must tell you of our fight the day we reached Ft. Donnelson. The Eighty-third Illinois was attacked by about 7,000 rebels and artillery. They fought from 2:30 P. M. to 10 when we came up with the gun-boats and immediately opened out on them, and they "skeddadled." The next day I saw many dead rebels. Ah! To know how dreadful war is you must see it yourself. At home you may talk of the horrors of the field of battle and its wounded and dying, but to realize, you must see it. Terrible is the responsibility and criminality of those begining a war, and such a war, to build a nation on the corner-stone of slavery. . . . .

March 6, 1863. . If I am not careful, my debts will consume my wages.

March 24, 1863. . Marched all day and night and next day. . . Have not slept two hours since we left and got into camp. Hard soldiering. . .

Camp near Carthage, Tenn,, March 29, 1863. . Awaiting rebels, he writes: No fire was allowed, and so sleep was out of the question, the night being bitter cold. We awaited the coming morn' for relief from our suffering. . . The rebels had disappeared. . . We marched twelve miles and then halted until sundown, and then marched till midnight, halting one hour and a half. . . Marched and scouted until next midday. . . Never was a boy gladder to get into camp than your son. My feet were in a blister, and every bone in my body was as sore as if beaten with a hammer. . . Yet I could only be satisfied in the service of my country, and as long as there is an armed rebel in the land, and a demand for men, I shall be on the field. . . There are some wishing our glorious Republic and her armies no good luck. Between them and me there can be no friendship. These men who would corrupt and demoralize our army have the bitter contempt of the soldiers. I shall do what duty calls for. If it should be my lot to fall by disease, or on the field of battle, I ask no sympathy from the enemies of my country. . . I like all my officers. . .

Camp near Carthage, Tenn., April 26, 1863. The longer I live the more I become impressed with the worth of character. Since I have been in the army I have lived right up to my duty. . . Major Glenn has been really a father to me. I never had better friends at home than here. . . . . . . Yours, BEN.

May 5, 1863. The prisoners say they have been drawing only quarter rations for months, and no coffee, sugar or salt. . . They all cry "peace," and that they will agree to come back to the Union as it was; but this war will not end until all realize this is a Nation, and for the colored as well as the white man. . . .

May 17. Burch at home. Does he look like the same dear old Burch that he used to? He wrote me you almost killed him with kindness. . .

Carthage, Tenn., May 27. MOTHER DEAR. * * You desire me to tell you about Jimmy Elliott, and what he said upon dying. * * His talk was most about his mother. He said he was willing to die, and was not afraid of death. He felt it would be all right with him. * * Will there be a camp-meeting this fall ? * *   Yours.   BEN.

May 31. * * A leave of absence of four days to meet Burch [his brother] at Nashville. It will be a glorious old meeting, you may bet your life. * * I wish mother was here to go fishing with me. * * Wouldn't mother's eyes glisten if she was to haul out one of the largest fish of this region. . . . Ask mother if she remembers the time she and I went fishing at the big rock, at the head of Spargur's dam. I can see her throwing them out, as fast as I could take them off the hook and string them. I was not bigger than a pound of soap then. What a change in our family. . . . But enough of this; it makes me sad. . . .

Murfreesboro, Tenn., June 13, 1863. If there is anything I despise it is a man holding a commission in the army and at the same time finding fault with everything the administration does to put down the rebellion. .

September 2. DEAR FATHER . . . I congratulate you in your becoming a captain of the Home Guards. If you want to know how to drill them, come down here, and bring a box of provisions along, and then I will hitch you in for about one week, and then you can go home with a good idea of the tactics. . .

Chattanooga, Tenn., Dec. 1, 1863. . . . Arrived just in time to engage in the fight. I found the regiment under arms. The army charged Missionary Ridge. Our brigade charged on double-quick over two miles and up an awfully steep mountain. I commanded two companies, A and B,— brave boys. I threw myself in front and told them to follow. They kept as pretty a line as I ever saw them make on drill. The rebs had two cross fires and a front one. They knocked us around. I reached the top of a hill without a scratch, but just as I leaped over their breast-works a large shell burst just before me. A small fragment of it put a hole in my cap, knocking it off my head. . . As soon as I got into the breast-works and the rebs began to fall back I commenced rallying my men. I had the company about formed when Capt. Curtis, Gen. Turchin's adjutant general, galloped up to me and complimented me   . . I never wish to see another fight. It is an awful sight to see men shot down all around you as you would shoot a beef. . .

Dec. 11. There is a hospital in the rear of our camp. You can hear the wounded screaming all through the day. Legs, arms, and hands lie before the door. . . They are cutting off more or less every day. . . War sickens me. . . I have about thirty men left out of the one hundred and one we started with over a year ago. The regiment does not look the same. . . Come what will, I shall stick to the company if I die with it.

1864.

Ringold, Ga., March 6, 1864. Foraker writes of the enemy taking a stand upon a hill after being pursued. He says: "More skirmishers being called for, I was ordered out with my company. I met the gentleman half way, and after pouring several decided volleys into his ranks, I prevailed on him to go back and let me have full possession. I regained all the ground lost, and kept it until relieved at 11 o'clock that night, though repeated charges were made on my line with a much larger number. * * Our regiment had done splendid fighting. * * Capt. Vickers is a very brave man. * * I have $200 to my credit. I owe brother Burch $35; credit him and discredit me with this amount.

Near Kingston, Ga., May 20, 1864. Within fifty-six miles of Atlanta. You have read of our fighting from May 7 to 17. We were under fire all day the 14th. . . The rebels commenced retreating last Sunday night, and we have been following them, fighting their rear-guard every day since. . . I write this letter within gun shot of the skirmish line. The sun is just rising above the tree-tops. If the rebels make a stand a bloody day's work will soon commence. . . My company stands up to the work like men. I wish no more honorable position than I now have.

South of Etowah River, May 25. Within forty-five miles of Atlanta. . . Awfully hard campaign. It requires all my strength and energy to endure it. . . . .

July 6. Ten miles from Atlanta. Going to have a hard fight. The enemy have their fortifications on the opposite bank of the river, and will make warm work for us in crossing; but cross we will one way or another. . . The fatigues and hardships of our campaign of sixty-one days, have reduced our thirty-four men to nineteen. . . . .

In the Field, Georgia, July 26, 1864. We are within two miles of Atlanta, the Gate-City of the South. . . War will end soon. . . I am not discouraged. I am only tired and worn out. Think of eighty days in the field under fire every day, and in a dozen heavy engagements besides. . . I can't compare myself to anything better than one of Jake Foraker's old horses about the time corn is laid by. . . . .

Atlanta, Nov. 6, 1864. Dear Brother Burch: Was relieved from duty at Marietta, by Lieut. Adams yesterday. Arrived here last night. Capt. Bachtell will accompany Gen. Sherman. He was ordered to select five of his best officers and transfer them Dept. Cumberland to Mil. Div. I was selected as one of the five. The rest of the corps are sent back to Chattanooga. . . . .

1865.

Savannah, Jan. 13, 1865. My Dear Father: A slight attack of the chills and fever, but am getting well. I am on duty in this city. . . Our next campaign will open in about a week. . . I wish I had my two horses at home. . . .

One letter to his father is marked "confidential." It begins: "You being more experienced in the world than myself, I come to you for advice . . . I have a chance for a cadetship at West Point. . . What say you? My strongest reason is that I am just the right age to get an education, and I can get one at West Point and still be in the army. If I don't go there I think I should go to school at some place. . . . Who will be the next President? Get a man who will not fear to make a draft.

I am tired of handling this thing with gloves. I say pitch in and wipe them out. We have the men and the means. So why not put a stop to this unnatural rebellion at once. . . . .

HIS ARMY LIFE.

His own speeches contain at times allusions to his army life. At Camp-fire, McCook Post, No. 30, G. A. R., April 28, 1881, Judge Foraker's topic was "The Soldier in Civil Life." He spoke of civil life furnishing the soldiers, of the dread of war through the north, of men giving up private affairs, business interests, and home and families; of repeated efforts at compromise; of the south regarding us as destitute of fighting qualities; of our finding what blood courses our veins and of our patriotism, of our grand army of a million, and of our men ready for every branch of service. He stated that a colonel, needing a locomotive engineer, announced to his regiment that any man able to run a locomotive should step out, and fifty men stepped to the front. He said:

"I remember that when Sherman, on his march from Atlanta to the sea, captured Milledgeville, which was then the capital of Georgia, our boys took possession of the State House, from which the Confederate Legislature had precipitately fled the day before, organized a mock legislature, elected officers, appointed committees, drafted a bill and enacted it into a law, repealing the ordinance of secession and putting the state back into the Union; and did it all as creditably, showing as much ability, as could any legislative body especially selected for the purpose. . . Thus we see that there is strength in popular government, and that government of the people, for the people, and by the people is no longer an experiment, but an established and demonstrated fact."

The Judge noticed the spirit of alarm that a military despotism with a favorite general for dictator would subvert our constitution and suppress our liberties, or that the country would be filled with an army of idle prowlers. He said:

"The soldiers in civil life to-day, are to be found in every field of usefulness, every art, every science, industry, and profession—with only enough exceptions to prove the rule, wherever you find an ex-soldier, you find a good, industrious, representative citizen. And not only are they toiling in the humbler walks of life, but they are honoring themselves and their country in the highest. As legislators, judicial officers, governors of states and presidents of the United States, they contribute to all the departments of government."

NEW DEPARTURE.

August 26, 1872, before the Grant and Wilson Club, of Hillsboro, Judge Foraker said: "For notwithstanding the new departures with which the Democracy have recently seen fit to edify themselves, and notwithstanding the nomination of the Chappaqua philosopher, there is absolutely no safety and security for this government, nor for republican institutions in general, the world over, but in the continuance of this government in the hands of the same men who saved it until every question of the war and every question that has grown out of the war, shall have been permanently settled on the side of the right.

MISSION RIDGE.

These new departures remind me of an incident of the battle of Mission Ridge,—an incident which I think I shall never forget. When we had pushed our lines up that rugged mountain side, until we had come within a few paces of the rebel trench at the top and when, as it was obvious to every one, we would in another minute sweep over their lines, bearing down everything that might stand in the way, I saw a rebel soldier thrust his musket out over their works and fire it at us, almost in our very faces, and then, jerking it back, throw it down into the ditch behind him, leap over to our side and run into our lines, crying out to us at the top of his voice for us not to shoot him, for he was a *Union* man, our friend, etc. Our lines opened and he passed through, and down that rugged mountain side to our rear something after the manner and style of a streak of greased lightning. It all happened in one-half the time I have occupied in relating it. I don't know that I have ever seen the gentleman since, nor do I know that I ever shall see him again, but I do know that I always have believed, and most likely always shall believe, that if, instead of passing him to our rear, as we did, our men had received him on the points of their bayonets and passed him into eternity, he would have gone up to the bar of God with a lie in his mouth. And yet, my friends, that rebel was doing just exactly what the Democracy are pretending to do. He was taking his new departure. But I did not believe then, and I do not believe now, that his professions of Unionism and friendship were sincere. They indicated a change of mind entirely too radical, too sudden, and suspicious in its character and surrounding circumstances. And as I have never believed that that rebel was taking any genuine departure, except such as he could take by means of his legs, so have I never had any faith whatever in these departures of the Democracy. And the reason why I have never had any such faith are the very same identical reasons why I disbelieved that rebel.

Here they come, many long years later than they ought to have come, to have been appreciated, and pledge themselves to maintain the Union. Yes. They wait till the war is over, till the Union has been preserved, till we are in a condition such as to render it a matter of but slight consideration whether they stand the one way or the other, and then they come forward with the pledge that they ought to have given the country in 1861. They in favor of the Union! What a great pity it is that they didn't find it out sooner! What a great pity it is that they did not see fit to come forward in 1861, and clasp hands across the little chasms that intervened between party organizations with the Union men of the country and pledge themselves before the whole world to so continue to stand to the end. It is a great pity because, had they done so, the war, if ever commenced at all, would have terminated long before it did. And, in that event, many brave and precious "boys" would not have gone down as they did in sacrifice. But, my friends, it is not only a great pity that they so neglected this important matter, it is also a gross crime. The blood of all such "boys" is upon the skirts of this Democratic party."

RECORD OF SERVICE

At the reunion of the the 89th O. V. I., Sept. 20, 1869, at Hillsboro, Judge Foraker, among other good utterances, said on our battle-flag are entitled to be written the following facts:

"Two years and eleven months in the service; more than three thousand miles traveled, over one thousand seven hundred of which were performed on foot, with knapsack on the back and the enemy in the front."

Hoover's Gap, Chickamauga, Mission Ridge, Rocky Face Ridge, Resacca, Kenesaw Mountain, Peach Tree Creek, Utoy Creek, Jonesboro', Atlanta,

Savannah, and Bentonville, are the battles, leaving unmentioned as too insignificant to be taken into consideration at least fifty such skirmishes as Phillipi, Rich Mountain, Scarey Creek, and Carnifex Ferry, which, in the beginning of the war, when they were fought, were thought to be great battles. And these are the *glorious* inscriptions which we are entitled to write upon our flag.

EIGHT HUNDRED FALLEN.

Next comes the recital of the *most terrible* price at which they were *purchased*. NEARLY 800 FALLEN! For, starting out with more than a thousand as hearty, strong, noble and patriotic men as ever obeyed a country's call, we returned to Camp Dennison at the close of the war numbering only 231, rank and file; and among them all there could scarce be found a corporal's guard who could not show where at least one bullet of the enemy had struck them. Not all of these 800 missing had fallen in battle, it is true, nor perhaps the half of them, for with us, as with all soldiers, the exposures and privations and over-fatigues were more destructive than the enemy's bullet. But whether they had languished and breathed their last on the couch in the hospital; or whether finally obtaining a discharge or furlough and reaching home, their pure spirits bade farewell to their tenements of clay, and winged their heavenward flight from among tender and weeping friends; or whether, as was the almost indescribably sad fate of so many of our brave boys, their bodies were wasted and their deaths hastened by a barbaric starvation in the still more barbaric prison pens of the South, far from friends, without even a shelter over them, denied the slightest attention and even the kindness of a decent burial; or whether the messenger of Death found them on the lonely picket and upon an ever-to-be-unknown spot, poured out their warm life's blood to sanctify, hallow and to make holy; or whether souls went up to God from amid the dust and smoke and shot and thunder of battle: it matters not. All must be alike enumerated in our mortality list; for all alike, though in so many different forms, fell victims to the same great cause. All alike, living sacrifices upon their country's altar that their country might live.

A PLEDGE OF FRIENDSHIP.

And now my comrades: we who were spared in this terrible havoc; we who stood, while so many of our number prematurely went down into the dust of death; we, who were permitted to survive the battles, the marches, the toils, the exposures, and all the other hardships and dangers incident to a soldier's life; we, who were of that fortunate few who were so highly favored as to be allowed to return home again, and enjoy in the bosom of families and in the midst of our friends that peace which our sacrifices and valor had achieved; we, who have all this to be thankful for, have gathered ourselves together to-day, not for the purpose of parade and glitter and show, but only that we may again stand in each other's presence and look upon each other's faces; that we may again clasp each other's hand, and while recalling and recounting the trials and dangers which we shared and passed through in common, have a recommingling of souls, and a refreshing and renewing of that friendship which, of all other friendships, is pre-eminently the first. And, this, the anniversary day of Chickamauga, is certainly a most appropriate time for our purpose; for, although duty called me elsewhere at the time, so that I do not have the honor of having participated in the engagement, yet, in common with every other member of the regiment, whether present or not, I can not but feel a glow of pride tingle down my cheek when I recall the heroic manner in which, from the beginning till the end of the fight, you battled almost to annihilation against most fearful odds, and finally, rather than desert your position, or yield an inch of ground, you yielded up that which is next dearest to life itself—*your own liberty.*

THE LAND OF THE FREE.

And it is because this day was one of such great disaster, as well as great glory, that we do well to so emphatically remember it as to make it our anniversary upon which to come together and repledge our friendship, and return our thanks to our Almighty Father, through whose omnipotent care we were saved harmless from the ravages by which so many of our most gallant officers and bravest men were swept from among us into eternity. But the preservation of our lives is not the only nor the great reason why we should to-day give thanks.

It is an unworthy selfishness that would prompt us to rejoice for no better reason than that the storms and dangers of war should have passed over and left us to bask, unharmed, in the sunshine of peace and the security of victory. Let us rejoice that our lot should have been cast in the day and land when and where the opportunity was afforded us of becoming the instruments, in the hands of a Divine Providence, with which to perform a work of such lasting benefit, not only to the present generation of mankind, but to those of all the ages which are to hereafter follow us. Yes, let the joy of our hearts be, that we can to-day recall that when the dark hour of peril and great responsibility came upon us, we were equal to the emergency and met it like men. That, unlike the many, who, under equal obligations with us, to the lasting disgrace of themselves and their innocent children after them, not only miserably, but most criminally, failed, we took our lives in our hands and went forth and stood as a wall of fire between the institutions of our Government and that enemy which, seeking the country's overthrow, were working the destruction of the country's people; and that in the performance of this duty we not only saved from destruction the works of our fathers and founders, but in addition brought them to a much higher perfection, by wiping out that great stigma, which, so long as it remained and received the recognition and protection of our laws, retarded our development and corroded our morals by giving the lie to our boasted professions that here was "the land of the free and the home of the brave;" where the oppressed and down-trodden of every country and clime could find a *welcome*, a refuge, and a *home.*

FORAKER AT HOME AND SCHOOL.

Before Ben Foraker was nineteen years of age he was mustered out of the U. S. service,—June 14, 1865.

The war over, the Union preserved, the slave at liberty, and young Foraker returned to farm, mill and school, studying at Salem, Ross County. He was two years at the Wesleyan University, at Delaware, Ohio, and then went to Cornell University, graduating in the classical course, July 1, 1869, and in its first class.

With his limited means he was not only assiduous in his academical studies, but at the same time he was also a student at law. A dear friend and class-mate says that not only did he study and read under high pressure, but on plain fare, at times boarding himself and thus reducing his expenses to the minimum that he might eke out his scanty means and finish his entire course.

He went to Cornell from the University, with a letter from the Rev. Dr. Merrick, the then President, honorably dismissing him and certifying to his character as a student and as a gentleman, "In all respects entirely unexceptionable."

His literary reputation at college may be somewhat determined by the subjects for essays assigned him. His essay upon "Macbeth," published in the Collegian, is modest and yet marks the thinker. The student, Foraker, asks why we should read Shakspeare? He refers to human nature all around, as well as in the plays of the bard, and that Duncans and Macbeths stalk over the land in broad daylight, and that were there fewer men with just sense enough to quote Shakspeare, and no more than to render themselves ridiculous by tentative efforts at imitation, our writing and oratory would be advanced in respectability. Foraker's analysis of Macbeth would do credit to an older essayist.

In 1869 he was elected as the proper person to write to Senator Sumner to deliver an address at Cornell, and to receive the great Massachusetts Senator upon his arrival.

Foraker is the only man who graduated first in the army, and then took college honors. As for his youth, "one ages rapidly," said Napoleon, "on the battle-field."

Major White, of Springfield, thus writes of his record at college:

"He was a recognized leader among the students; probably because of his long military experience before entering the college, as he came fresh from the battle-field to Delaware. In his studies he was one of the most exhaustive students I ever knew, as he always took up a branch of study with a view of getting the most complete and comprehensive ideas on it."

"He was probably the best debater in the college. He was a prominent member of the Zetegathean Society, a literary society of the college, and was one of the most prominent members in it. Foraker was always chosen to represent the Zetegatheans in any debate or contest in public, and in any literary or forensic contest with a rival society."

"From the time of entering, while not neglecting his literary studies, much attention was given to the study of the law, and his time, study and energy were directed toward this end. He was foremost in organizing a moot court and mock trials, and invariably acted as Judge, thus giving a prophecy of his future career."

"Foraker was not of the kind to make anecdotes. He was a lively, determined, studious young man, with a life object in view, and an indomitable will to obtain it. He was little inclined to joking, and was always earnest and serious. In the college tricks and pranks he took no part."

"He was head of his classes, and to show how great was his proficiency in his studies, I will simply state that he went from the Sophomore Class in Delaware, directly to the Senior Class at Cornell, thus jumping a class. He followed the classical course at both universities, but made an especial effort in all branches having a legal bearing or tendency."

"He was extremely popular with both pupils and professors. His studious, earnest bearing endeared him to all, and made him one of the most popular young men in the whole university."

Judge Vernon, of the Clinton County *Republican*, says:

"Foraker and myself were members of the same literary society while at college. In the debates, whatever side had Foraker, was almost certain to win. He was always a sure, strong fellow."

THE FLAG CAN'T COME DOWN.

A college mate at Delaware and lawyer at Dayton recalls an incident that well illustrates the effect of Captain Foraker's presence. Upon the college campus was a flag-staff brought from Camp Dennison, and erected at the expense of the students, who were Republicans almost to a man. After some election or national event, distasteful to the Democrats, the flag was hoisted to the top of the staff, by way of a glorification. In the afternoon of that day it was rumored that some Democratic citizens, not students, would lower the flag or cut down the pole that night. The boys arranged to have a couple of watchmen, and upon any hostile demonstration the chapel bell was to be rung. Sure enough, late at night some burly fellows made their appearance upon the campus and blustered about what they were going to do. While one watchman parleyed with them the other ran to the bell-rope, and in ten minutes the campus was black with students. Foraker was there, and although only a freshman or sophomore, and by no means one of the oldest students, they all instinctively turned to him for leadership. He confronted the disturbers, addressed them a few decided words in a dignified way, and told them that that flag would never be lowered nor the pole cut down. They departed. The pole was not thereafter molested. The circumstance shows the quality of Foraker, and the estimate in which he was held by his companions, and by his political opponents. When Foraker said the pole should not be cut down and the flag should not be lowered, all knew that Foraker meant to resist the insult to the flag with his whole physical power

MEN AND PHI KAPPA PSI.

We extract some choice periods from an address of J. B. Foraker, graduate member of New York Alpha, before the Phi Kappa Psi Fraternity, Columbus, Ohio, August 19th and 20th, 1874:

". . . . You are here as the representatives of the active working members of the fraternity! . . Only they who have experienced it can know how sweetly, grandly, and proudly will resurrect themselves in one's memory, bringing peace to the troubled mind, teaching its ever noble duty where the way is not plain, and lending strength for victory when the soul is tempted, those quiet, modest, but diamond-like words, "*Never forget that you are a member of the Phi Kappa Psi fraternity.*"

* * * * * * * * *

"Your duty is not a mere college pastime. Its objects are higher,—the symmetrical develop ment of our whole nature. It means men, men in the highest sense of the word, men who will depart from college to the battles of life with honesty of purpose, with appreciation of right, and with a power for work that will render the world better. Hence, be diligent, earnest, brave, honest, and God-fearing — a credit to yourselves, an honor to your society, a gain to the world — . . making the mind brighter, the heart warmer, and the soul nobler as you pass on to eternity.

* * * * * * * * *

It is plausibly argued that the world is full of bad people, that lying, cheating, and evil generally are prevalent, and therefore 'You must fight the devil with fire,' that success must come by the use of like instrumentalities. Is this not generally an apology for misguided conduct?"

* * * * * * * * *

"When Sir Francis Bacon bartered away the high honor of the great office of Law Chancellor of England, humiliation and disgust sickened every true heart of that proud realm. . . . But when the strong arm of the people was found sufficient, despite his mighty genius and influence to humble this great man, and strip him of the accumulations of his robberies, confidence in humanity revived and grew stronger, demonstrating not the retrogression of mankind, but the abuse of trust by one poor, weak public servant. . So with the discovery and punishment of our own faithless servants. . . Let us take cheer from the manifestations of virtue by which the people turn their backs upon their idols, rebuking sin and encouraging righteousness."

After giving much useful advice the Judge said:

"You may not thus gather wealth — you may not win fame, but your mind will know a serenity, your heart a sunshine, and your soul an assurance, compared with which all the riches and honors of the world are veriest baubles. Not because you shall be free from storms of trouble, but because you shall have the anchor of safety. . . You may be in advance of many as to your opinions. Don't seek to avoid censure and criticism and to destroy your self-respect in an outward approval of the errors of the many. Boldly and unhesitatingly maintain your own sentiments. The most disgusting, demoralizing, and discouraging feature of entire political systems is the abominable demagoguery of truckling to popular sentiment."

* * * * * * * * *

LET POLITICS ALONE.

"Let politics alone" is sounded in the ears of the college graduate. . . In this Democratic country of ours every man is charged with a voice in the Government. . . If the wicked are put in power, and disaster overtake us, will it be a sufficient excuse for the good man that he takes no part in politics? . . We must not sleep on guard and be criminally unmindful of our highest duty. . . Have all to do with politics, both understanding and controlling. . . Our surest safety in politics lies in the exercise of honesty and intelligence in the formation and presentation of public questions."

DISFRANCHISEMENT OF STUDENTS.

The Judge in 1868, himself a student, gave to the press his views of the disfranchisement of students by the Democratic legislature.

"There are about four hundred students attending this university (Delaware), about two hundred are voters. Not more than twenty of all are Democrats. The remainder are unqualified Union men. I do not know that this is the case with *all* the colleges of the state. It is so with most; and I presume the Legislature thought it so with all, for in their very great *wisdom* and exceeding *patriotism*, they have thought best to *disfranchise* us, while here as students, hoping thereby to cheat a few Republicans out of their votes, discourage education, and retard progress and enlightenment, the most deadly enemies with which the Democratic party has ever had to contend.

"But, aside from this view of the matter, the law is certainly one of very great injustice and hardship to the students of both parties. For why should not the student enjoy the same rights that are extended to any other description of temporary inhabitant? The *clerk* and the *mechanic* have but to remain here the time required by the statute, and their right to exercise the elective franchise becomes unquestionable, whether they are here temporarily or permanently. And so it should be with all classes of persons, and any enactments to the contrary are uncalled for and unjust. So we must pronounce this act, when we take it by itself; but when we couple with it the circumstances and facts to which it owes its existence, it becomes particularly offensive, and our disapproval ripens into contempt for a body of men who are so lost to duty, lost to honor, and lost to conscience, as thus to legislate away the dearest of all American rights—the ballot."

AS A LAWYER.

He entered the law office of Judge James Sloane, then practicing in Cincinnati. He was admitted to the bar of Hamilton County in the fall of 1869, and at once began practice, with no influential friends in the city and without the usual aid of membership in some secret or social club.

"Slow rises worth, by poverty depressed."

Thus it was with him for a season; but his genial manners, indomitable energy, great ability, and stern Christian integrity eventually secured him practice, in every court, from that of the local magistrate to the supreme court of the United States.

Hon. Ben. Eggleston says it was but a short time before the people of that great city saw that he was not an ordinary man; that there was something in and about him more than there was in ordinary young men.

Judge Foraker, at the beginning of his law course, wrote, June 1870, an essay for a Wilmington journal, in which (unintentionally) he gave his personal views of the law as a profession and the spirit with which he entered upon its duties. He had no apology for the "infamous Jeffries," nor for "Noy, who by his technical quibbling evaded and delayed the ends of justice;" nor for "Eldon, who perverted his legal knowledge and powers to prevent more good than any other man had accomplished in a life time." He claimed and felt (and thus entered upon his work) that "the work of the lawyer is in harmony with, and part of the great labor of carrying humanity forward;" that his work is not only of pecuniary benefit to mankind," but that the "lawyer's great work, properly viewed, is most closely allied to that of the clergy;" that lawyers should check and not promote the "perturbations of society;" that they should be leaders in contests for truth, liberty, and progress, and be ever on the side of the oppressed.

HIS MARRIAGE.

October 4, 1870, Judge Foraker, with the memory of a blessed paternal home, married Miss Julia A. P. Bunday, a daughter of Hon. Hezekiah S. Bunday, of Jackson, Ohio; the intimate friend of Lincoln, and a member of Congress in the most eventful period of our history. This lady he met while she was a scholar at the Ohio Wesleyan Female College, at which she graduated in 1868, and where she was noted for her high literary attainments.

God has blessed this sacred union with one son and three daughters.

Mrs. Foraker often urged her husband to prepare an *autobiography*. The Judge wrote the preface thus:

"I never liked the idea of *autobiographies*. For a man to write disparagingly of himself cannot be commendable. "It is a mean bird that fouls its own nest." If one's career deserves disparagement, there will be others to afford it. If not, it is at least well enough, if not better, to let it go unwritten.

On the other hand, if praise is merited, others should sound it. To praise oneself will appear egotistic—no matter how deserved. To avoid both disparagement and praise is difficult, if not well-nigh impossible.

It might be thought these objections could be avoided by a mere naked statement of facts, but that is not really true, since the mere statement of any given act must carry with it the idea that, accordingly as its nature may be, the author suffers it to redound to his credit. Entertaining such views, it is in the nature of an unpleasant task that I enter upon this short work, and yet I undertake it, contradictory as it may seem, in another sense, with very great pleasure. I do it at the request of a loving, admiring and devoted wife; a wife who by ten years of fidelity, affection and devotion to every duty, and by four as bright and beautiful children as ever graced any union, has merited and won for herself all the confidence and love that belongs to the several and hallowed offices of wife and mother. These statements must be my apology for these pages.

The Judge wrote a few lines and never resumed the task.

FORAKER AT HOME.

Our public men should not only be moral and upright men, but men who appreciate home life and are examplars of family, as of patriotic sentiment. What would our nation be without its homes?

Upon entering the home of Judge Foraker, with the home-spirit, and not with that of impertinent intrusion, in lifting the purple curtains where his weary brain reposes, we find a true home, a true husband, and a true father. We exercise no distasteful scrutiny; but, we can not but see a true religious and American home. The country more and more demands of our statesmen that they erect for themselves, pure, virtuous homes.

The Judge has no sympathy with the sentiment or the law that destroys the individuality of the wife, or which awards greater punishments to a woman for the same vice, or which classes women with infants and idiots; yet he values the intellectual filtering through the moral nature, giving power, maintaining virtue, exercising that subtle influence which makes every moment a seed-time of future good, and finding scope for mind and heart in the education of the children. He esteems the wife as companion, lover, friend and counsellor, having her especial duties as he has his—a division of labor.

JUDGE OF SUPERIOR COURT.

In April, 1879, he was elected a Judge of the Superior Court of Cincinnatti. He held this office for three years. The kind of record he made is best shown by the expressions elicited by his resignation. One decision selected at random out of the many that have been published will illustrate his logic and style of expression:

SUPERIOR COURT OF CINCINNATI.

GENERAL TERM, JANUARY 1882.

MARGARET R. POOR, Plaintiff.

vs.

SARAH S. SCANLAN AND MAURICE J. SCANLAN, Her Husband.

Foraker, J.:

This case was reversed upon the evidence. It is an action for rent.

From the pleadings and the evidence it appears that March 1st, 1857, the plaintiff, being then the owner thereof, leased a certain lot on the north side of Third street in the city of Cincinnati, to George Selves, for ninety-nine years, renewable forever. The certificate of acknowledgement of the lease was not written on the same sheet of paper that the lease was written upon, but on a separate sheet attached to the paper the lease was written upon, by a common paper fastener. All parties seem, however, to be ignorant of this fact until after this suit was brought. Selves held possession of the premises under the lease, paying the rents reserved therein: $250 every quarter, until his death in 1862. When he died he left a will by which he devised to his widow Sarah Selves, now Sarah S. Scanlan, the defendant herein, all his real estate for life. She elected to take under his will, and at once took possession of this leasehold estate. She remained in possession continously until after this action was commenced, paying the rents reserved according to the covenants of the lease, until June 1, 1878, when she refused to pay the quarter's rent then falling due, and offered to surrender the premises, which offer was not accepted. She had not paid anything since. In 1869 she married her co-defendant, Maurice J. Scanlan, who, jointly with her, has occupied and used the premises since, until they quit possession in 1881.

This action was commenced in 1879, to recover four installments of rent that had become due, amounting to $1,000. The petition simply alleged that there was due the plaintiff, from Sarah S. Scanlan and Maurice J. Scanlan, for rent of the said premises, $1,000, and prayed for judgment against the defendants. Nothing was said, either in the style of the case or the body of the petition, about the defendants being husband and wife. No reference was made to the lease, and there was no allegation that the wife had a separate estate. The case stood upon this petition and a general denial filed thereto, by the defendants, when it came on for trial. The facts above mentioned appearing, the plaintiff was allowed to re-file an amended petition which she had previously filed and withdrawn, in which the facts above stated, except as to the defective acknowledgment of the lease, were fully set out, together with allegations that the wife had a separate estate, followed by a prayer for judgment and appropriate relief. The defendants excepted to the re-filing of this amended petition, and thereupon answered, denying all the allegations of the amended petition, except that George Selves occupied the premises at his death, that Mrs. Scanlan was the devisee of all his real estate for life, and that she entered into and held possession of the premises in question until 1881, and that she married Scanlan in 1868, also that she held for life, under the will of Selves, the real estate described in the petition, as her separate estate. Defendants claim that the amended petition ought not to have been allowed, because a departure.

It is not pretended that defendants were surprised or placed at any disadvantage by it. The provision of our code on this subject is that such amendments may be made when in furtherance of justice, and when they do not substantially change the claim or defense. Section 5114. In the case of *Spice vs. Steinruck*, 14th O. S., 213, it was held that this did not refer to the *form* of the remedy, but only to the general identity of the claim, and, consequently, that it was permissible, as was done in that case, to so amend the petition as to change the action, which was to recover damages for a malicious prosecution, to support which malice and want of probable cause had to be shown, to an action for damages for an illegal arrest, to sustain which it was not necessary to show malice or want of probable cause, but only a *void* process. The amendment in this case certainly does not change the claim that is made in the petition. At most it but changes the form. It can scarcely be said to fairly do even that. It is really nothing more than a statement of the facts of which we have the naked legal effect set forth in the petition, with some allegations about a separate estate, which according to our view of the case, are only so much surplusage.

Considering the case upon its merits, there are two general propositions relied upon by the defendants. In the first place it is claimed, that because Mr. Scanlan was the devisee of this leasehold only for life, she took less than the whole term, and she was consequently a sub-lessee, and not an assignee, and if but a sub-lessee, not liable to the lessor for want of privity of estate.

For a second defense it is insisted that the defendant, Mrs. Scanlan, has done no act to authorize her separate estate to be charged.

Either of these propositions would be sufficient for the defendants if it could be applied to this case. But in our opinion, neither one has application.

The first has not, because the instrument intented for a lease to Selves was invalid, as such, by reason of the acknowledgment being written on a separate sheet of paper. Winkler vs. Higgins, 9 O. S., 599. It did not pass the term to Selves. It was, consequently, at most but an equitable lease, giving him a right to occupy and enjoy the premises upon the terms and conditions named in it, and binding him, as upon personal covenant, to comply with is terms and conditions, so long as he remained in possession. Bridgeman vs. Wells, 13 Ohio, 43. This equitable right was all that passed by the devise. And this right defendant took without assuming his personal covenant. Her undertaking was by an implied contract to pay for her use and occupation, so long as she enjoyed the same, according to the terms of the lease. This contract was between her and the lessor; hence there was privity of contract at least,

The second proposition would be unanswerable, if the plaintiff's right to recover a judgment depended upon a right to charge Mrs. Scanlan's separate estate upon such a contract entered into during coverture. For we fully agree with the claim of her counsel, that in such a case it must be shown that she intended to charge her separate estate, and that such intention was relied upon. But, in our judgment, this is not such a case. This is merely an action to recover a personal judgment, and whether or not such a judgment shall be rendered, does not depend upon, and is not affected by, the question whether or not she at all has a separate estate.

Mrs. Scanlan was a *feme sole* when she took possession of these premises.

She was therefore competent to contract, and as we have seen, did, by implication, contract to pay, according to the terms of the lease, so long as she remained in possession. Her continued possession, after marriage, as well as before, must be referable to her original entering, and must have been therefore in pursuance of the contract to which we have alluded as thereby made for her by operation of law. Especially do we think so in view of the fact that she took possession for life, and hence did not have occasion to periodically consider, whether or not she would continue there. This being true, she held the premises at the time the rents accrued, for which she is now sued, under a contract, which the law made for her when she took possession, and which was in force when she married her co-defendant, whereby she was obliged to pay the same. It is upon that contract that this action is based: a contract therefore substituting at the time of marriage; not made during coverture, but before.

This view is not affected by the fact that her occupation, after marriage, was jointly with her husband, since her interest and rights in the property under our statute, section 3108, remained her separate estate.

The case is, therefore, properly stated, an action against husband and wife, to recover rents that have become due, during coverture, upon a contract made by the wife before marriage, and existing at the time of marriage. At common law, marriage made the husband liable for the existing obligations of his wife. But in all actions against him to enforce them, she must be joined as a co-defendant, without regard to whether she had a separate estate or not. *Drew vs. Thorne*, Aleyn, 72, 7 Term, Rep., 348. If, therefore, we had no statute on the subject, this action would lie against the defendant for a money judgment.

In such case however, *i. e.* if there were no statute, the separate property of the wife could not be taken to satisfy the judgment. But in such actions we have instead of a common law rule that the *wife* must be joined with the husband, sec. 4996, of rev. statues, which requires the husband to be joined with the wife. And instead of the wife's separate estate being exempt from liability to be taken to satisfy the judgment we have it expressly made liable by section 3110, which provides that "the separate property of the wife shall be liable to be taken for any judgment rendered in an action against husband and wife, upon a cause existing against her at their marriage, etc."

The language of this section has been changed somewhat since the case of Westerman *vs.* Westerman, 25 O. S., 500, where it was constructed to mean that the wife's separate property was not only liable to be taken in such case, but that as between her, and her husband's property, it was primarily liable, but the change has only made it more apparent that the legislative intent agreed with the construction of the Court.

Our conclusion is that this is an action against Mrs. Scanlan and her husband on a contract obligation of hers, existing at their marriage, that it is immaterial whether she intended to charge her separate estate or not, and that judgment should be rendered for the plaintiff; Jas. H. Perkins and D. H. J. Holmes, attorneys for defendants.

THE TRUE MAN.

We desire not to study Joseph Benson Foraker as a lawyer, soldier, or scholar, but to discover the man in the conduct of the lawyer, judge, soldier, and scholar. We study his briefs and charges and speeches to see how he links himself with broad humanity, to discover why men and women, citizens and soldiers trust him, and honor him. Thus we present the remarkable address that Judge Foraker delivered in memoriam before the District Court at Hillsborough, Ohio, upon the death of Judge Sloan, with whom Judge Foraker was formerly a law student.

JUDGE SLOANE.

Among his embarassments in delivering the address he said, "that Judge Sloan was unlike any man of his acquaintance."

"On account of some of his peculiar traits of character, I know him to be a greatly misunderstood man by a majority, I think, of the people who professed to be acquainted with him. And knowing him to have been thus misunderstood, I fear there may be those who will regard at least a part of what I shall say in praise of his character as mere empty and fulsome eulogy, instead of earnest and honest testimony.

I have no desire, or interest either, to speak in this matter aught save the strictest truth; and I know that he for whom I speak had so much truth in his heart, that he would utterly despise the slightest deviation therefrom, no matter how much that deviation might favor his memory in the estimation of men.

Therefore, I feel perfectly free, as well as conscientiously obligated, to say here to-day, as I have frequently said to the deceased in his lifetime, that there were certain striking features in his outward character that were objectionable, in the most serious sense of the word; for I considered them immoral and pernicious in their influences.

But for these things Judge Sloane is not answerable to us. That settlement must take place between him and that highest, wisest, and kindest Judge of all. . . . Let us remember that humane injunction of the Savior, "Judge not, that ye be not judged."

It was my fortune to know Judge Sloane well. I knew him for a number of years, and in a variety of relations. I think the majority of even this community, where he lived and died, never knew him except as I first knew him, and by all such Judge Sloane was not really known at all; for I first knew him only as a great, intellectual, legal giant, upon whom, when he went forth into public places, I, in common with others, was at liberty to look; and, if he chanced to pass my way, the compliments of the day might perhaps be deferentially exchanged. Closer than this I felt that I dared not, and I know that I desired not, to go; for there seemed to be a kind of Ishmaelitish coldness and bitterness about the man that rendered him uninviting to all except his personal friends, who knew him well, or such as might stand in need of his splendid talents.

In short, as I have already stated, I thought him only a cold, selfish, ambitious, intellectual giant; and had I never come closer to Judge Sloane, his loss would not now concern me much; for I have long since learned that there are giants in *these* as well as in *those* days, and that the places of giants simply are easily supplied.

FRIEND, PRECEPTOR, ASSOCIATE.

But I shall always be glad that it was within God's providence that I should know Judge Sloane better. His great abilities as a lawyer led me to sufficiently subordinate my objections to him personally to enable me to take a place as a student in his office. My association and connection with him, in some manner, was uninterrupted from that time until the day of his death. And I can say now, that in all the relations of a friend, a preceptor, as associate, and as opposing counsel, I have ever found him to be the very soul of honor.

He was the very body of truthfulness itself. I don't believe the man ever told a lie in his life. And when I remember how my daily experience teaches me that "the world is given to lying," I feel that absolute truthfulness is a rare and an extraordinary virtue to be ascribed to any man.

But Judge Sloane was not simply a *truthful* man. He was as honest.

I don't mean that Judge Sloane was honest merely in money matters. The country is full of people who pay back all they borrow, and pay for all they buy, and take not, unlawfully, that which belongs to another. There are a thousand reasons why a man should be honest in these respects, and a thousand reasons why a man deserves no credit for such honesty.

Judge Sloane was honest in that higher, and better, and *braver* sense of the word. He was honest in the sense that honesty is the equivalent to truthfulness. There was no sham about him—no hypocrisy—no deception—no false pretense—no borrowed capital—no sailing under false colors. Whatever he pretended or appeared to be, that he was. If he manifested a spirit of friendliness toward any one, it was a genuine spirit, and the person toward whom it was manifested could rely on it to the fullest extent. And on the other hand, if he disliked any one, it was a genuine dislike, but the person disliked need have no difficulty in learning the facts in the case.

In other words, whatever he was that he was earnestly, fearlessly, and outspokenly, and whatever he believed, he believed earnestly, and what he didn't believe earnestly he didn't believe at all. He was no reed to be shaken by the wind.

Judge Sloane was also a kind and generous man. I do not mean kind and generous to the rich, for that would be easy for any man to be; nor to his equals, nor to the well-to-do classes—from all which sources he might reasonably have expected some benefit in return. Nor do I mean that he was kind and generous in public places, where his acts of kindness and generosity would be seen and known of all men. But he was kind and generous in a way that showed his kindness and generosity to be genuine. He was kind and generous privately rather, and to the poor and lowly, from whom he could not possibly expect anything in return.

HIS CHARITY.

I well remember, and shall never forget an incident that occurred in his office at Cincinnati, while I was a student with him. Hardly a day passed without from one to a half-dozen beggars coming into the office, with their various stories of poverty and destitution.

The city of Cincinnati cares and provides well for all who are really needy, and on this account it is rarely the case that any one who knows it, as Judge Sloane did, gives anything at all to that class of mendicants.

It was to my surprise, therefore, that day after day I observed that he never refused a single application, but patiently and kindly listened to the appeals of all, and gave something to every single one.

One day I ventured to call his attention to the matter, and to suggest that perhaps he was being imposed upon. There was a perfect sermon of genuine religion and Christianity in his reply, that, "he had long since come to the conclusion, that it was better to be imposed upon in many cases, than to turn away empty even one worthy applicant."

But Judge Sloane was kind in another respect. He was kind to the young practitioner. And standing here to-day, as in some measure the representative of the younger members of the bar, you will excuse me if I ask a special remembrance of this trait of his character. . . . .

It should not be any uncommon virtue, yet we all know that it too truly is. Every young man who starts in the profession of the law must encounter difficulties and perplexities, and troubles of various kinds. . .

. . When the country was imperiled and brave hearts were needed at the front, he was the first of all our citizens to appreciate the situation and to step forward with both his services and his blood. . . . .

Of Judge Sloane as a lawyer I shall say but little. We all know how he towered among us; and how his mind was exceptionally remarkable for its power of discernment, analysis, and logical reasoning. . . . . .

. . We know, too, how, with an almost uncommon fidelity, he at all times maintained the interests of his clients. . . . But for that "grievous fault," for which he was continually "grievously answering," he would in all probability have risen to national importance. . . . . .

When we consider the turbulent times through which we have just passed, the great fields of national usefulness that they presented, and the rich honors that have been therein gathered by others; and when we further consider his splendid abilities, his scrupulous honesty, and his unswerving patriotism, who can feel otherwise than that it was a genuine misfortune both to the country and himself, that Judge Sloane did not figure in national affairs. . . . . . .

. . . But regrets are vain. His life has been lived; his record is made. . . By his sad loss let us be freshly and impressively reminded of the importance of correctly living while we do live, of making the most of time while we have it, both for this world and eternity.

AN HONEST OFFICER.

In the fall of 1876, Judge Baxter, of the U. S. Circuit Court, appointed Foraker to the delicate and responsible position of Chief Supervisor of Elections for the Southern District of Ohio. Again he made a personal sacrifice of feeling and business in the interest of his country and party, and of the purity of the ballot. He administered its duties so fairly that even the Democrats, in their Congressional investigations, made record of his honorable integrity as the officer of the law.

Judge Foraker, by common consent, was agreed upon by men of all parties, and endorsed by the Judge for chief supervisor by reason of his purity, integrity, and courage, as "worthy, honorable and true in every respect, who would desire nothing but a free, fair, straightforward election, and as down on all fraud, and down on all men who undertake to cast an illegal vote, or import votes from any State to Ohio, or from any ward or precinct to any other."

It is remarkable that in the canvass to be hotly contested, and amid the anxieties of candidates and parties for victory, Judge

Foraker was the only person upon whom all, Democrats and Republicans could harmonize. It is an enviable tribute to honest and moral worth.

In the spirit of eminent fairness, Judge Foraker, as chief supervisor, asked Mr. Sayler, as chairman of the Democratic elective and campaign committees, to present the names of Democrats as supervisors. He said that he desired to have "all parties fairly represented, and by only good, honest, representative men, who will perform their duties solely in the interest of an honest election, and without regard to partizan advantages."

In the course of the correspondence with the obstructives of the law to promote pure elections, Judge Foraker took occasion to declare that the government of the United States could not only protect itself against an armed rebellion, but could protect itself against fraud and abuse at the ballot-box.

The character of Judge Foraker is seen in his instructions to his subordinate supervisors. After a minute examination of their duties and methods so as to cover almost every conceivable case, he declares that their duties are " to secure an honest, full and free expression of the voice of the people. This is of far greater importance than the success of any party or candidate. You are the representatives of all parties and all candidates, and your work is in the interest of the whole people—for law, order and good government. You will, therefore, carefully abstain from all electioneering, discussion and controversy."

Such an administrator of law may be safely trusted in any executive position.

Foraker was nominated for Judge of the Court of Common Pleas, in 1867, but was defeated by the notorious Eph. Holland frauds of that year. The confidence of the Republican Community in Judge Foraker was again evinced in his nomination for County Solicitor, in 1868. This was without his knowledge and against his wishes, but he served his party and his country, when he knew that he would suffer defeat.

RESIGNATION.

Upon the announcement in Cincinnati that Judge Foraker contemplated leaving the bench, the strongest remonstrances were made by the legal fraternity and by lay friends, without regard to party. They insisted upon his retaining the position, and the taking of a long vacation until his health had been regained; that his health had been lost in public service and that the vacation was his right. But his sensitive nature would not permit his receiving the least portion of salary for which no current equivalent was rendered. After the resignation had been forwarded to Columbus, telegrams were sent to the governor urging its non-acceptance. Among them were those from Hons. Force, Hoadley, Perry, Kettredge, and Warrington.

NO WORK, NO PAY. FORAKER'S MAXIM.

Mr. Eggleston thus describes his interview with Judge Foraker as to his resignation:

"No, Mr. Foraker, they [Democrats and Republicans of the bar] say they will not permit you to resign; that you must take a six month's vacation, and keep your seat. What do you think that honest young man said? 'Why,' said he, 'Mr. Eggleston, it would look like stealing for me to take the salary and be absent from my duty; and I can not do it.'"

From many letters upon Judge Foraker's resignation we select but a few to furnish appreciatory extracts.

From Judge Harmon:

". . . Sorrow was the first feeling; and it still fills my mind. . . I can only say, God go with you wherever you go, and compensate me by many years of friendship for the few years of official companionship I am to lose. . . . In the three years we have spent together here I have come to love you as a brother. I long since passed the point of mere respect and admiration. I consider you as one of those friends a man rarely makes when he has reached our age—a friend who not only fills the romantic idea of youth, but meets the requirements of mature judgment. . . I am sad and lonely . . . Knowing it can not remain a secret, I mentioned it to some friends of the bar. The feeling is unanimous that the bench and bar sustain a great loss in your leaving the bench. They talk of petitioning you to reconsider, etc. . . Judge Hoadly and others have telegraped the governor . . ."

From Judge Worthington:

". . . I can not express my regret, and that of every member of the bar I have met and they have been many. If in one year of judicial service that opens before me I can gain the confidence and respect of the bar to one third of the extent that it has been given to you . . . I shall feel highly gratified."

Judge O'Connor, who expressed his regret at the resignation of Judge Foraker, and the cause of it, hoped that he would recall it, and take rest and travel; that "the superior court is so advanced in work that absence would be without the slightest detriment to the public, or if at a slight disadvantage, the public loss would be nothing compared with its loss" if the resignation is persisted in. The Judge said:

"I know the feeling among the bar is unanimous that there would be irreparable injury in losing you from the bench; and they are also unanimous in wishing you to take the necessary rest and vacation. Therefore I hope you will regard these earnest wishes of your friends, the bar, and the public and withdraw your resignation. Do not hesitate on account of any idea of false delicacy about receiving your salary while absent from the court house. The public, not only would not so regard it, but would look upon it as the only proper course to take The public could far better afford to pay you many months salary than to lose your services, when you will, in all probability, be able to resume your duties, with all your ability, vigor, and usefulness, in the fall."

Judge Force telegraphed Judge Foraker from Washington City:
"I have telegraphed the governor not to accept your resignation. Judge Harmon and I will keep up your work."

From an eminent lawyer of Cincinnati:
". . . Your leaving will be a great public loss. . . I would comfort you in this hour of need and of peace. I can only lead you to Him who has said, 'Come unto me and I shall give you rest.'"

From another lawyer of Cincinnati:
". . . I always found you to be the same good-hearted friend, trying to help every one."

The *Gazette*, (Cin.) April 12, 1882: "Judge Foraker has earned the admiration of the best practitoners at the bar by his promptness and ability."

The *Commercial* said, April 12th: "One of the ablest and most popular men on the State Bench. * 'His retirement is a public loss.'"

The *Enquirer*, April 12th: "Able, fair, and universally respected. His loss will be deeply felt and deplored."

Law Bulletin: "Industrious, pains-taking, conscientious, . . . working out with care and good discernment all the questions submitted to his judgment."

Penny Post: "An able, conscientious, upright judge.

Times-Star: "Very sincerely and generally regretted."

Volksfreund: "Regretted by judges, lawyers, and the whole public. . ."

FORAKER'S BRIEFS.

Foraker's briefs as a lawyer are remarkable for seizing the salient points and presenting his case with no superfluous verbiage. His decisions as a judge are eminently perspicuous, composed in pure English, conforming to the use which is natural and reputable and present, and manifesting a remarkable disposition to state the whole case, using the methods of logic leading to the conclusion. A learned jurist remarked that for a judge of his few years in life and at the bar, his decisions and their presentation are unexcelled, and are indeed models of their kind; that he is " able to see the point in a case and to state the conclusions in a clear and concise manner. He is a sound, forcible reasoner, and has good judgment. He has never debased himself or degraded his friends in seeking office."

His charge to the jury in a case of popular interest has been quoted as a remarkable example of legal and evidential analysis. Its conclusion illustrates the character of the man, in whom the public is now much interested:

"I need not say that you have nothing to do with consequences. I will not call your attention to the fact that you are not to consider the person of the plaintiff, nor of defendant. Courts and juries can accomplish the purposes of their creation by only conscientiously doing their duty, without regard to parties or results."

Thus spoke the incorruptible judge, uninfluenced by wealth of the parties or by popular considerations.

ALWAYS A REPUBLICAN.

Foraker was a Republican youth and his first vote was cast for Republican candidates.

Senator Sherman says Judge Foraker has carried the Republican banner in war and in peace, without halting by the wayside.

Judge Foraker did not regard the Republican party as an association to obtain the spoils of office, but as born of the conscience of the people; its motive, justice; its purpose, to restore the government to it original lines, moving forward with the boldness of earnest conviction, denouncing slavery as an outrage and a crime, assailing the doctrine that capital should own labor, seeing in the constitution abundant power to repress slavery, promote education, foster industry, encourage internal improvement, establish free homesteads and promote free discussion. He did not regard the victory of 1860 as a transfer of power from the Democratic to the Republican party, but as the beginning of a new life, which conquered the great rebellion, raised an army, constructed a navy, maintained the public credit, destroyed slavery, and provided for development. He says our wonderful prosperity has not come by chance, but is the effect of the political logic of the Republican party of 1860.

NO SPOILS OF OFFICE.

Judge Foraker could not consistently vote with the Democratic party, as he did not seek the spoils of office. He could not vote with the Democratic party, because of its views of the States and the Constitution; because the Democratic party asserted state sovereignty at the command of the slave power; because the Democratic party brought on the war of secession; because the Democratic party (though many individual Democrats were patriotic) opposed the subduing of the rebellion and enforcing the unity of the Republic; and because Democratic organizations resisted the measures of the Government. He could not join the Democratic party because its last administration of affairs brought the government to the verge of bankruptcy, had defied the constitution in eleven states, and arrayed an army against the nation; because the party had never apologized for its errors nor retracted its opinions; because this party was the enemy of free elections and of a pure ballot, the enemy of American industry. He realized that the patriotic element of the Democratic party had largely come into the Republican party, and that the Democratic party had become an artifice for office — controlled and manipulated by office-hunters; that the Democratic party had ceased to exist, in the sense of a body of citizens formed around a political question to effect a political object by united action to that political end, and that the last act of the party organized to uphold and enlarge the area of slavery, was to organize a rebellion of slave provinces in support of its political idea, and that the Democratic party was without reason of existence after the rebellion was crushed and now it exists by force of habit, inherited prejudice, or appetite for office.

FREEDOM AND CIVIL RIGHTS.

Supporting the war as a soldier, in times of peace he favored reconstruction measures to secure the fruits of victory and to establish the freedom and civil rights of the late slaves. In 1874, Judge Foraker, at a Republican mass meeting at Cincinnati, on the civil rights question, said:

"The object of this bill is to prevent masked marauders from burning negro school-houses, shooting negro school teachers, and keeping this innocent and inoffensive people in a state of terror, which retards their development and corrupts and demoralizes society and politics in a hundred ways. And it is right, and the Republican party is for it because it is right.

"When in Columbus the other day, I stood in our capitol building and looked with admiring gaze upon that magnificent painting, which adorns its walls, of "Perry's Victory on the Lake." There, in the midst of the death-storm of that terrible conflict, as gallant looking as any one of the brave faces surrounding the Commodore, is a full-blooded representative of the African race. And thus it has always been since our government was founded, on land and on sea, in adversity and prosperity, through peace and through war, this race has been ever present with us, and never once has its faith faltered, its devotion lagged, or its courage failed.

"They have justly earned their citizenship, and they have earned it in such a way as that for us not to protect them in it would be the basest ingratitude and wrong—ingratitude and wrong for which the nation would deserve to sink to rise no more."

* * * * * * * * *

JUDGE FORAKER'S NOMINATION

Judge Foraker's nomination for governor was spontaneous in southern Ohio, and soon became popular throughout the State as candidates were canvassed. It was not sought for by Foraker. No efforts were made to secure the nomination. No whiskey nor unworthy devices, and no money were employed to affect votes. No certificates was furnished that he "satisfied his appetite for spirituous liquors," and that he was "neither a temperance man nor a Sunday fanatic."

When it came to the serious determination of the large and able convention gathered from all over the State, there was but one voice and but one unanimous acclamation for the farmer and soldier boy of Rocky Creek.

NOBLE TESTIMONY.

The following extracts from an interesting correspondence between the colored people and Judge Foraker, shows the grateful regard of the former and the noble sentiments of the Judge, who places suffrage upon pure manhood, and who bears his testimony for the Christian religion and for a pure domestic life.

The Judge regards the building up of families as the epitomized history of the American people for more than two hundred years—the central idea at Jamestown, at Plymouth Rock, at Charlestown, at Philadelphia, at Baltimore; by the Puritans, by the Cavaliers, by the Quakers, and by the Roman Catholics; the family, the social, and the political unit of America.

The colored people invited the Judge to a camp-meeting. They said, (June 19, 1883):

* * * * * * * * *

"We are religious people of color, and are Methodists. We remember those who have labored for our cause in the political field and on the field of battle. Joshua Giddings was not a Methodist, yet he was an Ohio champion of our cause. Salmon P. Chase was an Episcopalian, yet he never wavered in his devotion to the cause of our emancipation and elevation. We shall never forget the late Speaker of the House and our Republican Representatives, who carried on the memorable struggle for a fair count and a free ballot, and which seated our brethren, Smalls and Lynch. We are not ignorant as to your history and your early devotion on the battle field to the cause of our race. We have read your speeches and we trust you.

We know your mother to be a plain, old-fashioned Methodist, and we believe you to revere her religious principles.

Now can you not come up and give us an address of advice and encouragement?

* * * * * * * * *

To this the Judge replied:

CINCINNATI, June 23, 1883.

REV. AND DEAR SIRS:—Your kind letter of June 19, I find before me upon my return to the city. Make my apology to your associates for my seeming neglect.

It is now so very late in the week, and my previous engagements for this day and to-morrow are of such a character, that it is impossible for me to accept the invitation so kindly extended. Please return my thanks to your associates and the laity assembled, and express to them my appreciation, not only of their courtesy, but, also, of the good work in which they are engaged.

If our colored brethren will but continue in the future to cultivate religion and morality as they have in their free past, the day is not far distant when they will have conquered all prejudices that may have arisen, because of their being changed from serfs to citizens.

Religion and well-ordered domestic life, are the foundation of good and stable government. Without them the blessings of liberty and prosperity may be lost to us in anarchy and despotism.

The purity of the ballot box must be preserved. The franchise bestowed upon the men of your race because of their manhood, and not because of their color, must be enjoyed by you without fear or menace all over our land. With sentiments of regard, I am

Yours truly, J. B. FORAKER.

Robert Harlan wrote June 15, 1883:

"I know of my own personal knowledge that he has always been an earnest friend and supporter of my race in its struggle for its rights.

I remember well to have heard him make a speech to a mass meeting at Lower Market in this city, in 1874, when the civil rights bill was pending, in which he took a strong ground in favor of it, saying it was right, and that the Republican party could not hesitate about making it a law."

This is a portion of the speech of Judge Foraker alluded to by Mr. Harlan:

CIVIL RIGHTS BILL.

Another question about which the Democratic soul is troubled, is the Civil Rights Bill. This is not to be wondered at, however, for the poor, innocent colored man has always been a "bugaboo" to the Democracy. They have always been the enemy to this unfortunate race, and I suppose we can always count upon their opposition in advance to any proposition looking to the improvement of their condition.

The Civil Rights Bill does not confer upon the colored man a single legal right which he does not already possess.

For every colored man in this country has already the full legal right to sleep and eat in any hotel in the land, ride upon any common carriage, attend any public school, in short, do and enjoy any and all things that any other American citizen as such, can enjoy. Here in the North he enjoys these rights. The Civil Rights Bill does not therefore affect us here. But throughout the south the colored man is still called a "niggah," and he is not only denied these rights, but he is unceremoniously and unhumanly murdered and outraged if he dares to insist upon them.

The negroes have been made free and have been made citizens, and clothed with all the rights and powers that pertain to the American citizens. It is unnecessary to rehearse the process and causes whereby this result has been reached. Sufficient it is to say that even the Democracy, in order to secure any favor whatever before the people, have been compelled to recognize the propriety and justness of this action, so earnest are the people in their approbation of it. And even the Democracy have been compelled to pledge themselves to maintain this condition of things, and take no step backward. If it was right then, as the whole country says it was, to make a citizen out of a negro, it is not only right now, but the duty of the government to secure him in the enjoyment of all that the title carries with it.

YOUNG MEN'S CANDIDATE.

Judge Foraker, as the young men's candidate, is a bright example to young men of the fruits of an honest, industrious, studious, temperate, patriotic, filial, and even religious life; that there is something that gives success earlier than strong liquors, money, and demagoguism. Our first voters, our young men, will judge of Foraker by his life and his acts as they will judge of the party of which he is now the accepted leader in Ohio. Judge Foraker with his party fought for and maintained the integrity of the Union against secession and state-rights. He with the Republican party declared slavery a curse; was with it for the freedom of all men and in clothing more than four million slaves in the garb of liberty and the full rights of citizen manhood. He was on the battle-field, when the party now opposing him declared the war a failure and was demanding an ignoble peace. He fought against the party that would have purchased peace at any price, at the expense of justice and the freedom of the slaves. He represents a party that turned out the rascals twenty years ago—turned out those who stole the money in the treasury; the rascals who rifled the arsenals, and who attempted to annihilate the Union. He is to day opposed to turning in the rascals who have caused the distress of our war, taxation, and the life sorrow of our households by the loss of father and brother and son.

IS HE UNKNOWN?

It will thus be seen that Judge Foraker is not an unknown man and is not without an enviable record; that he is known to the soldiers for his gallant bravery; that he is known as a lawyer at one of the strongest bars in the United States; that he is known as an able and careful jurist; that he is known to the colored people for his bold and strong advocacy of their rights; that he is known as the friend of the mechanic and of the laborer and of the farmer; that he is known among the students and graduates of colleges; that he is known where sweet domestic life is valued; that he is known as a man of Christian integrity and of Christian principle; that he is known as the incorruptible politician, who seeks no office and wins no distinction by vile methods and the improper use of money; that he is known in his own county, in the chief city of Ohio, throughout the state, and is becoming known all over this land, not as a rich man and not as a mere politician; and that he is unknown as Lincoln was, as Grant was, as Hays was,—and to be known as the next Governor of Ohio!

A Georgia paper candidly admits that Judge Foraker "has proved that he has in him the stuff of which governors are made. He is not afraid of the people. He appeals like a man to their reason and conscience, and discusses public affairs with the power of a master in reasoning and debate.

Senator Sherman thus spoke:

"Judge Foraker, the nominee of the Republican party, is a Republican soldier, who, as such, served his country when he was young. He has since been educated by his own efforts, and has attained an honorable distinction as a lawyer and a judge. His speeches are clear, bold, and manly, and express without evasion the principles of the Republican party—in favor of the protection of American labor, and in favor of the taxing the traffic in liquor and beer. In his speeches there is nothing evasive or uncertain."

Hon. Mr. Townsend, thus:

"Foraker, by his clear, practical, plain, common sense reasoning, is taking wonderful hold of the people. He is a fine stump-speaker. He never utters what can embarrass him or the cause of truth."

Gen. Gibson, thus:

"I regard him as one of the most successful campaign orators Ohio has ever produced. He speaks with ease and grace, his words are well chosen, sincere and impressive, and have an effective influence upon his audience. He comes before the public unpreceeded by a great reputation, and his hearers are astonished that they never knew him before. His character is perfect, his record clear, and his ability large. He is the cleanest and best man for Governor the State has known for thirty years, and, possibly, excepting John Brough, the ablest stumper. I told Hoadly when he was at my house in Tiffin, a short time ago, that he would suffer defeat if he allowed himself to go before the people in a joint discussion with Foraker.

Hon. General Noyes, late minister to France, said to the people of the Scioto Valley, in mass meeting assembled:

"The Republican party on the other hand, proud of its past and confident of its future, has consistently placed in nomination a man who was born a Republican, and who has remained one all his life; a Union soldier who has fought for his country, with a gun to his shoulder and a knapsack on his back; one who did not seek the nomination for Governor, but whom the office sought; a brilliant lawyer, an able debater, an upright, patriotic gentleman. Having called him away from a successful practice of his profession, we propose to elect him. What the future have in store we can not tell, but we may be sure Judge Foraker will deserve whatever honor may be in reserve for him."

THE PEOPLE IN EARNEST.

As we go to press, these are specimen reports from the meetings Judge Foraker is addressing:

LANCASTER, O., Sept. 3.

"Judge Foraker addressed one of the finest and largest mass meetings here this afternoon that has been held in this city for years. Everybody was surprised at the great crowd, which exceeded any meeting held during the last Presidential campaign. The City Hall was packed to its utmost capacity, hundreds being turned away for want of room. The Judge's speech was another of his masterly arraignments of the Democratic party, and held the vast audience enrapt until its close. He explained at length and to their satisfaction the wool issue, showing just what it was, and what the opposition were trying to make of it. He also showed by his matchless argument just how impossible it is for Democratic success to be permanent.

One old Democrat who was an attentive listener to the Judge's address, said he did not wonder that Hoadly was sick; his only surprise was that he was alive at all.

He told what he had seen and heard among both Republicans and Democrats throughout the State, and gave the people a clear understanding of the true status of affairs. Foraker's facts and figures consummately upset the Democratic wool bugaboo, and clearly demonstrated what a ludicrous farce the whole thing is. It was a splendid speech, and has left a telling effect."

From Zanesville, Sept. 4:
"Judge Foraker addressed the greatest hall meeting ever held in this city. Never before in local annals have voters manifested so great a willingness to endure the discomforts of a crowd."

We now supplement the foregoing by extracts from addresses of Judge Foraker, further illustrating the man and his principles.

The following was delivered at a Banquet at the Burnett House, given to the Loyal Legion of Philadelphia, Pa., February 3, 1883, in response to the toast:

"OHIO."

MR. COMMANDER AND FELLOW-COMPANIONS:

No matter what the occasion may be, it is always a great pleasure to an Ohio man to talk about Ohio. Particularly is this true of what may be termed these war occasions, such as this to-night. For great as our state is considered to be in area, business, population, art, and education, in all that pertains to the civilization and improvement of mankind, she is transcendantly greater still in all that relates to the part taken by her in the great struggle. From the firing of the first gun on Fort Sumter, until the surrender of Lee at Appomattox, she was continually at the very fore front, side by side with Pennsylvania, and the best and bravest of her sister states. Her sons displayed their valor, poured out their blood, and laid down their lives on every battle-field of the war. And I need not repeat in this presence that she contributed to our cause in that contest vastly more than her two hundred regiments of gallant fighting men. There are some names that have become as familiar as household words, the world over, in which she claims an especial interest—names around which cluster all the dazzling glories of triumphant war,—names, also, at the mere mention of which is suggested all that is implied by the highest, purest, and most successful accomplishments of enlightened statesmanship. For while Pennsylvania was giving us Mead and Hancock and brave John Reynolds, Ohio was giving to the country, and to the cause of humanity, not only Grant and Sheridan, Sherman and McPherson, but Chase and Wade and Stanton, also. And these illustrious names I have mentioned barely begin the long list of her scarcely less distinguished soldiers and statesmen who in that great trial won imperishable renown in field and cabinet.

OHIO EVER DISTINGUISHED.

As proof conclusive that our success then was based on merit, that the war was merely an exceptional opportunity, we have been no less distinguished since. This is shown by smaller as well as by greater things.

When a year or two ago the Messrs. Scribners undertook the issue of campaign histories of the war, to be written by different persons, in twelve volumes, and cast about to see who from the thirty-eight states of the Union should be selected as the most fit for the important work, the result was that four of the twelve volumes were allotted to Ohio.

"Continually since the war, of our Supreme Court, the highest, judicial tribunal in the land, consisting of nine members, we have had two of the number, and one of them the Chief Justice. And during all this while we have had both the General and the Lieutenant-General of the Army; and during almost all this time we have held at least a fair share of the most important heads of departments, and of the most important posts of representation abroad.

And, notwithstanding this every excess of favor, we have been twice called upon, without the place being sought in either instance, to furnish a chief magistrate for the whole people; and twice we have responded,—with what eminent success you all do know.

GARFIELD AND HAYES.

"So long as the history of the American people shall be read and known among men, so long in the tenderest recesses of the heart will be held in grateful recollection and proud esteem the name of James A. Garfield.

"It would not be in good taste to speak in the presence of our other ex-president the warm words of praise with which all would be pleased to hear to his many virtues recounted. Suffice it to say, he regards it as one of the highest honors of his distinguished life to be present with us to-night as simply *companion* Rutherford B. Hayes.

"I think I can truthfully say for Ohio that her past, at least, is secure; and I know whereof I affirm when I say that we have confidence in the present, and hope for the future. We may not be called upon to furnish any more presidents, generals, chief justices, secretaries, or foreign ministers; but if so, that will be *your* fault and not *ours*. For I assure you we will not be discouraged thereby from keeping constantly on hand, and well advertised, an inexhaustible supply of the very best material. [Laughter.]

"I sincerely hope that these remarks will not excite apprehension in the minds of any of our visiting companions; for I am sure this Ohio acquisition has not as yet any designs upon the honors of this organization. On the contrary, I am quite positive that none of us expect offices right away. We expect to be required; and we shall be content with that—to patiently wait for all such matters until at least a reasonable probation shall have expired. I warn you though that we are a progressive class. We claim to be representative of our state; and being such, it is only fair to assume that when the expiration of this probation shall have come we will desire to be useful. From all I was able to learn from the speech of General Owen of the principles and purposes of this order, it is my judgment that it affords a first-class chance for the display of the talents of the average Ohio man. With its espousal of principles and its proclamation of purposes I know him to be entirely familiar. They have been his meat and drink all his life long. In fact, ever since good old Frances Dane wrote it down in his first organic law—the ordinance of 1787—for the government of the territory lying north-west of the river Ohio, that 'religion, morality, and knowledge were necessary to good government;' and that 'civil and religious liberty lay at the basis of all our constitutions and laws,' our Ohio man has had for his polar star what the charter of this order declares its principles to be. First, a firm belief and trust in Almighty God, under whose beneficence and guidance the triumphs of the war were achieved; and second,—and only second,—true allegiance to the United States of America, founded on fidelity and devotion to the constitution and laws of our government. [Loud applause and laughter.]

"With such antecedents as I have referred to, such an education as I have

described, and such aspirations as all concede us, I confidently predict that the future will afford us a chance, both in this order and outside of it, commensurate with the glorious grandeur of the past; and that as the years go gliding by, the name of Ohio, linked with and second only to that of Pennsylvania, shall continue, like that of Ben Adhem, to lead all the rest."
[Prolonged applause.]

THE BOYS IN BLUE.

A prophet is sometimes honored in his own home. Judge Foraker was so by the "Boys in Blue," at the soldier's reunion and fourth of July celebration of this year (1883), within the borders of his native county. Old veterans and their wives, not away from their neighborhood since the war, went twenty miles to see this Highland private, this hero of Atlanta.

How like a true man, with domestic and popular sympathies, how like Lincoln breaking forth, "why should the spirit of mortals be proud," was Foraker in his speech of this day among the neighbors, the friends, the men once boys on Rocky Creek. He spoke without notes, from a full heart. He spoke as Lincoln, and Garfield spoke, men poor in this world's wealth, but rich in the treasures of a noble heart. He said:

"Here I regard myself as in an especial sense in my own country; for here I am within the borders of Highland County, and when I come within the boundary lines of this county, I feel as though I had come within the walls of my own home, and on this account I can say, in response to the kind words of your chairman, that if there is any place on the face of the earth where I would rather enjoy the confidence and esteem of mankind than another, it is here; in this county where, as he has said, I was born and reared, and where for that reason I am better known than I can ever hope to become at any other place, and where I have friends that I know will always remain such without regard to any difference of opinion that may exist as to temporal concerns, and without regard to the varying fortunes and changes of life. For me to come into your midst is like gliding into a veritable haven of rest where all the frictions and buffetting contentions of an anxious and busy life, are for the time being, shut out by a general amity of feeling, and by sentiments of a kind and mutual regard.

.   .   .   .

"We are here to-day not only to celebrate the Fourth of July, but we have come here to perform this work in the name, in the honor, and under the direction of the Grand Army of the Republic.

"We are here, therefore, not only to pay honor to the initial work of the founders of these institutions of government, in the enjoyment of which it is our happy privilege to live, but also to pay honor to the men by whose services and sacrifices, patriotism and valor, these institutions of government have been preserved to us from the threatened wreck and ruin of rebellion. But for the works of the fathers, there never would have been any occasion for the services of the sons, and but for the services of the sons, that which the fathers did would have been done in vain. . . . .

"One hundred years of successful experience under a republican form of government, has taught us not only to regard the ideas and truths and principles embodied in the Declaration of Independence, as fundamental proposition with respect to the character of government and the rights of man, but it has also brought us to the point where it is well nigh impossible for us to realize that there ever was a time in the history of the world when they were not so regarded. . . . .

MAGNA CHARTA AND LUTHER.

"And yet, notwithstanding our fathers were lacking in these respects, notwithstanding they were without precedent, and without anything in the way of experience to guide them, they were not without the essentials of success. On the contrary, they had that without which there could have been no success, but with which success was inevitable, for they had that which nerved the hearts of the old Lords and Barons when they wrestled Magna Charta from King John, at Runnymede; they had that which filled the soul of brave old Luther, when he said: 'Yes sir, I will go into that city of Worms, though there be as many devils there as there are tiles on the roofs of the houses.'

"They had just convictions of right, and they had the courage of their convictions, and that was the key to the whole situation.

"For when men have a just and proper sense of duty, and then fearlessly undertake its performance, Providence never fails to lead them safely through, whatever consequences may result." . . . .

MEN MUST BE RIGHT.

That which they accomplished makes the most striking and brilliant illustration that has ever been given of the truth to which I adverted a moment ago, that all political movements must succeed when they are based on just convictions of right, and are fearlessly and boldly espoused and upheld. Their works make a fitting frontispiece for the grand career that this Nation has run. It was a work that never has and never will fail to impart inspiration and honesty of purpose to political organizations when called upon to grapple with those insidious evils that affect the morality of the people, and sap at the foundations of government. It was an example that exerted a most salutory influence on us while we were passing through the great struggles with slavery. It is a good example to bear in mind in connection with the contests now going on in this country, and no matter what may be the growth and complications of the future, we can always turn to this beginning of the fathers, with pleasure, pride and profit.

After describing the grandeur of our country, its present population, and its vast capabilities, the Judge continued:

But I do not make these suggestions for the purpose of exciting vanity. On the contrary, I make them to bring about a properly serious appreciation of the great trust that is confided in us—a trust that involves for all these millions of people and billions of property the preservation of our form of government, our constitution, our civil and religious liberty, our popular education, our equality before the law—a preservation, in short, of all that which makes us free, and makes us great, and makes us safe in the protection of our property and our lives.

In replying to the proposition that our institutions are not adapted to the conditions of the future, he said:

And remembering, as all must who passed through the trials of 1861-5, how this whole land was made to fairly blaze and burn by the unparalleled demonstrations of loyalty, patriotism and devotion to duty which we then witnessed, I can not doubt either the capacity or the determination of the people of this country to preserve its government and its institutions

PRACTICAL PATRIOTISM.

And yet, to do so, we must be for the future as we have been in the past, true to ourselves. I believe in a practical patriotism. I believe in taking care of America. To this end we should discard sentimental theories and pursue an administrative policy that is based on sound common sense. We should make this country independent of every other to the fullest extent that our situation and advantages will admit. We must take care of our labor and laboring men, to the end that they may have a just reward and an even chance in the race of life for those better and higher things that come with education and culture. We must develop our resources, multiply our industries, and make as much diversity of employment as possible, thus creating a domestic commerce that will make all the different parts of our country virtually dependent on each other, and lead on to the construction of railroads and canals, and other facilities for traffic and travel, thus tying ourselves together with the bonds of trade and interest which are far stronger and more enduring than any that can be forged by constitutional provision or legistative enactments.

WASHINGTON AND DANE.

And not only that, but man can not live by bread alone. Our fathers recognized this fact when they framed our government. They, therefore, framed it so as to encourage not only the greatest material prosperity possible, but also so as to encourage the highest intellectual and moral development of which mankind is capable. Washington reminds us of this in his farewell address, when he warns us to remember that the people are the sovereign power—that all rightful authority must emanate from them, and that, consequently, if we would have a good government, we must have a good people, and that to that end we must ever labor to inculcate among the people a disposition for knowledge and morality. Another of the greatest men that this country ever produced was Francis Dane. He was the author of "the ordinance of 1788 for the government of the territory lying nothwest of the River Ohio." This was the first organic law that the people of Ohio ever had. In it is expressed the idea to which I refer in the declaration that knowledge and morality are essential to good government. All the founders and all the great men of this government, from Washington to Garfield, have impressed upon us the same truth.

And above all things let us remember to preserve and inviolate the dignity and majesty of law. As Washington said, we have no sovereignty in this country except only the people. Law is their expressed will, and the officers of the law are only their agents. Whosoever undertakes to strike down law in this country, either by open violence or by exciting distrust, is aiming a deadly blow at the very life of the Nation.

GRAND ARMY—A FIRST BOOK.

Thus spoke this soldier to his comrades of the Grand Army of Republic in his own native county, July 4, 1883:

"I remember that one of the first books my father ever gave me was a history of the Revolution, bound in which was a *fac simile* copy of the Declaration of Independence, including the signatures thereto of all the signers. I can never forget how, in my boyish ambition, I envied those men the honor of having signed that instrument. I have no doubt you had the same kind of experience. But you didn't know then of the compensation that was in store for you. Your names can never be read on the Declaration of Independence, but they will be read so long as that declaration is remembered on the muster rolls of that grand army of a million men that sprang to the Nations rescue and stood like a wall of fire between the country and the country's danger. And to have your names written there is the highest honor that your country's service has permitted you to achieve in your day and generation. As I said a while ago, but for your services all that the fathers did would have been done in vain. The men who inaugurated the rebellion put themselves beyond the pale of reason at the outset. They wouldn't listen to argument. All the logic and all the eloquence of Webster, although absolutely unanswerable, were nevertheless unavailing. They wouldn't be convinced, and couldn't be persuaded. They had made up their minds that if they couldn't rule this Union they would break it up and destroy it. They invented their doctrine of State sovereignty for that purpose, and when, in their judgment, the time was ripe for it they invoked it, and involved this whole country in war to sustain it. But that which argument could not settle, shot and shell did. On three hundred bloody battle-fields, and in the blood of three hundred thousand of our slain fathers and brothers and sons it was written with the bayonet amid the storm-clouds of war that this is a Nation. Webster was vindicated and the Union was preserved. The character of our Constitution was taken out of all controvesy, and there was established for it, as one of its elementary features, that it was just what on its face it expressed itself to be, not a league between States, but the organic law of a great people, and as to the rights and powers by it delegated supreme over States and people alike. There were many good results of that war, but this was the richest prize we brought out of all that bloody struggle. Let us hold on to it. Let us keep it to the forefront.

1798.

Divide as we may about other matters, let us ever remember to stand shoulder to shoulder for this. When you hear a man talking about the reserved rights of the States and the resolutions of 1798, as we occasionally do, set him down as a man that no soldier can afford to listen to. So much we owe to the brave comrades we left behind when we marched home in victorious triumph. We owe so much to ourselves, and we especially owe it to our country and our posterity. Not that we would keep alive any of the animosities or prejudices of the war, but simply that we would have no foolishness about the preservation of what we won. We were in serious earnest then. There has been too much blood shed to permit of our becoming otherwise now.

No soldier wishes to keep alive any animosities or prejudices. On the contrary, it is our earnest hope that they may all perish with the hated doctrine of secession that originated them. We fought the South and compelled them to stay in the Union, not because we hated and despised them, but because they belonged to us, because they were part and parcel of us, because their country was our country, and their destiny was our destiny. We compelled them to stay in the Union, not that we might live together in jarring discord, but that we might have a perpetual peace and a common prosperity.

THE SECESSIONIST—THE REGICIDE.

We can rejoice to-day in the fact that the chasms of the war are being rapidly bridged over. You couldn't to-day give slavery back to the South as a free and gracious gift. They appreciate as keenly as anybody else can that the abolition of it was a great blessing for them. Their country is now everywhere prospering as it never did before, and the day is not far distant when the secessionist of 1861 will be known in this country only as the regicide is known in England. We will have a Union in fact as well as in name, and every section will vie with every other in a common devotion to a common flag, by which we will all be led in a common prosperity to a common destiny.

THE GALLANT UNKNOWN.

From the decoration-day address of 1869, at Hillsboro, which was delivered, says the *Highland News*, "with deep and earnest feeling, with grace and dignity, impressing all with the great ability of the young orator: "

"There are many graves in this land to-day, equally as deserving as the ones we have honored, about which no kind tribute-payers are gathered. Not all the bodies that fell by the ravages of our war sleep in our cemeteries.

"Far away in the woods, the thicket, the mountain gaps; on the barren plain, the deserted field, in a hundred kinds of hidden, obscure, and unfrequented places, wherever, on the hard-fought field, the deathful missil of the enemy reached and struck them down, lie and sleep another band—*the gallant unknown.*

"God, in his infinite wisdom and goodness, as though jealously reserving it unto himself, has thus deprived us of the pleasurable privilege of decorating their graves. But while he has done this, there is another pleasurable privilege and pleasurable duty, of which he has not deprived us, and that is of constantly remembering them, and praying him that he may annually stretch forth his hand and causing to descend "the earlier and the latter rains," make to grow thereon flowers even more luxuriant, more fragrant, and more enduring, than the ones which to-day have been scattered by the fair hands of these beautiful little girls upon the graves of our known; scattering there, I shall add, only that they may fade and whither, and perish, and pass away, typifying, as it were, the untimely snapping, and perishing, and passing away of the lives of those whom they are intended to honor."

CHEAP TRANSPORTATION.

From Judge Foraker's address at Cincinnati:

Although the question of cheap transportation is of vast importance, I can say but a word:

The Constitution of the United States confers upon Congress the power to regulate commerce among the states. No restrictions are placed upon its exercise. We contend that the provision was framed in the way, intentionally, that it might be broad enough to cover all times and circumstances. And hence, notwithstanding the fact that railroads were not known when the Constitution was framed, yet, inasmuch as they have become a chief means of commerce among the states, they are within the purview of the provision, as well as rivers, lakes and harbors.

Fortunately, before it ever entered into politics, this question was, quite a number of times, raised and passed upon by the courts, and in every such instance the provision was construed as we contend it should be. So far then as the right to exercise the power is concerned, it is no longer an open question. The democracy, true to their natural instincts, have doggedly arrayed themselves on the wrong side, and are amusing themselves with their ancient political Shibboleth, "unconstitutional."

The propriety of exercising this power is a question to be determined by the particular facts of a given case.

But when the facts are that millions of bushels of grain are raised in this country which never get to a market, and consequently never result in any profit to the producer, simply because the lines of railway passing through the different states lying between the markets and the points of production, charge unreasonably large freights, I think Congress should look after the matter and correct the evil, if there be any remedy, because so long as such a condition of things exists, agriculture is discouraged throughout vast territories of our country, and all kinds of improvement and progress are delayed and hindered.

This is the position af the Republican party, and it is the right position, for it is upon the side of the correct construction and a proper enforcement of a good law, framed by the wise fathers who made our constitution, to protect the people and aid the prosperity of the Government.

The financial platform of the Republican party to-day, as in the past, is nothing more nor less than a pledge that we will continue in the future as we have done in the past to retrench and economize, and cut down the expenses of the Government to the lowest possible sum consistent with a wise and intelligent policy. That we will lighten the burdens of taxation resting upon the people just as rapidly, and just as much as proper regard for the highest interests of all will allow. That we will continue to faithfully and diligently collect the revenues, and honestly and promptly apply them to the satisfaction and diminution of the public debt, until, in this honest, straight forward, practical, common-sense way we have, by easy and natural stages, and without shock, precipitation or derangement, led the country back, as we have been leading it, to the solid basis of specie payments, and then on to an entire discharge of this enormous indebtedness.

We propose to pay the debt simply by paying it, and by paying it dollar for dollar until every obligation of the Government has been fully redressed, to the last farthing.

To this end we propose neither expansion nor contraction, but the application of every surplus dollar we may be able to get into the treasury to the payment of interest bearing bonds held by private individuals in whose hands they are non-taxable, and yield no support whatever.

NO PATIENCE WITH TREASON.

At Spring Grove and Wesleyan cemeteries, Cincinnati, May 31, 1879, Judge Foraker said:

"If any man think there is less patriotism in the country, less devotion to the Union, less love and affection for the old flag—let him look abroad over the land on this National Decoration Day and be undeceived. Let him witness the impressive spectacle of a whole people gathered in sorrow, but with the choicest flowers of spring time in their hands about the graves of their dead soldiers. Let him listen to the patriotic hymns that will be sung, the fervid sentiments of patriotism that will be expressed, and from these things let him learn that the loyalty of this people is as unquestioned as ever. Yea, let him learn more than that! Let him learn, especially if he be a Confederate Brigadier in Congress demanding that every vestige of war legislation be torn from the statute book, or a so-called "silver tongued orator" from the Blue Grass regions talking about the rebel dead being martyrs to a holy cause that is to be revived and vindicated in the near future, let him I say, especially, if he be one of these classes, learn that by so much as we mourn these lives by so much is there less of patience for treason than ever before.

* * * * * * *

Abraham Lincoln was elected President of the United States. There was no pretense that any section of the country, or any individual even, would be interfered with in the enjoyment of any right or privilege guaranteed under the Constitution and the laws of the land. But that did not matter; the galling fact still remained that the control of the government had passed out of the hands of the South. The North had gained ascendancy in national affairs, and was likely to maintain it, and that was enough. The chivalric sons of the South wouldn't submit to any such outrage as that. The time against which the conspirators had plotted was come. A practical application of the doctrine they had taught was now in order.

SHORT WORK WITH TRAITORS.

And, consequently, in braggart speeches, for which the authors ought to have been then and there arrested and hanged by the neck until dead, we were told that the Union of the fathers was dissolved, that the Constitution was torn into shreds and tatters, that the South had seceded, and that all they asked of us was that we would quietly remain at home and behave ourselves while they went their way in peace. Not until these initial proceedings in the great drama of secession were actually transpiring, did our people awaken to anything like a proper appreciation of the infamous character of the doctrine that had been invoked. But then it was, as in bewildered amazement and astonishment they found themselves confronted with the necessity of a choice between the calamities of a civil war or a dissolution of the Union, that the fires of patriotism began to burn in their bosoms—fires of patriotism that found fitting expression at the lips of that gallant old patriot when he commanded, "If any man attempt to haul down the American flag, shoot him on the spot." Fires of patriotism that were shortly to blaze into a flame that would astonish and excite the admiration of the whole world. For the same match that fired the first shot against old Fort Sumter, and the stars and stripes waving over her, at the same time fired the patriotic hearts of the loyal millions of the North, and there followed the most magnificent demonstration of patriotism and devotion that the world ever witnessed. Business pursuits, private interests, family and social ties, the pleasures and comforts of home, attachments, endearments, affections—everything that stood in the way was instantly sacrificed by a million gallant heroes who sprang to the nation's rescue."

ONE COUNTRY—ONE FLAG.

At the Camp Fire, October 5, 1880, of Geo. H. Thomas' Post No. 13, G. A. R., the subject of Judge Foraker's address was "One Country and One Flag." After giving the history of the two civilizations, that from Plymouth Rock and that from Jamestown, the Judge proceeds:

BOYS IN BLUE.

"Jealousy ripened into hostility and hostility brought blood. 'One country and one flag' would no longer answer. Slavery demanded two countries and two flags. They claimed it as a legal and constitutional right. Webster met their claim, annihilated their arguments, and showed conclusively that they had no such right. . . . He appealed to the recollections of the past, when Massachusetts and South Carolina stood shoulder to shoulder acknowledging Independence. But they steeled their hearts and the clash of arms came. When the boom from the guns at Fort Sumter rolled up over our land its reverberating echoes filling our valleys and breaking against our mountain sides, it was as a long roll calling a nation to duty—a long roll that was answered by a million men; a million men who were not educated and professional soldiers; a million men to whom war was no opportunity to work out individual ambitions and aspirations; but a million volunteers—citizen soldiers—a million men to whom war was only a horrible and bloody evil to be resorted to only for the accomplishment of great purpose, and then only when nothing else would answer; a million men who were working out their individual ambitions and aspirations in the peaceful pursuits of civil life; a million men who had homes and families and professions and farms and work shops to leave behind men, therefore, who sacrificed all these things and stepped between their country and their country's danger with that solemn and determined resolve that only men can take who are actuated by a sense of responsible duty; a resolve that come what would—come separation from home, from wives, from children and loved ones; come exposures, come hardships, come sickness, come battle, come death, come whatsoever God in his providence might send there should be in this country but one government and one flag, and that should be the government of the constitution and the flag that our fathers gave us.

"These were the 'Boys in Blue,' and when the boys in blue thus took up the discussion it meant there was to come an end of it; that we were to have no more unavailing arguments; that if words wouldn't convince shot and shell should; and they did.

* * * * * * *

ONE NATION.

"If there be anything at all that soldiers cannot afford to listen to argument about; about which they cannot afford to admit that there is room for argument; anything which they are under obligation to at all times treat with impatient indignation, it is that damnable heresy that is eternally arraying the State against the Nation.

"If the war accomplished anything at all it was the overthrow of that idea, and the establishment upon its ruins of that other idea that the American people are an American Nation. A nation for Ohio or New York or

Massachusetts, nor yet for South Carolina or Alabama or Georgia—not a nation for the States at all, but a nation for the people and the whole people of all the States of the whole Union.

* * * * * * * *

INFAMOUS IDEA.

I hope the day is not far distant when it shall be established that the general government may lawfully stretch forth its arm of protecting power to unprotected citizens at home as well as abroad. It is an infamous idea that the national government can not go into any State of the Union and compel any citizen to render its service against its enemies, and that when he shall have faithfully served it and been discharged, and shall have returned to his home, his State lines are to rise up so high about him that the government he has protected at the peril of his life cannnot cross over them to his protection in the enjoyment of all the rights to which he is entitled under a Republican form of government.

"It is not enough to answer that it is the duty of the State to afford this protection.

"It is not enough, because by unpunished barbarities, horrible enough to shock and disgrace savages, we have been afforded most abundant as well as most painful evidence that the State may not do its duty. I hope the bloody outrages of Hamburg, Coushatta, and the murder of the Chisholms will never again be repeated to disgrace our land and civilization, but should the misfortune of their re-enactment be visited upon us, I earnestly trust there may be no counterpart to the great crime for which we, as citizens, must bear the responsibility, in a lack of power on the part of government somewhere to visit speedy and fitting justice upon the perpetrators.

"I want to see, therefore, not only one government and one flag for our whole country, but I want that government to be strong enough to go into every nook and corner of the whole land, not simply to collect its revenues, its taxes on whisky and tobacco, but what is infinitely more important and more to our credit, to protect the lives of its citizens and redress their wrongs and grievances. And I want the flag that is to stand for this government to symbolize all this to every man who looks with allegiance upon its folds. With such a country and such a flag there is nothing of patriotic reverence and affection that they will not enjoy. With such a country and such a flag, there is nothing of strength that will not be added unto us as a Nation. With such a country and such flag we can press forward into the future with a confident assurance that there is a destiny for us commensurate in grandeur and magnificence with the advantages we possess."

Of Judge Foraker's Decoration day Address at Springfield, May 30, 1881, the Springfield *Republic* said:

"The mention of names of well-remembered commanders brought the applause of the audience every time; and frequently was this repeated at other periods of the grand effort of twenty-five minutes' duration. Attention was really strained at times. At affecting passages, particularly the references to mothers and wives of our dead soldiers, many eyes filled involuntarily. The address was in full keeping with the spirit of the hour, unambiguous, often impassioned, and delivered with impressiveness which had a marked effect. Although a comparative stranger in Springfield, the gentleman will be remembered with affection and admiration by all that vast audience. He unmistakably created a very favorable impression among the most intelligent class of people.

The Judge said:

"This imposing demonstration has a wide and an inspiring significance. It means more than that these men were brave. It means more than that they were our fathers and sons and husbands and brothers. It means more than that we loved them. It means more than that we owe them a debt we can never discharge for a nation preserved by the lives they surrendered. It means more than a tribute of honor and gratitude and affection for the dead. Its chief lesson is for the living.

SOLDIER'S SACRIFICES NOT FORGOTTEN.

"It means that the sacrifices of that time are not to be forgotten; that they are to be kept in perpetual remembrance as the price paid for a nation purified and preserved; kept in remembrance, however, not to keep alive any bitterness or hatred or prejudice that may have been engendered by that strife, but kept alive to cultivate and strengthen and cherish in our recollections that spirit of patriotism, loyalty, and devotion to duty that inspired our heroic dead.

"It means that these men died for the cause of all mankind, and that their lives and sacrificial deaths are worthy to be held in perpetual remembrance and continual honor as bright examples for the emulation of the living. It means that we do not propose to have to do that work over again. It means that here is the most sacred spot that can be found; here in the most solemn presence that can be invoked; here on these graves, as upon the altars of our country, we come to pledge ourselves anew to the preservation of that nationality and those eternal principles of truth and justice for which these men were slain. Then,

"'Cover them over with beautiful flowers,
Deck them with garlands, these brothers of ours,
Lying so silent by night and by day.
Sleeping the years of their manhood away;
Years they had marked for the joys of the brave,
Years they must waste in the moldering grave.
All the bright laurels they wasted to bloom,
Fell from their hopes when they fell to the tomb.
Give them the meed they have won in the past;
Give them the honors their futures forecast;
Give them the chaplets they won in the strife;
Give them the laurels they won with their life.
Cover them over—yes, cover them over—
Parent, husband, brother, and lover;
Crown in your hearts these dead heroes of ours,
And cover them over with beautiful flowers.'

It is a grand and inspiring work in which we are engaged. Let us be careful not to abuse its privileges or pervert its purposes. Let us not permit ourselves to be blinded or misled by that sickly and inconsistent spirit of sentimentality that has been here and there manifesting itself in a disposition to blot out all distinctions by scattering flowers alike over the Blue and the Gray.

NO BITTERNESS.

"Toward the dead soldiers of the South no heart can hold any bitterness, but it does not follow that we should pay them honor. We know they were brave; we know they fought gallantly, and, for the sake of argument, we can afford to admit that they believed they were right. But all that does not and can not change the everlasting fact that they were not right, but wrong, and criminally and treasonably wrong, too. All that does not change the fact that they made this land to run red with rivers of blood, and filled our homes with widows and orphans, and weeping and morning, in a causeless and wicked endeavor to tear down and destroy the best government the wisdom of man ever devised, simply because its genius was Liberty, that they might establish for themselves, in its stead, another, based upon and inspired by human slavery. In their graves with them we can bury everything except, only, a vigilant watchfulness against a repetition of their treason; but to decorate their graves, at the same time and in the same way we decorate the graves of our fallen Union soldiers, would be to do an act that would be worse than a crime against the dead, and to teach a lesson that would be worse than meaningless to the living.

BOYS IN BLUE NOT TO BE DISHONORED.

"Whatever else we may do, may God save us from a criminal stupidity that would dishonor the boy in blue, who fought for the Union and the Constitution, the equality of all men before the law, and all the other great and grand ideas that underlie and vitalize our institutions, by holding him up to posterity as on an equality with the men who fought to uphold treason, destroy our nationality, and make shipwreck of all the bright hopes of self-government. Let us not do ourselves the injustice nor posterity the injury of indicating by such an act that we no longer know any difference between the men who saved us and the men who would have destroyed us.

GLORIOUS OLD MOTHERS.

On the contrary, when we are done decorating our Union dead, if we have any flowers to spare, instead of destroying all the good we have done by throwing them upon the Confederate dead, let us rather, in God's name, intensify the lesson we teach by lovingly scattering them over the glorious old mothers of the war; the glorious old mothers who followed us down into the smoke and fire of battle with fervent prayers to heaven for our preservation and for the success of our cause; the glorious old mothers who, with heroic words of patriotism, steeled the hearts and nerved the arms of the gallant boys with whom they now are sleeping; or over the tender and loving wives who, with hearts broken with grief, have prematurely followed down into the damp, cold grave the husbands they kissed farewell forever amid war's wild alarms; or let us weave them into bright chaplets with which to crown the children of our patriot dead—the children to whom the preservation of the nation meant orphanage and poverty and destitution; or in some other way let us do something that will be patriotic—something we can respect ourselves for —something that will redound to the honor of our dead, the credit of ourselves, and the good of our country.

Until the time shall come when all talk about the right and truth and justice of the "lost cause" shall be hushed forever—until equal and exact justice is freely accorded to every American citizen in every state in the Union—until the exercise of all the rights, privileges, and franchises of citizenship is as free and untrammeled wherever the flag floats as our slain heroes intended it to be, let us have a jealous care as to what we do, even with our flowers. Not, as I have already said, because of any feeling toward the dead, but for the effect upon the living. We must never forget that our Government is a Government of the people. It will be whatever the people make it, and they will make it whatever they are themselves; and what the people will be depends upon what they are taught.

Because of the teachings of our fathers the war found us ready to meet it. We have made the country free; we have made it a fundamental idea that the constitution is the organic law of the whole people; that the

General Government, as to the powers and functions delegated to it, is supreme from ocean to ocean, and that the American people are an American nation. These are grand results. They are worth all the blood and treasure they have cost. It was our highest duty to secure them then; it is our highest duty to preserve them now.

A PATRIOTIC IRISHMAN.

A patriotic Irishman, who had lost his mother while he was in the patriotic army, was so affected by the Springfield address in its allusion to decorating the graves of the mothers who had given their sons to the war, that he walked many miles to see and hear the man, at Leesburg, who had heart enough to make such a speech. He went away from the Leesburg address saying, "That's the man for me, with a head level enough to command an army, and a heart big enough to capture the soldiers."

THE UNITED STATES—OUR COUNTRY.

Judge Foraker made an address January 13, 1881, before the society of Ex-Army and Navy officers, whose names are a synonym of valorous deeds; the theme being "The United States—our Country." The Judge adverted to our vast domain; to our self-government; to our civil and religious liberty; to our thrift, ingenuity, enterprise and industry; to our illustrious past, the inspiring present and the grand future, and to our grave and increasing responsibilities: He concludes:

"Grave, therefore, as are the responsibilities that rest upon us, yet I confidently predict that they will be fully and faithfully discharged, and that as the years go by we shall not only continue to increase in numbers and grow in wealth, but that we shall see all sectional prejudices and animosities forgotten and swallowed up in a generous rivalry and a common pride; that we shall continue to be one people, maintaining one government, supporting the same Constitution, and following a common flag to a common destiny, thus verifying the prophetic assertion of the lamented Lincoln when he said, at Gettysburg, in those beautiful, impressive, and ever memorable words: "Government of the people, by the people and for the people, shall not perish from the earth."

LAW AND ORDER.

Judge Foraker presided Sunday night, 1882, at a meeting of citizens in the Methodist church, Walnut Hills, in the interest of law and order. In his address he said that the majesty and dignity of law must be preserved. * * He had an abiding faith in Providence and the common sense of the American people. * * Morality is the foundation of the Republic, and thus morality is dependent on religion.

THE LAST DOLLAR TO BE PAID.

Before the Lincoln Club of Cincinnati, June 23, 1883, the Judge said:

"You all remember how, under the name and banner of the Democratic party, especially here in Ohio, all the disloyalty, faithlessness and demagogy of this country seemed to clasp hands, and join in a common effort to besmirch and disgrace and dishonor that country and that government which the enemies of the government on the field of battle had failed to overthrow and destroy. You all remember how it was through long years of earnest argument and effort that the country was finally led back and placed on the firm rock of specie resumption, and the people were brought to a settled determination that all the obligations of the government should be faithfully paid to the last dollar. * * * *

PROGRESS FOR THE RIGHT.

But the mission of the Republican party is progress—and progress for the right; and where right and justice demand it, there is always a way to reconcile differences and conquer difficulties. We have never failed to find that way in the past; we shall never fail to find it now. Yea, we have already found it, and, as in the past, the defeats we have sustained have but served to the point, and give effect to the victories that have followed in succeeding years, so, too, will it prove that the defeat of last year will but serve to give emphasis and lend brilliancy to the magnificent triumphs of this. [Long and enthusiastic applause.] * * * *

GERMAN REPUBLICANS.

I say it is a slander upon the German Republicans of Ohio to say that they will withhold their support from the Republican party in this campaign. [Applause.] I think I know something of the German Republicans of Ohio. I went soldiering with some of them twenty years ago. [Tremendous applause.] With the old Ninth Ohio, made up of German Republicans living here in Cincinnati, I helped to carry our flag up the side of Mission Ridge. I was with them in such a way that I know what they endured of the privations and hardships of a soldier's life. I know how they bared their breasts to the storm of battle, and with what loyalty, devotion and patriotism they at all times stood by the flag, the country, and the cause of their adoption. [Ringing applause repeated several times.] Yes, I know, too, something about them since the war, and in time of peace. I know that the German Republicans of Ohio are an intelligent, fair-minded, liberal-minded, and honest-minded class of people, who have cast in their lot with us in good faith and for good purposes. I know that they believe in good government, in the protection of society, and in advancing the welfare and best interests of their commonwealth, as much as do any other class of people we have in the State of Ohio. [Great applause.] And being of that class of people, I say it is a slander, and a libel upon them, to say and print it of them, that they will withhold their support of the Republican party simply because it has enacted legislation that is manifestly just.

On August 2, 1883, before an audience of 2,000 people the Judge spoke at Corning, Perry Co., Ohio: * * * *

PERRY'S VICTORY.

"There is something in the name of *Perry* County, for, when that name of Perry County is spoken it instinctively recalls one of the most illustrious heroes that this country has ever produced. ["Good!"] And along with the recollection of the old hero comes back fresh to our minds one of the most brilliant achievements of which the naval history of this country gives us any account.

THE COLORED REPUBLICANS.

And I want to say to these colored men whom I see so well represented here to-day that they do well to come up to this Convention along with the other Republicans of Perry County. [Applause.] Let me say to you, colored men that the next time you go up to the State House at Columbus —that place where I expect to hold for—for two years after the next election [laughter and applause]—you will be pleased if you will go into the rotunda and look at that magnificent oil painting which adorns its walls; the title of it is "Perry's Victory on the Lakes." You will be pleased because you will see there in the boat, along with the old Commodore, in the thickest of the hail and storm of battle, and as brave looking as any of them, a fit representative of the African race. And thus it has ever been from the very formation of our Government — in war and in peace, in prosperity and in adversity alike—the colored man has stood side by side with his white brother. He has been with us in war; he is with us in peace. He has been with us to share our adversities; he has been with us to participate in the triumphs that we have been permitted to enjoy.

LITTLE PHIL.

Another reason why it is a pleasure for me to be present here to-day is in the fact that within the boundary lines of Perry County is to be found the birth-place of another illustrious American citizen—a man who was as great a Captain on the land as Perry was on the sea—a man whose name is a familiar "household word" the world over—a man whom fifty thousand of us followed, with an admiration and confidence that no language can describe, as we carried that flag [pointing to the stars and stripes waving above him] up the rugged sides of Mission Ridge, sweeping Bragg and his regiments from off its crest, capturing more than sixty pieces of artillery and more than three thousand prisoners, and breaking forever th backbone of the rebellion. [Applause.] I need not say that I refer to gallant little Phil. Sheridan! [Great applause. A voice: " Bully for the Irish !"]

A county which so reminds us of two such men as these is a county to be congratulated. Patriotism is safe here. * * * *

THE TARIFF.

" How are you to tell in this month of August, 1883, how much tariff this country will need in 1884? How are you to foresee the expenses of Government? How are you to foresee a year ahead whether you will have an expensive Government or an inexpensive Government ? Whether you will be put to a great expense or a little expense in administering the affairs of this great Nation ? And if you can not foresee that, how can you tell how much duty to put on this, that or the other thing, to the end that you may raise just enough revenue to meet the wants of the Government economically administered ? And then another thing—are you to change this tariff every year? It costs some years more than it does others to administer the affairs of Government. We have more pension bills to pay some years than others. We have more Indians to feed some years than others. We have more expenses of various kinds some years than others. If we are to regulate our tariff by the expenses necessary to be met, we must, necessarily, each year, vary the duties that are to be levied on our imports. And what kind of an effect will that have on the business of this country ? If a man must buy a product that is to be imported for him from another country, to be used in his business in this country how can he tell what he is to pay for it when he does not know that the tariff may not be changed in the time intervening between his order and his receipt of his article? Therefore, I say it does not affect the objection I make to the duplicity of this platform for Judge Hoadly to turn and ask me whether I want a tariff levied that will be more than enough to sustain the Government when it is economically administered. It only shows its weakness.

Of his New Philadelphia speech, Aug. 5. 1883, the Journals said that "Although the Judge spoke in the open air, in the broiling hot sun, the audience of thousands remained attentive to the last word. The Judge never slacks speed or rises in the air, pays no attention to wayside 'funny business,' but makes straight for his goal." The Judge thus spoke:

THE NATIONAL GOVERNMENT SUPREME.

"What lawyers and the statesmen of the country could not settle satisfactorily—the constitutional question as to the character of our government, the North contending that the Constitution was the organic law of the whole land and people, and that our National Government was supreme over States and people alike—that question "the boys in blue" settled in the storm of battle. They wrote a decision upon it; they wrote it with the bayonet; they wrote it with blood; they wrote it where it would do the most good—they put it into the Constitution of the United States, and they put it there to stay. [Enthusiastic applause.]

And thus it was that the heresy of secession, the infamous product of the resolutions of 1798, and one of the most vicious of heritages to the people of this country, existing as a continual threat and menace to our institutions and prosperity—that idea of secession, I say, perished, and I trust passed away from American politics forever amid the burning glories of the triumphant victory at Appomattox. [Immense applause.]

FOUR MILLIONS ENFRANCHISED.

Well, as a consequence, in that great struggle which the Republican party came into existence for the purpose of carrying on, we had the shackles stricken off of four millions of people, and as a result of the reconstruction measures that followed, four millions of people and their colored brethren everywhere throughout the United States were lifted up to the plane of citizenship. They were enfranchised. Thus, for the first time, we had in this country "personal liberty" for every man and equality of rights for every citizen; so that every man who looked upon the folds of that flag (pointing to one floating before him from the staff in the public square) with the allegiance of citizenship, looked there knowing that it was symbolical of defense for him and of protection for all his rights. * *

CONVICT LABOR.

We don't believe in putting our laborers into unjust competition with foreign laborers, or into unjust competition with degraded home laborers; for we believe that the honest laborer outside the penitentiary—who has never committed any crime, and who has to support himself and family—should not be brought on a level 'as to his labor with men who have been confined in the penitentiary for the commission of offenses. For that reason, while we say these men should be made to work, we also say they should be made to work in such a way under the supervision of the State so me manner to be devised, as to prevent their work being brought into an unjust manner with the labor outside.

APPENDIX.

THE DEFEAT.

When it was ascertained that Judge Foraker had been defeated in the contest of 1883, the sentiment was concurrent, universal, and spontaneous that it was in no way attributable to the ticket. The defeat, as in the case of Lincoln by Douglass, only endeared Judge Foraker to the people. It was felt that it was not a just and honorable defeat; that the judge was the real victor.

A GRAND CAMPAIGN.

Judge Foraker made a grand campaign two years ago, and if any Republican could have been elected then, he would have been—*Ashtabula Sentinel, April* 30, 1885.

THE KIND OF TIMBER NEEDED IN OFFICE.

Let no one wear crape for Foraker yet. So far from being a dead man, politically, he is the livest man in the State. The history of politics does not chronicle a more gallant fight than he has made.

THE DEFEAT DID NOT HURT HIM,

and we deem him one of the strongest men in the State to-day. We ask nothing better than Ben Foraker two years from now, and feel confident that if then nominated for governor he would sweep the State. He is the kind of timber that is needed in office nowadays, and the kind that will get there too. The people of Ohio are honored by having such a man among them, and they will see to it that he is yet put where he belongs.—*Scioto Gazette*, 1883.

A CLEAN CANDIDATE—NO RING—NO UNHEALTHY ALLIANCES.

Joseph B. Foraker was a man of mark before he made his famous canvass in 1883. He was known for his services in the Union army, for his brilliancy as a lawyer, and his learning as a judge. His contest in 1883 was

THE MOST MEMORABLE IN THE HISTORY OF THE REPUBLICAN PARTY OF OHIO,

and was watched with great interest in every State in the Union. The conditions were particularly unfavorable in 1883. The Democrats had swept the State in 1882, and were already in possession of half the State offices. Republicans were disheartened or indifferent, and believed that they would be defeated. Men who had in other years subscribed freely to pay campaign expenses cut down down their contributions, or refused to give anything. Judge Foraker accepted the nomination, and made the most able contest in the history of the Republican party. He did not deserve defeat. He was a clean candidate. He belonged to no ring, and was free of all unhealthy alliances. But every man who had a grievance against the party singled out Judge Foraker as the head of the ticket, and determined to stab him. Those Republicans who were disgusted with the Pond law cut Judge Foraker, although he had no voice in the passage of that law. Republicans who objected to anything the Republican general assembly had done, held Judge Foraker responsible, because he was the head of the ticket. Yet, had the election of 1883 been held two weeks earlier, Judge Foraker would have carried the state. The Second Amendment contest in the last two weeks cost the Republican ticket ten thousand votes.—*Sandusky Register.*

DEMOCRATIC TESTIMONY.

The Cleveland *Plain Dealer* (Democrat), 1883, rising above partisan prejudice, said: "The fact must be conceded that Foraker made a good campaign. He was a new man in politics, but he acquitted himself well. He made a strong, earnest fight, and if he comes out defeated, he comes out with a clear record."

CREDIT AND HONOR.

Hon. Mr. Jordan, in his speech at Cincinnati at the celebration of the Democratic victory, said: "Judge Foraker conducted the campaign courageously and honorably, with great credit to himself and honor to his party."

NEW YORK TESTIMONY—A MAN OF COMMANDING WORTH.

Judge Foraker was not elected governor of Ohio, but in the long and arduous campaign closed last Tuesday, he made a record as a speaker and a candidate which commands

GENERAL ADMIRATION.

His one hundred and five speeches delivered throughout the State were all models of sense, substance, and manliness. Without being exceptionally strong in point of *physique*, he underwent the tremendous strain of the canvass, speaking always twice a day, six days out of the seven, and sometimes oftener, frequently riding sixty miles a day in a buggy, and in a hundred other ways taxing his strength as a Sullivan or Slade could not do, with his voice stronger and his eye brighter the last night than they had been when he started. The Republicans of Ohio have introduced to the country a man of commanding worth, and one who must hereafter be given a prominent place among the Buckeye leaders available for national honors. —*Albany Evening Journal, October* 11, 1883.

TENNESSEE—UNIVERSAL ADMIRATION.

His canvass was conducted in the face of most trying obstacles, and was one of the most brilliant in the history of his party in that State, and at the time commanding universal admiration. His speeches were able and masterly, and exhibited a variety of mental resource which could only be

COMPARED TO THAT OF GARFIELD OR BLAINE.

It was an off year in Ohio, and he was left to make his canvass almost solitary and alone, and to bear the big end of the expenses of the fight. When the sure promise of victory was turned to defeat, he accepted the result gracefully and manfully.

Two years ago the Republican party of Ohio was as proud of him as of any leader they ever had, and by his dignified and manly course he has earned their further esteem.—*Knoxville (Tennessee) Journal, April,* 1885.

ILLINOIS—HE WITHSTOOD EVERY ASSAULT.

The Ohio Republicans have done the wisest possible thing in renominating Judge Foraker. Two years ago he made a splendid canvass, and proved himself well fitted, personally and politically, for the post of leader. At the close of the campaign of 1883, the Ohio Republicans were practically unanimous in the opinion that Foraker was one of the strongest candidates they ever put in the field. It is a strong man who can sustain defeat in this way. So well satisfied were the Ohio Republicans with Foraker as a leader, that with one accord they determined at the first opportunity to put him again in the field and defy the Democracy to defeat him a second time. He was accordingly selected as the man of all others to snatch victory from defeat.

Judge Foraker must appreciate the splendid compliment the Ohio Republicans have paid him in the manner of his renomination. In the campaign of two years ago he more than met every expectation, and his ability on the stump attracted attention and admiration throughout the country.

HE WAS A LEADER OF SPIRIT, BRAINS, AND COURAGE.

His record, too, was of a character to withstand every assault. He entered the army as a sixteen-year-old boy, and showed the stuff he was made of by writing to his mother that he did not want to lay down his gun until every slave was free. In civil life he has won his way by sheer force of merit and brains.—*Chicago Tribune.*

DEFEAT—JACKSON—VAN BUREN—LINCOLN—DOUGLAS—LUCAS—TRIMBLE—TODD—TOM CORWIN.

The following statement of votes for Republican nominees of Ohio since 1873 shows that Foraker in 1883 received 30,000 votes more than any candidate on a Republican ticket ever received in Ohio:

Year	Candidate	Votes
1873	Edward F. Noyes	213,837
1874	A. T. Wikoff	221,204
1875	R. B. Hayes	297,817
1876	Milton Barnes	317,856
1877	Wm. H. West	249,105
1878	Milton Barnes	274,120
1879	Charles Foster	336,261
1880	Charles Townsend	362,021
1881	Charles Foster	312,735
1882	Charles Townsend	297,759
1883	J. B. Foraker	347,164

The Sandusky Register says:

"He polled 50,000 more votes than Townsend polled in 1882, and more votes than were ever polled in a state election, save in the presidential year of 1880, and but for a deceptive circular sent out six days before the election to 30,000 spiritualists by the Democratic committee, Judge Foraker would have polled more votes than the state ticket received in 1880, and would have been elected.

Andrew Jackson was defeated in his first contest, and twice thereafter elected. Martin Van Buren was "defeated" by the United States Senate as minister to London, and was afterward elected President. General Harrison was "defeated" in 1836 for president by Van Buren, and then overwhelmingly elected over

Van Buren in 1840. Lincoln was "defeated" by Douglas in the senatorial race in Illinois, and in turn "defeated" Douglas for the presidency. Allen Trimble was "defeated" in 1822 and 1824 by Morrow, who had himself been "defeated" in 1820 by Brown. Then Trimble was elected in 1826 and re-elected in 1828. Robert Lucas was "defeated" in 1830 by McArthur, and elected in 1832. In 1840 Tom Corwin "defeated" Wilson Shannon, and the same Shannon in 1842 "defeated" Tom Corwin, the idol of the Whigs. David Tod was "defeated" in 1844 by Bartley, and in 1846 he was "defeated" by Bebb, and then elected in 1861.

DELEGATE AT LARGE TO CHICAGO. — CLEVELAND CONVENTION, 1884. — HE REPRESENTS THE REPUBLICAN PARTY OF OHIO.

Candidates for delegate at large being called for, Hon. Amor Smith of Cincinnati arose to present the name of J. B. Foraker, of Hamilton County. The convention anticipated the nomination and cheered lustily. Mr. Smith said:

"Mr. Chairman and gentlemen of the Republican Convention: I wish to place before this convention for delegate at large to the Republican convention at Chicago the name of a wise counselor, a brave soldier, and the leader of the late gubernatorial contest in this state. [Applause.] I nominate Judge J. B. Foraker." [Applause.]

Judge J. R. Johnston, of Mahoning County, moved that the rules be suspended, and the nomination of Judge Foraker made unanimous by acclamation.

Judge L. W. King, of Mahoning County, rose and said:

"Mr. Chairman: On behalf of the Blaine men in eastern Ohio, I want to say that we recognize the fact that Judge Foraker represents as

NO OTHER MAN REPRESENTS THE REPUBLICAN PARTY OF THE STATE OF OHIO.

I hope that no Blaine man in this convention will feel called upon to vote against Judge Foraker. In our section of the state, where all of the people are willing to vote for Mr. Blaine for President, we are willing to vote for Mr. Foraker." [Applause.]

The motion of Judge Johnson was carried unanimously. It would be hard to imagine anything more unanimous than the manner with which Judge Foraker's name was agreed upon.—*Commercial Gazette.*

Judge J. B. Foraker, chosen in the convention by enthusiastic acclamation as delegate at large, is one of

THE REPRESENTATIVE YOUNG REPUBLICANS

of the state. His speeches and general conduct of his campaign in the last gubernatorial contest won him the highest regard, and made for him thousands of new friends among the people whose representatives so heartily indorsed him yesterday.—*Cleveland Leader.*

GARFIELD AND WADE.

At the Cleveland convention in April, 1884, Judge Foraker was chosen to head the Ohio delegation to Chicago, and he did it with honor to himself. * * Here Foraker made a national reputation, and was given the honor which in former gatherings had been bestowed on Garfield and Wade.—*Times Star.*

A CORNELL TRUSTEE.

Under the original act by the New York legislature granting land to the institution as an "agricultural college," it is provided that the alumni shall elect one of the trustees, and that all nominations must be made in writing before April 1st, and each signed by at least ten of the alumni.

Judge Foraker was asked to become a candidate, but declined, owing to pressure of business. Despite his declination, his name was put in nomination by members of the Alumni Association all over the country. After a spirited and friendly contest, his election was made unanimous, June 18th, 1884. He is

THE FIRST TRUSTEE ELECTED

from any other state than New York. He thus addressed the alumni:

"LADIES AND GENTLEMEN:—This morning I had occasion to thank you for the honor of being made

PRESIDENT OF THE ASSOCIATION

last year, and now I must thank you again. Under ordinary circumstances this honor should be sufficient to make me proud, but when the rivalry was between myself and such noble men as were my competitors, it is doubly appreciated by me. I shall endeavor to faithfully discharge the duties of the trust with my best ability. * * * I remember the language of Goldwin Smith, in 1869, when he said Cornell was too sanguine—that it requires one hundred years to make a university. The university is entitled to our earnest support. * * * I esteem it more than ever my duty to give to it all the labor, time, and intellect that the duties of the place may require." [Hearty applause.]

THE NEW YORK "WORLD"

relates an incident in the judge's career in this connection:

"THREE HUNDRED LAWYERS."

The story of the career of Judge Joseph B. Foraker, of Cincinnati, the recently elected trustee of Cornell University, is interesting; and one phase of it is unique. He was graduated from Cornell in 1869, one year after the university was founded, and for several years afterward buffeted against adverse circumstances, the most irritating of which was poverty. He had been compelled to borrow money to carry him through the year, and had worked so hard at his studies that his health failed in April previous to the June when he was to take his diploma. With a shattered constitution and little money in his purse, he started in the spring for his country home in Ohio. Next to the thought of graduating was that of what he should do after leaving the university. Having decided to devote his attention to the legal profession, he stopped on his way home in the spring of 1869 to visit a young lawyer friend in Cincinnati, intending to ascertain what opening there was in that growing city for a young man to commence in the profession of law. While walking along Third Street he was struck by the great number of signs of lawyers, and asked his friend how many lawyers there were in Cincinnati. The answer was, "three hundred." In his physical and financial condition those two words fell upon

YOUNG FORAKER'S EAR WITH TERRIBLE EFFECT.

He continued his journey home, still thinking of his future in connection with those words, "three hundred." At home he found himself exhausted, and was put to bed, where kind friends devotedly attended him. While alone one day his mind wandered back over his experiences of the previous week, and his doubts and fears as to whether he would be able to join his class on graduating day alternated with his Cincinnati friend's answer. These thoughts chased each other through his mind until he could bear them no longer. He jumped out of his bed, where he had been ordered to remain, sat down at a table and wrote in three hours a first-class graduating thesis on the subject 'Three Hundred Lawyers.' That was the conquering act. His mind was relieved, his purpose fixed. He returned to Cornell, graduated with his class, settled in Cincinnati, almost pennyless, determined to add one more to the three hundred. His rapid advancement to the front rank of lawyers in the whole West has been owing to his untiring energy and integrity in practice, and calm, cool, good judgment in legal as well as political work.

JUDGE FORAKER AT CHICAGO.

In nominating John Sherman, Judge Foraker received an ovation. He was listened to with great attention. Nobody who heard Foraker could doubt his loyalty to Sherman. Foraker spoke of Arthur. There were a few cheers. He expressed his admiration for the brilliant chieftain of Maine. Foraker gave Blaine, merely by an incidental reference, the largest boom he has had yet. The galleries were uncontrollable. The white plume was seized and put on top of a starry flag, and amid the wildest imaginable scenes it was carried around the center aisle. Foraker

CONDUCTED HIMSELF AMAZINGLY

under the ordeal. He made a good point when quiet again reigned over the convention by reminding his hearers that they should not shout until they had cleared the woods.

Foraker's speech was not ambitious in its style, but was the best that was made.—*Commercial Gazette, June 6, 1884.*

Foraker's management showed that he is quick to seize the opportunity at the supreme crisis, as he is a hard and unflinching advocate of his preference.—*Commercial Gazette, June 7, 1884.*

THE SYMPATHY OF THE CONVENTION.

Judge Foraker, who presented the name of John Sherman, won the sympathy of the audience by his manly attitude. He did not beg the nomination of a citizen of Ohio by reason of its being a doubtful state, for he frankly conceded that it was sure to go Republican the presidential year. * * He set forth in superb detail the statesmanship of John Sherman, eliciting enthusiastic applause.—*Chicago Inter-Ocean, June 6, 1884.*

ADROIT—PLEASING—EFFECTIVE.

Judge Foraker's eulogy of Senator Sherman was adroit, pleasing, and effective. The Ohio lawyer is a graceful man, possessed of a good voice, and very evidently of a keen intellect. His figure on the stage was the best of all. "I wish," he began, "to speak a few plain words in behalf of a plain but very good man." It was a good start. He kept the same plane throughout, never lowering his voice, but perhaps a little elevating it all the while. Foraker was a popular man when he had finished. That speech, with an eastern man, is likely to make Foraker the vice-presidential candidate.—*Chicago Evening Mail, June 6, 1884.*

The *Chicago Tribune* of May 31st called attention to various plans and propositions to nominate Judge Foraker for the vice-presidency.

Ohio came here for harmony. Even in the selection of the vice-president she gracefully waived all claims, though Judge Foraker's name had been prominently mentioned.—*Chicago Tribune.*

The soldier element were vociferously for Judge Foraker.—*Chicago Times.*

The judge had no wish for the vice-presidential nomination, and gave his ardent support to General Logan.

JUDGE FORAKER'S REPARTEE.

General McLaren was introduced to Judge Foraker at the Grand Pacific, Chicago.

"What, is this Judge Foraker?"

"It is, sir."

"What, Judge Foraker of Ohio?"

"The same sir."

"Not the late candidate for governor?"

"Yes, sir."

"But, judge, you are so young. I——"

"Oh, interrupted the judge, "I'll get over that in time."

Ex-Senator J. B. Chaffee, chairman of the Republican National Executive Committee, says the

"YOUNG MEN MUST COME TO THE FRONT.

A new generation has sprung up. The old factions have worn the party threadbare. It was so with the Democratic party. But their young men got hold of the machinery of the party. They nominated an obscure man, practically without a record, and elected him. The same things are working in the Republican party to force us to follow this road."

RATIFICATION AT TURNER HALL, CINCINNATI, JUNE 11, 1884—TREMENDOUS OVATION.

The chairman introduced Judge Foraker as the young gallant leader of Ohio Republicans. Judge Foraker received a tremendous ovation. Hats and handkerchiefs were waved, and it looked like a small edition to the Chicago Convention.—*Commercial Gazette.*

EXTRACT FROM THE SPEECH OF JUDGE FORAKER.

* * * "He (James G. Blaine) has done his work by twenty-five years of arduous public service. He has done it by an illustrious

career that has been run in the presence of the American people—a career that has endeared him to the hearts of this people. * * We see this by the bonfires lit on every hill top, by the cannon thundering all over this country, by the ratification meetings all over this land. * * * We are in favor of Republicanism, for that means human liberty and equality of rights. We are in favor of Republicanism, for that means nationality as opposed to state sovereignty." * * * * * * *

ONE OF THE COMING MEN OF THE COUNTRY.

The *Portland Advertiser*, June 21, 1884, said of Judge Foraker upon his visit of ceremony to Mr. Blaine:

"Judge Foraker of Ohio looks to be about thirty-three, though he must be forty. He is a clean-cut, level-headed man, who makes a good showing, and is one of the coming men of this country. He began life low down, and grew from a private soldier into a good place during the war. Since the conflict, he has educated himself, been an excellent judge, candidate for governor, and is waiting for greater honors. He makes a good speech, and in the recent convention at Chicago, as in the present gathering of which he is a central figure, he has more attention than any other single man."

SOUND, GOOD SENSE.

At Portland, Maine, June 27, 1884:

CHAIRMAN REED.—To say that I have kept the best speaker for the last would be invidious to the distinguished men that have addressed you. * * But you must have noticed among the foremost figures of the Chicago Convention a gentleman distinguished not only for his eloquence, but for sound, good sense. That gentleman I introduce to you,—Judge Foraker."

NATIONAL REPUTATION.

The Lewiston (Maine) *Journal* said of Judge Foraker that he "is a young man of national reputation. His address was one of the most telling in the campaign. * * * He is an orator of force and directness, holding the closest attention of the audience to the last."

Extract from the speech at Lewiston:

"As your chairman has said, I come to you from the State of Ohio. It is a long distance from that State to this. I have journeyed through many of the States of the Union, each one of which has had much interest for me. The States, however of Virginia and Massachusetts have occasioned particular interest. These are much more interesting because they are the two states that have given us the two parties now before the country. On the one hand we were given by Massachusetts that civilization propagated by the Pilgrim Fathers from Plymouth. On the other hand Virginia gave us that of Jamestown. Both were marked by most characteristic acts in their early life. That of the Plymouth Colony was marked by the establishment at Cambridge of a seat of learning that is to-day known and honored throughout the world by the name of Harvard University. The first characteristic act of the other civilization of the South, was the purchase at Jamestown, Virginia, of a cargo of slaves. The first civilization cast across the entire northern half of our republic a golden ray illuminating it with the sunlight of a glorious liberty; the other cast across the entire South the dark blight of the curse of human bondage. The one civilization taught men to be self reliant, to depend upon their own resources, to act their own responsibility.

"As time passed those two civilizations invaded the field of politics. It was early forseen by the statesmen of the South, that it was only a question of time when the civilization of the North would outstrip them in the race. So they began their war on States."

Judge Foraker made a review of the various disputes, invasions, and demands of slave power.

"Then it was that the Republican party came into existence, and it met at the threshold of its existence the same Democratic party of to-day. In 1860, under the lead of the immortal Lincoln, [applause] it took charge of the government."

Judge Foraker reviewed the history of the war.

"It was with great surprise when we were entering on the career of peace to hear that the

MISSION OF THE REPUBLICAN PARTY

was ended. We were told that with the completion of the work it ought to step down and out, and let the Democratic party resume the work.

"The people said 'No.' The debts of this great war must be paid. They said 'No' in 1868, and so they repeated it in 1872, and again in 1876, and once again in 1880. And now they are getting ready to do it again in 1884, by the election of James G. Blaine to the Chief Magistracy. [Applause.] And they ought to do it. There are several reasons why they should. The mission of this party is not done, not until all through this land there is a free ballot and a fair count." [Tremendous applause.]

The speaker dealt briefly with the right of the Nation as such to take charge and examine into the legality of the votes in the States. In his opinion it is objectionable to relegate this matter wholly to the States. It seems strange that the United States can come into a State and lay hands on us and compel us to go forth to battle for her on fields of war and then, that war over, the State line should rise up so high that the United States government can not come in and protect the people in the right and majesty of their ballot. Judge Foraker referred to Hamburg, Danville, and the murder of Print Matthews in Copiah County. "What I want, what you want, is a man in the chief magistracy of this nation who can not only punish these outrages, but prevent their recurrence."

JUDGE FORAKER AND THE NARROW GAUGE.

The character of the man is shown in the following letter. It will be seen that some one had started the report that he was in some way responsible for the fact that the *employes* of this road had not been paid their wages for the month of July, 1883; but that the attack only served to bring out the fact that he had been the means of the men getting one months' pay for October, 1883, and that he had gratuitously, for mere sake of seeing justice done to the laborers of the road, gone outside of the duties imposed upon him, to argue to the court the case of these men, and that it was upon his advice that the efforts are being made that are to secure the men their money eventually as it is hoped. And so it is in this case, as in all others, that assaults upon his character or conduct only serve to develop new features that add to his claims upon the confidence of all.

The following was sent to the editor of the *Dayton Journal*, in response to his inquiry as to the Democratic charge that Judge

Foraker was responsible for the delay in the *employes* and creditors receiving their dues on account of labor and supplies furnished the road before and after it went into the hands of the receiver, and that Judge Foraker advised and defended the course which led to this. The judge wrote:

"The trouble with the article is that there are no 'facts' whatever in it.

"I never was attorney for the 'Narrow Gauge,' and had nothing whatever to do with the making of any of its debts.

"After the road had been put into the hands of a Receiver I was appointed by the court to represent him in such matters at Cincinnati as demanded the services of an attorney.

"In pursuance of this employment I represented Mr. Craig the Receiver, in a great many very important suits, about which he was almost constantly occupied for more than a year.

"Instead of opposing the payment of the laborers and other claimants, I did all in my power to secure their payment. At the time Mr. Craig was appointed Receiver, November 1, 1883, there were due to the laborers two months' wages, namely, July and October, 1883.

"The court at first refused to allow Mr. Craig to pay the men for either month, holding that the Receiver should not be required to pay any debts, except those of his own making. Finally, however, *upon the application of Mr. Craig and myself*, Judge Sage made an order allowing him to pay the October payroll.

"But the court still refused and yet refuses to allow him to pay for the month of July. As attorney for the receiver, I had nothing to do with any matters except such as the receiver consulted me about, and when the court decided a question, of course I was bound by it as well as everyone else.

"Notwithstanding all this, I have at different times, when the matter has come up, done all in my power to induce the court to change its ruling, and order the wages of July, 1883, to be paid. When all such efforts failed, I then advised the men (such of them as applied to me) to combine and make up a claim amounting to $5,000, so as to give the Supreme Court of the United States jurisdiction, and on such a test case endeavor to reverse the ruling of the court here. In pursuance of this suggestion I understand such a case is being made up.

"On the 6th day of last February I wrote to Ed. L. Spencer of Chillicothe, Ohio, in regard to the claims as follows:

"'With respect to other claims for wages for July, 1883, I have always been anxious to see them paid, and have frequently brought them to the attention of the court, in the hope that some provision might be made, and that they should be paid, for while it is true that they are not debts of the receiver, yet they are debts for which the bondholders who own the road got the benefit. All claims for labor, at least, ought to be paid, but of course I am powerless in the hands of the court.'

"I might made similar quotations from many other such letters, but deem it unnecessary. In confirmation, however, of all I say I respectfully refer you to the Hon. John A. McMohon of Dayton, and to Wm. J. Craig, the receiver of the road, both of whom are Democrats.

"The 'fact' is, therefore, that in the first place I have nothing whatever to do with the contracting of the debts of the company. I did not, in fact, know there was such a railroad in existence until I was sent for by the court and told that it had been put in the hands of a receiver, and that I had been appointed to act as counsel for such receiver, a man I never before had heard of. I did the best I could to satisfacorily discharge the duties thus imposed upon me, but never at any time opposed the payment of the claims against the road for labor, or anything else, but on the contrary, did all in my power to get the men their pay for both October and July, and regretted very much when I failed as to July. Very truly, etc..

J. B. FORAKER.

THE ELECTION FRAUDS OF OCTOBER, 1884.

The Committee of the Lincoln Club on Elections, affected by the frauds by which the election of April, 1884, was carried in Cincinnati, gathered the evidence and submitted it to Judges Foraker and Bateman for examination. Judge Foraker and his associates said:

"We are satisfied that the voice of the majority of the legal voters has been clearly overborne by corrupt practices and illegal voting. The evidence shows systematic frauds, organized and paid for, and directed by political agents. It shows the existence and use of professional repeaters, hired in gangs, and voting from poll to poll. In many of the precincts the election was a farce. It is clear that if the use of the ballot-box is to be preserved this crime must be resisted at once before the vilest classes shall have handed the city government and public offices wholly over to their kind, and frauds upon the electors at the polls shall become the recognized and necessary means of party success."

The frauds of the spring led to legal efforts to prevent their repetition in October. These efforts were largely successful. Judge Foraker felt that southern methods were being employed in Cincinnati, and he ranged himself openly and firmly on the side of the purity of the ballot.

THE DEMOCRATIC HOUSE OF REPRESENTATIVES

ordered an investigation which seemed mere political strategy. Charges were made against Lot Wright, United States marshal, of "usurpation of power," and "violation of law." Judge Foraker entered with spirit upon the defense of Marshall Wright, which meant the defense of the purity of the franchise. In his brief, Judge Foraker said:

"And in this connection, to show what might have happened had not the influence of these deputy marshals been felt, we call the attention of the committee to the testimony with regard to what is known in this record as 'the Hammond Street outrage;' for, notwithstanding all that was said by counsel at the hearing, and notwithstanding all that was testified to by Mullen, the convicted perpetrator of that outrage, there never was such an outrage perpetrated north of the Ohio River on citizens of the United States with respect to the exercise of their right of suffrage.

"That testimony shows that at midnight the

HOMES OF PEACEABLE COLORED CITIZENS,

many of whom had lived there for years, were invaded, and they were marched bodily by the police officers, under the direction of Mullen, to the station-house, where they were shut up and kept from about midnight preceding the election until after six o'clock the day of the election, and for no other purpose than to deprive them of the exercise of their right of suffrage—a right they were as much entitled to exercise at that election as Lieutenant Mullen himself; and all this without any charge whatever against them.

"This testimony was so convincing and overwhelming that at the trial of the case Lieutenant Mullen entered into a compromise agreement, which was in its effect a confession of his guilt, to the effect that the jury should find him guilty of having thus deprived one hundred and fifty-two citizens (as the court found) of their right to vote. This outrage of itself is enough to show the desperate purposes and designs of the Democratic party with respect to that election in the city of Cincinnati, and to warrant all that Marshall Wright did in the appointment of deputies and in the arming of these deputies to prevent such outrages, and to preserve the peace and purity of the ballot-box."

IN THE DEFENSE OF THE PURITY OF THE BALLOT

there were associated with Judge Foraker in this gratuitous service the Hon. Mr. Morey, ex-member of congress, of Hamilton, and Hon. Messrs. Goodhue and Probasco.

After Mr. Follett had for days attempted to smirch Mr. Wright with the Nettle gang, Judge Foraker adroitly demonstrated that the gang were all Democrats. The judge made it manifest that not a Democrat had been deprived of his vote at the October election. The Kentucky witnesses for the Democrats became self-convicted and justified Marshal Wright in his preparations for the Bourbon invasion.

When Foraker had suffered unjust treatment for several days in behalf of the marshal, he felt it his duty to the country and the ballot to put a stop to this, which he did effectually. Mr. Springer made a confession, and the judge and the cause of a pure ballot were not snubbed thereafter. We extract from a report of the proceedings in the *Commercial-Gazette*.

Judge Foraker asked the witness if he "was not aware that he bore the reputation, whether deservedly or not, of being at the head of a notorious gang of repeaters who had long carried on their nefarious work?"

Before the witness could answer, Chairman Springer said in a louder tone of voice than he had been heard to use before during the entire investigation:

"No witness in this investigation shall be permitted to be insulted by counsel for defense, and the witness need not answer that question."

[It will be noted that Mr. Springer made an exception against counsel for the defense. He is particular that counsel for the *defense* must not insult witnesses, no matter what counsel for the complainant may do.]

And then occurred something of a breeze.

Judge Foraker asked with emphasis: "Do I understand the Chair to charge me with intending to insult the witness?"

Mr. Springer, otherwise Follett's counsel, lifted up his voice again and said, "I believe you did."

"Then," said the judge, "I shall at once withdraw from this investigation."

Then Follett's counsel (otherwise known as Springer) said with as much impertinent suavity as he could command, "You may act your own pleasure as to that, Judge Foraker," adding with indecent haste, "I wish you a very good-morning."

Judge Foraker then closed his book of documents, folded his papers, and made preparations for retiring from the committee.

Governor Stewart here interposed and said, "I think the Chair will allow me to say that I believe he acted hastily. Judge Foraker certainly did not offer an insult to the witness, though perhaps the question should not have been put in that form."

Then Follett's counsel, who is such at the expense of the national government and the tax-payers, said again, "Nothing shall be said to any witness at this investigation which may tend to offend him or affect the freedom of his testimony."

By this time Judge Foraker had prepared to retire. With hat and coat and documents in hand, he thus addressed the flippant congressional official, *i. e.*, Follet's counsel:

"It was offensive to ask the witness if he had been in the penitentiary, but no lawyer will deny my right to question him on this point. I consider

THE LAWYER A COWARD WHO TAKES ADVANTAGE

of his position to unnecessarily offend a witness who is powerless to defend himself. I never permitted it when I was upon the bench, and I emphatically resent the imputation now cast upon me—the first in sixteen years' practice. I asked the witness 'whether deservedly or not'"—

Springer, by this time, had become dizzy from the unusual height to which he had climbed, in the hope of plucking feathers from an eagle. He began to want to get down. He had got above the reach of Follett and Baker. They had never ventured to reach such a height. Follet wouldn't venture after his counsel, for he knew from late experiences that he couldn't come within 1,609 of it. Baker was already all dazed from looking up to where Springer had taken his aerial flight. So Springer began to back down himself, and when he got to where the atmosphere was not quite so thin, he asked of the Judge:

"Did you say 'whether deservedly or not?'"

"I certainly did," was the reply, "and I appeal to the stenographer's notes."

He was corroborated by the stenographer, and then Judge Foraker delivered himself of an eloquent protest against the unjust treatment he claimed to have received from the committee all through this inquiry. Mr. Springer made a humiliating confession of hasty conduct, and there was molification all around.

The congressional official, alias "Springer," alias "Follett's counsel," had scarcely shaken down his feathers after his perilous flight and subdued his nerves of the dizzy sensation than he was further humiliated by Van Alstyne, who asked:

"Well, Springer, shall I take the chair?"

SPRINGFIELD PRE-CONVENTION NOTES.
NO MANAGEMENT BY JUDGE FORAKER.

In the two years that have passed, Judge Foraker has given some time, during the presidential campaign, to the discussion of public questions, but he has been busy in the labors of his profession.

When the question of his nomination for another gubernatorial race came up, he declined to take a personal part, but frankly said he could not refuse the nomination if it were tendered him.

His friends have not been organized in his behalf, not even in his own county—and the delegates from Hamilton were not chosen so as to make a suggestion to the rest of the State. There has been no management. JUDGE FORAKER HAS MAINTAINED HIS DIGNITY AND EASE OF ATTITUDE.—*Commercial-Gazette, May,* 1885.

NO CANDIDATE.

"What about your own candidacy, judge?"

"I am not a candidate for the Republican nomination for governor, and will engage in no contest for it. If it comes in the nature of a compliment from the Republican party I would be flattered, indeed. * * * I am not standing on a pedestal waiting to be struck by lightning, and shall not feel disappointed if I am not nominated. I will make no fight. I will have no struggle with Republicans before the campaign opens."
—*Interview, Enquirer, April,* 1885.

PERSONAL POPULARITY.

Foraker is one of the coming men of this country, and the sooner Ohio pushes him to the front the better for her. He attracted the attention of all present by his fine speech at the Chicago Convention, and it was a question whether it was not the best speech delivered on that occasion. Foraker has personal popularity.—*Cleveland Leader, January* 22, 1885.

OFFICE NOT SOUGHT.

The canvass of Judge Foraker was of marked ability. No citizen should seek the nomination to an office and strive to obtain it. This Judge Foraker has never done.—*Bucyrus Journal, February* 29, 1885.

HIS OPEN, FRANK, MANLY WAY

of meeting measures and questions pleases the Republicans of old Knox.—*Mt. Vernon Republican, April* 17, 1885.

NO BLOT, NO BLEMISH.

There is not a Republican in Ohio who can find a blot or blemish on the personal or political character of Judge Foraker. He meets all requirements—*Sandusky Register.*

NO BETTER MAN IN THE STATE,

and no one who can win more votes.—*Georgetown Gazette, January 21, 1885.*

In 1883 the nomination for governor

MOST EMPHATICALLY SOUGHT JUDGE FORAKER.

He rose into a most popular candidate. * * * No one attributed the defeat of the party in 1883 to him. * * * He is not, either openly or secretly, scheming to obtain the nomination. Before the scrutiny of all men, he is strictly attending to his own professional business. * * Captain Foraker believes that a citizen should not be insensible to the distinguished honor conferred by a re-nomination, yet he has too high a sense of honor to permit him to seek it.—*Bucyrus Journal, January 16, 1885.*

Foraker is leaving the matter altogether to the Republicans of the State. In 1883 he led a forlorn troop in gallant style. Politicians agree that

SHERMAN OR BLAINE WOULD HAVE MET

the same fate.—*Commercial-Gazette, January 11, 1885.*

JUDGE FORAKER IS REMAINING QUIETLY AT HOME

attending to his law business, and is making no effort to secure the nomination for governor. He has everything to lose, in a pecuniary sense, if he should be nominated and elected. He has a remunerative law practice to which he devotes his whole attention. He has no desire to abandon his law practice for politics. If he receives the nomination, which there is every probability of his doing, it will be because the Republicans *want* him as their standard-bearer in the coming political contest in this State. Judge Foraker has NO CONSUMING AMBITION TO BE GOVERNOR OF THIS STATE.—*Miami Union.*

Foraker's conduct during the campaign of 1883 was so vigorous and manly, that defeat did not lower him in the estimation of the people. In the campaign of last fall, Foraker was

THE FOREMOST IN THE FIGHT,

and by his vigor, wisdom, and eloquence, he achieved a national reputation. No other young man in Ohio is as widely and favorably known.—*Circleville Union Herald, February 5, 1885.*

We have had the most thorough faith in

JUDGE FORAKER'S INTEGRITY,

in his loyalty,* in his Republicanism, in his humanity.—*Sandusky Register, February 6, 1885.*

---

* NOTE.—Ben's parents came to Ohio from Virginia because of their love of liberty and of their whole country. Ben was born loyal. He was bred a loyal boy. "Carp" in *Cleveland Leader* tells of

FORAKER'S FIRST FLAG-RAISING.

Young Foraker was raised on a farm in southern Ohio, and his patriotism developed rather early. During the Freemont campaign, when flag-raisings and mass-meetings were setting the country wild, young Foraker's parents went away on a visit, leaving Ben, who was ten years old, at home. The boy concluded

FORAKER HAS NOT THRUST HIMSELF TO THE FRONT.

He has asked no man in Ohio to advocate or promote his nomination. He has written no line of solicitation for votes. He thinks that the office should seek the man. He is

ABOVE EVERY TRICK OR ARTIFICE.

He is a man of pure methods. Judge Foraker is an almost perfect type of the best Republicanism of the nation.—*Dayton Journal.*

The *Albany Evening Journal* (N.Y.,) regards the campaign (1883) of Judge Foraker as not only brilliant, but under the circumstances that he should have been "defeated" by only a few thousand in a poll of a million as the most striking evidence of

HIS WONDERFUL POLITICAL AVAILABILITY.

Two years ago, when Judge Foraker captured the State convention he surprised the older heads and made the

MOST AGGRESSIVE CAMPAIGN IN THE HISTORY OF OHIO.

He was beat owing to a mistaken attitude of the Prohibitionists and wool-growers. The peculiar causes of Foraker's defeat after such a brilliant canvass were recognized, and he became at once the most popular man in State politics,

REVERSING THE USUAL CONDITIONS

incident to a defeat. At Chicago he was chairman of the Ohio delegation, and placed Sherman in nomination with a speech that thrilled the convention.

Judge Foraker represents the hearty feeling as well as the deliberate preference of the party.—*New York Tribune,* April 27, 1885.

Foraker has made

WONDERFUL PROGRESS

for a new man. I remember quite well when he first came prominently to my notice as governor of Ohio. It was when he resigned as judge of the Superior Court in Cincinnati. Half a dozen of the leading attorneys of the city telegraphed to take no action on the resignation until they could see the judge and make an effort to induce him to reconsider. He would not, however. Later I offered him

---

to have a flag-raising of his own, and he found on the other side of the Rocky Fork a tall, straight sassafras-pole which he considered the very thing for the purpose. He cut it down with a hatchet, dragged it to the Rocky Fork, threw it in the water and swam across, pushing it in front of him. The story of his expedients to get it up the hill on the other side shows his perseverance. His little sister helped him, however, and the pole was finally planted after a week's hard work. He then took a couple of child's petticoats, one red and the other blue, and with these and one of his father's best shirts he made a flag and hoisted it to the top of the pole. When the family returned they found young Ben triumphant, and the red, white, and blue flag waving over their farm-house.

A SEAT ON THE SUPREME BENCH

when a vacancy occurred, but he declined. I remember well the origin of the effort to nominate him for governor. It was at the State-house in Columbus. A number of Ohio and Cincinnati gentlemen were talking about a probable candidate. They said Judge Foraker would be a good man. He was a clean man. The people of Cincinnati admired him and loved him. The Republicans of Columbus and from various parts of the state immediately coincided, and exclaimed, "Foraker is just the man we want in this fight. He has no record behind him that would make him objectionable to any faction." Other men who had been canvassed were dropped after that, and Foraker was decided upon by men from all portions of the State as the standard-bearer for the coming campaign.—*Governor Foster.*

The *Cleveland Plain-Dealer* (Democrat) published an interview at Columbus, which shows what the duty of the people is. The private objection to Foraker as therein exhibited is

THAT " HE HAS NO MONEY,"

that " it would not be wise to nominate him because

" HE. IS NOT WEALTHY.

" The candidate must have funds. We must strike a man that has funds."

This is a libel upon the Republican party and the people. May the day never come to the Republic when poverty is a disqualification and wealth a qualification for office.

Foraker's nomination means

THE NEW ERA

in our later politics.

Judge Foraker's whole life has been one of

REMARKABLE PURITY OF PURPOSE AND METHODS.

He has never had any connection with rings. He has not used the ordinary nor indeed any devices for securing nominations. Without any assumption of superior purity, his official life encourages the young in quiet, steady attention to duty, leaving results to God and the people.

He has never sought an office, and has never accepted any compensation or any office for which he has not rendered a full equivalent.

NO NOMINATION BY SOLICITATION.

The following private letter (published by an admirer of clean methods) was written to a comrade of Captain J. B. Foraker at the Soldiers' Home. A member of the same regiment in the war addressed him a note expressing a desire to help him obtain the nomination for governor. Judge Foraker replied in the following characteristic terms:

CINCINNATI, May 30, 1885.

Geo. W. Doughty, Esq., National Military Home, Ohio:

DEAR SIR:— * * * I would gladly comply with your request to extend you some aid, as you suggest, if it were not that

I have determined if I am to be nominated at all it shall be as always heretofore, without doing anything whatever personally to bring about such a result, and especially without expending a single cent of money.

I know that you would not use any money save in a legitimate way, and aside from the fact that you will use it only in that manner, I would be glad to give it to you on account of old friendship and comradeship; but already in yesterday's newspapers I see the charge that I have emissaries traveling over the State upon money that I have furnished them. This is all false. I have not furnished anybody a cent, and do not intend to. Neither have I any emissaries or agents of any kind in my employment anywhere. The truth of the matter is, I do not want a re-nomination unless it is the wish of the party to give it to me without my asking for it.   *   *   *   *   *   *

Hoping that you will fully appreciate my situation, and knowing that you will approve my feeling and determination in regard to the matter in this respect, I remain

Very sincerely yours, etc.   J. B. FORAKER.

THE SPRINGFIELD CONVENTION.

Judge Foraker, though telegraphed for Tuesday and Wednesday morning, declined going to Springfield. When the noon train arrived, great was the disappointment at Foraker's non-arrival. It was said that Foraker had doubts about going at all. Upon continued urgent requests he consented, reaching Springfield in the evening of Wednesday.

The meeting was similar to that of Blaine's in 1884.

Reaching the steps, Foraker was relieved from the jam and started for his rooms; but the cheers of the crowd called him to the balcony, and when order had been restored he said:

MY FELLOW-CITIZENS:—I sincerely thank you for this very kind, cordial and complimentary greeting, and I trust that about this time to-morrow afternoon I may have occasion to thank you again. I have come here, however, and with just this I shall excuse myself for the present—that I might attend this convention, and with you help to give expression to the Republicans of the State of Ohio. [Cries of "Good."] Whether you shall see fit to intrust our party banner again to my hands or give it to my worthy and esteemed friend, General Kennedy, or to my equally worthy and esteemed friend, General Beatty, or to any one else of the gentlemen who have been named in connection with that honor, I pledge you that no man in Ohio will be better satisfied with the result than I shall be; [cheers] and I say to you also, that whether you give it to me or give it to any one of them, the ticket nominated by this convention will have no heartier support from any man than that which I shall give to it from the first to the last day of the campaign. [Loud cheers.] It is a matter of but little comparative consequence what one of the gentlemen who have been mentioned shall have that honor conferred upon him. But it is a matter of the highest moment that the campaign which we have come here for the purpose of inaugurating, shall be made a triumphant success. [Loud cheers.] What we want to do, and upon that I congratulate you, is to keep up from this time until October the enthusiasm with which you have inaugurated this campaign, to the end that when the election has been held there may go to the rest of the country as the verdict of the Republicans of Ohio, that sort of message which will inspire and give new life to Republicanism throughout the whole United States of America. [Loud cheers.]

Leaving the balcony, he was escorted to rooms 52 and 54, which had been established by Cincinnati delegates, where a crowd of friends pressed forward to grasp his hand.

In a few minutes he was again summoned to the balcony to greet the Montgomery County delegation.

This delegation, on leaving the train, formed as quickly as the rush would permit, marched into the Arcade, and called for Foraker. He responded:

GENTLEMEN:—I very much appreciate the compliment of being called a second time to address this audience. If there are any friends I would prefer to greet it would be the friends that come from Dayton. If you desire to listen to a speech, I know that there are many distinguished gentlemen within who would be glad to address you. Please excuse me with the assurance that I appreciate your kindness.—*Dayton Journal.*

Returning to head-quarters, he was greeted by a host of delegates, and at 9 o'clock was serenaded by the *Colored Foraker Club, of Springfield*, led by Mr. Dewell, the colored attorney who was on the other side of the school case. He said:

GENTLEMEN OF THE SPRINGFIELD COLORED CLUB:—I am informed that you have come here for the purpose of serenading me. I do greatly appreciate the compliment, coming as it does not only from the colored men but the represesentatives of colored men—not, however, as a compliment to myself but as a compliment to my party that has placed colored men *on the same plane of equality* with white men.

Coming here as Republicans, entitled to a voice with all other men to select a ticket, you are typical of the grandest work the Republican party ever accomplished. It reminds me of thirty years ago, when Republicanism meant hatred to human slavery. It reminds me of the war, which was not only to preserve the constitution, to preserve the unity of the States, but to strike the shackles from the arms of bondsmen.

It causes me to remember, with pardonable pride I trust, that when as soldiers before Chattanooga, although we were poorly fed and suffering privations; and anxious as we all were to return to our homes, yet we felt and wrote that now the war was on, it should not be concluded *until every slave was free.*

I remember when I cast my first vote, in 1867. I voted the Republican ticket because the Republican party was in favor of the colored man voting, and the Democratic party was opposed to it.

Only in this day's newspaper we read of the removal of Lot Wright, removed because last fall when in the crisis of an election it had been determined by the Democratic leaders that the scenes of Danville and Copiah counties should be introduced into Ohio. Lot Wright said that no such outrage should be permitted north of the Ohio River.   *   *   *

You are invested with every right, every immunity that the laws give to other citizens.

OUTBURST OF POPULAR ENTHUSIASM.

Foraker received a glorious greeting when he stepped from the train, and it was with the utmost difficulty that he could push his way to the hotel. Shouts were made of "Here comes the winner," and there was a row of hands stretched on either side to grasp his. There was a volley of salutations. Some called him "Foraker," some "Judge," some "Captain." But with those who personally knew him the favorite salutation was "Joe" or "Ben."

Headed by their brass band and the banner of the Republican Club, of Precinct A, Twelfth Ward, Cincinnati, the Montgomery County delegation marched through the Arcade. The jam in that passage-way was very great. Calls were made for Foraker. He stepped out on the balcony, and was received with rousing cheers.

With no desire to magnify the matter, I must say that I never saw *such an outburst of popular enthusiasm* at any State Convention crowd as that on the present occasion.—*Commercial-Gazette.*

When the train came in the crowds about it reminded one of

THE BLAINE TOUR.

"Where's Foraker?" "We've got him here," came the response from the car platform as the Hamilton County delegates crowded down. There was a hush of expectancy, and then Foraker came out, lifting his hat to the yelling thousands. A double escort line was formed by common consent, and through this he was almost carried into the hotel. Then the crowd fell back into the Arcade and the band marched through adding to the enthusiasm.

In a minute Judge Foraker appeared on the balcony and stood watching the surging crowds below him. He looked as he did a year ago at Chicago while nominating Sherman. He made a neat little speech, and made a long, glorious stride over the ground which his enemies declared he had lost by his absence.—*Times-Star.*

NO CLAIMS—NO PLACE ASKED FOR.

During the evening the enthusiastic multitude demanded another appearance of Foraker. The demonstration showed the hearts of the vast crowd of the people were with Foraker. He said:

"I have come here only to thank you for this kind compliment. I come to Springfield only as the rest have come, to take part in the counsels of the Republican party of Ohio, and help to prepare for a grand victory this fall.

I HAVE NOT COME TO VAUNT ANY CLAIMS. I HAVE NO CLAIMS.

"It has ever been my pride to be simply a member of this party. I do not ask for any place, knowing that any place no matter how humble, that the party may give me, will be full of honor. No matter what the result may be to-morrow, no man will labor for our cause with greater zeal than myself."

THE YOUNG MEN'S BLAINE CLUB OF CINCINNATI,

men of high moral worth, showed their enthusiasm for Foraker.

They arrived at 10 o' clock, two hundred strong, and headed by the First Regiment, O. N. G. Band, marched from the depot to the head-quarters of the local clubs, who acted as an escort. While the Blaine boys were passing the Convention wigwam the Hamilton County delegates recognized them through the open door, and gave them a rousing reception. Immediately after dinner they formed in procession at the Court-house and marched through the two principal streets. They carried the Starry Club flag and a Foraker banner, with an excellent oil-painting of the judge. On the back of the latter were the words: "Vim, Vigor, and Victory." There was an immense crowd in the Arcade, and as the club poured in to the jubilant music of their band, they were greeted with loud cheers. Foraker appeared on the balcony. It reminded one of the ovation to Blaine by the same club in Cincinnati. When quiet reigned, Foraker said:

"Gentlemen of the Young Men's Blaine Club of Cincinnati, and fellow-citizens generally: — I sincerely thank you for this complimentary serenade. If there is any club in Ohio from which such a serenade could come with more welcome than another it is your club—the Young Men's Blaine Club of the city of Cincinnati. I have an especial admiration for you because of the fact that having been organized during the last year's campaign you took it upon yourself in the hour of defeat to turn a temporary into a permanent organization, and to enlist for life in the cause of Republicanism. Republicans of that character are the kind of Republicans we want in the State of Ohio. With such Republicans victory is sure. Again thanking you, I bid you good afternoon."—*Commercial-Gazette.*

GOD—FEARING PROTECTOR.

Ben. Butterworth's eulogy of Foraker was brilliant and unusually sympathetic, and his happy allusion to Judge Foraker as one with whom he would trust the

WELFARE OF HIS FAMILY AND LITTLE ONES,

and die contented in the knowledge that they would have a conscientious, careful, and God-fearing protector, touched the popular heart.

THE WIGWAM.

Mr. O'Neal, Chairman of the State Committee, in the opening address to the convention said:

Let us go hence with the determination to win victory whether the nominee be the gallant, courteous, hard-working Judge Joseph B. Foraker, who in response to the call of his Government, though but a boy sixteen years old, went forth as a private soldier to fight the battles of his country; who two years ago at the head of our ticket made a most brilliant fight, and who, though defeated, has never sulked in his tent, but who has responded to every call and worked earnestly for the success of the Republican party.

Hon. J. D. Taylor, temporary chairman, said:

GENTLEMEN OF THE CONVENTION: Accept my profound thanks for the distinguished honor you have conferred upon me, in making me temporary chairman of this, THE LARGEST AND MOST ENTHUSIASTIC CONVENTION ever held in Ohio.

YOUNG MEN THE STRENGTH OF REPUBLICANISM.

Miller Outcalt, of Cincinnati, in presenting the name of Hon. J. B. Foraker, was received with unusual demonstration at the mention of the name of the candidate, the convention jumping to their feet and waving hats and fans in the wildest confusion. Mr. Outcalt spoke as follows:

MR. CHAIRMAN AND GENTLEMEN OF THE CONVENTION: * * * * * The giants of mythology typified the strength of young men, and to-day the strength of the Republican party is in the young men of this country, of whom it possesses a vast majority. Such were Blaine's words to the young men of Cincinnati last fall, and to every one who heard them and to every one to whom they were repeated they gave new life and vigor and the rich promise of victory. Were those words idly said? Hamilton County spoke then. She can and will speak again. Could truer words be said to-day? Then it was a hope,—a promise, a purpose; to-day it is equal with the stars—immortal history and immortal truth. It is, therefore, in keeping with the spirit of this truth that THE VAST MAJORITY OF THE YOUNG MEN OF THIS GREAT COMMONWEALTH present the name of J. B. Foraker. [Applause.] Honored and respected in the councils of the young as well as the old, possessing that integrity of purpose and energy of political life which alone characterizes

A GREAT AND PURE MAN;

young because, as Ingersoll said, standing at his brother's grave, he has not yet reached that point in life's highway where the shadows are falling to the West, yet old enough to have shouldered the musket, and wearing the private blouse, marched to his country's defense twenty-five years ago, honored and respected for brave and valiant service as a soldier, and of pure and upright life as a good citizen, a conscientious lawyer, and a just judge. I do not make him greater than other men; his worth as pictured in his every walk of life serves but to reflect the intelligent high-minded,

GOD-FEARING MAN THAT HE IS AND THAT HE IS UNIVERSALLY KNOWN TO BE.

I have said that he was honored and respected in the councils of the old as well as the young. Need my words further confirmation to the knowledge of men and things common to us? Need I recall the facts and circumstances of his selection by our own illustrious Senator, John Sherman, to present his name at the national convention in Chicago last year? Need I recall the fact and circumstances of his selection by that convention as one of the committee to formally notify Mr. Blaine of his nomination? Need I go further and recall the fact and circumstance of his selection, most wisely bestowed, to meet and escort Mr. Blaine on his trip through Ohio last fall? Need I go still further to assert the fact that he enjoyed the confidence and esteem of Mr. Blaine himself, to whose judgment upon our state matters during that memorable campaign Mr. Blaine was glad to defer? These are but a few of

THE SHADOWS ON THE DIAL

which point instinctively to his appreciation and recognition by the grandest leaders of our party. That he enjoys the confidence and respect

OF THE COLORED AS WELL AS THE WHITE MAN

you know full well. Devoted to the absolute equality of the two races, casting his first vote for the right of suffrage to the negro, fighting for that right with musket and bayonet when but a boy, writing to his home that this war would never end until all realized that this was a nation, and for the colored as well as for the white man, so does he now with all his strength and manhood struggle for the same cause; and it is a most significant fact that since his candidacy has become known, clubs and organizations of colored men have been founded all over the State glad to wear his name and proud to do him honor.

I have not yet spoken of his candidacy two years ago. Then, as we all know, the cause of Republicanism in this state was at the most but a forlorn hope, yet in the face of an admitted fact,

LIKE A MARSHAL OF OLD,

stimulated by the same courage and hope, he accepted the nomination at your hands and infused a vigor and enthusiasm into that campaign which surprised even his most ardent friends and supporters. For the result he certainly, above all others, was not responsible. It was not Foraker's defeat but the defeat of the Republican party. Conditions and complications of State issues involving legislative action controlled the election then. Those complications do not now exist. Then he was almost a stranger to the great mass of people of this State. Though

LOVED AND HONORED AT HOME,

he became the party's leader two years ago, and the splendid canvass he made throughout this entire State steadily advanced him in popularity and public confidence; and though unsuccessful then, he is to-day the most popular young man in Ohio.

His speeches were statesman-like, scholarly, logical, and convincing. Free from all blundering, inviting no malevolence, destroying all bitterness of feeling, it was conviction, truth, good-will. Friendship he regards as sacred, convictions as moral principle, and public duty well performed

THE PRICELESS JEWEL OF MAN'S RENOWN.

Do not let it be said that he has earned this nomination, that he seeks or begs it, but rather that he is deservingly worthy of this high honor; for the Republican party, clothed in the garment woven from its splendid achievements during the past twenty-five years, rises above man or men. Then such is the man, such are the reasons which Hamilton County, the key and figure of the coming campaign, with its solid seventy-seven votes, presents to the Republicans of this State, and with a majority of ten thousand asks the nomination of J. B. Foraker for their Governor.

MOST BRILLIANT CAMPAIGN SINCE TOM CORWIN — THE SPLENDID FELLOW.

Ex-Governor Noyes said: "No more brilliant campaign has ever been made in this State by any man since the days of old Tom Corwin.*

"Judge Foraker is a scholar, an able lawyer, a wise and distinguished judge, a patriotic boy who without shoulder-straps put his blouse upon his back and shouldered his musket in the hour of our supreme peril, and went out to fight and help save the government of the nation. I say that his name is

AN INSPIRATION TO THE REPUBLICANS

of this State. * * * There is no name which

CAN MORE INSPIRE THE PEOPLE OF THIS STATE

than that of Joseph B. Foraker. The legislature next winter will select a successor to the Hon. John Sherman—whether it be himself or another, it would be convenient to have the fourteen members of the legislature from Hamilton County Republican. If you want them by 8,000 or 9,000 majority nominate the soldier, the statesman, the wise lawyer, the splendid fellow J. B. Foraker. [Tremendous applause.]

Judge West said: "I am proud in the past to have done, I shall be proud in the future to do honor to that gallant gentleman, J. B. Foraker."

The first great demonstration of the convention was made when Mr. Covert (nominating Mr. Rose) mentioned the name of Judge Foraker. Then the great assemblage flew up, and did not get down for five minutes, floating high in air all that time upon the wind of wild yelling, hoarse cheering, and stentorian howling.—*Commercial-Gazette.*

---

*Foraker's campaign of 1883 was the most brilliant in Ohio since that of Tom Corwin.—*Judge Haynes of Dayton.*

"MARCHING THROUGH GEORGIA."

When it was announced that balloting would begin for governor, there was a settling into seats and a preparation for the struggle, even as the old soldiers used to pull down their caps, tighten their belts, and draw a long breath when the order came to charge.

It was apparent almost from the beginning that the day was Foraker's, and as the votes crept up regularly and swiftly to the necessary four hundred to nominate, it became harder for the red-hot Foraker men to restrain themselves, and when at last, with but three votes wanted to nominate, gallant old Trumbull County came up with a solid thirteen votes for Foraker, and settled the matter, the devil broke loose in the wigwam, and the scene was scarcely less in noise and imposing display then than it was at Chicago when James G. Blaine's nomination was accomplished. The Band started up "Marching through Georgia," and everybody joined in a tremendous chorus, fairly making the walls rock and drowning out the very vigorous tooting and hammering of the band.—*Commercial-Gazette.*

THE GREATEST DEMONSTRATION.

When Trumbull County was reached in the call nearly the entire convention jumped to their feet, and the greatest of all the demonstrations of the day ensued. Those who had been keeping tally knew at this point that the leader had secured over four hundred votes, and enough to nominate. It was some time before order could be restored, and the call of counties finished. Meantime, the band played "Marching through Georgia," and the convention joined in the chorus.

On motion of John C. Covert (representing Rose), the rules were suspended, and the nomination was made unanimous by acclamation. The motion was heartily seconded by Judge West (the blind orator representing Kennedy), and a delegate from Franklin (representing Beatty).

THE NOMINEE APPEARS.

Colonel Robert Harlan, Hon. Wm. McKinley, and Colonel Allen Miller were appointed as a committee to bring the nominee before the convention, and Miller Outcalt, L. S. Bumgardner, and A. T. Brinsmade were appointed as a committee to perform similar service and escort Generals Kennedy and Beatty from their room to the convention hall.—*Enquirer.*

ANOTHER BIG HURRAH.

It took a long time to get the convention down to a basis of comparative quiet and common sense from the clouds of enthusiasm.

When Foraker appeared there was another big hurrah, and then, in his even, cooling tones, with his graceful manner and way so perfectly described by the word "taking," the judge for the second time accepted the leadership of the Ohio Republicans.

There was at once evident a feeling of relief and gratification upon all sides at the outcome. And well might such a feeling arise.

No party in any State ever marched under the leadership of a man more splendidly equipped for his duty in

STERLING MANHOOD, IN HONEST AND PURE RECORD, IN FRESH AND
CLEAN. PERSONALITY,

in rousing energy and fruitful resource, in ready and telling eloquence, in devoted and unswerving Republicanism, in heroic battle and high official record, animated by an ennobling ambition, and guided in private life by the best and truest aims of the citizen.—*Commercial-Gazette.*

Judge Foraker said:

MR. CHAIRMAN AND GENTLEMEN OF THE CONVENTION:—For this renewed expression of your confidence I sincerely thank you. I should regard it as a great honor to receive this nomination under any legitimate circumstances, but I deem it especially such coming to me, as it does today, after the defeat of two years ago, and in preference to the claim of such distinguished men as have been my competitors for your favor. I appreciate something other and more than what may be termed the mere personal compliment involved in this matter, for I appreciate also the fact, of which I am only too well aware, that the acceptance of this nomination necessitates the assumption by me of some important responsibilities. * *

In this work I invite and insist upon the hearty co-operation of every Republican in the State of Ohio. [Applause.] I wish you to go away from this convention impressed with the idea that this work is your work as well as mine. Your candidate, unaided, can do but little, but with your united support we can easily defeat the Democratic party, and inspire Republicanism with

NEW LIFE AND COURAGE THROUGHOUT THE WHOLE NATION.

* * * As we start out upon this work we are encouraged by the most auspicious circumstances, our position in this respect being in marked contrast with that when we were assembled in Columbus two years ago. It is perhaps true that at that time

I WAS THE ONLY MAN IN ALL THE STATE OF OHIO

who confidently expected an election; but to-day it would be difficult to find anywhere within the borders of our State any man of sound judgment, Democrat or Republican, who has any serious doubt but what our entire ticket this day nominated will be in October next victoriously elected. At that time our Democratic friends had at the preceding election swept the State by a majority of more than 20,000. They were flushed with victory, and united and emboldened by confidence, wh le we were weakened with dissension and discouraged by defeat. But to-day the situation is reversed; for while it is true that we have a Democratic administration at Washington, the first we have had for the last twenty-four years, and the last we will have for the next twenty-four years to come, yet it is also true that no part whatever of the blame for it attaches to the Republicans of Ohio. On the contrary, our party banner in this State was was never more loftily carried than when it followed the unsuccessful but gallant and brilliant leadership of James G. Blaine. Hence it is that we go into this campaign without the depressing recollection resting upon us of a Democratic victory of more than 20,000 at the last prior election, but, on the contrary, with the recollection of the most inspiring State victory ever recorded. It gives us assurance that since 1883 there has been a revolution of political sentiment in Ohio. The duty resting upon us is to take advantage of these circumstances and give practical effect to this change of sentiment by the election of a Republican legislature and a Republican United States Senator. And after we shall have victoriously gone through this contest, it will be the proud privilege of Ohio to carry the old Republican banner of Ohio once more to the head of the column and lead it on to a grand and triumphant victory for the whole country by the election of a Republican president in 1888.

This is not the time nor the place, gentlemen of the convention, for me to discuss or even to allude to the many issues and questions that enter into the campaign. * * * * * *

Foraker's speech was a

SINCERE AND MANLY EFFORT,

and did credit to his head and heart.—*Enquirer.*

LIEUTENANT-GOVERNOR.

The theatrical event of the day was the nomination for Lieutenant-Governor. Foraker, Kennedy, and Beatty had all made speeches to the convention after the nomination for the first place, Beatty quite gracefully accepting the situation and Kennedy making the speech on "general principles." *

When there was a general call for Kennedy for Lieutenant-Governor he declined. The call was vociferously renewed. Kennedy reappeared, Foraker was sent for and suddenly placed by the side of Kennedy in the presence of the crowd. Foraker took his late competitor by the hand and the two stood in an attitude of friendly greeting and silent under deafening applause.—*Enquirer.*

General Kennedy stretched out his hand to begin his speech of declination. Just then Judge Foraker stepped out, stood by his side, and touched him on the shoulder. Kennedy let his hand partly fall, and turned half around to see who had interrupted, Judge Foraker put out his hand and stood smiling in Kennedy's face. Kennedy looked in his face, turned with an uncertain air toward the people, turned hesitatingly back, looked in the judge's smiling face and down at the outstretched hand, and then slammed his right hand into the judge's, and the two, hand in hand, swung around facing the multitude, which immediately became a

SCREAMING, DANCING, SINGING MOB.

Said Kennedy, "It is the first time I was ever drafted."

The nomination of Kennedy was received in the same spirit as that of Logan's at Chicago. * * * * *

---

* NOTE.—Hon. Wm. G. Rose, of Cleveland, was not at the convention. He thus wrote of Judge Foraker: "His defeat two years ago was no fault of his. He made a splendid campaign then, speaking at about one hundred meetings and never saying a word *for which he or his friends had to apologize* or make any explanations. Then last summer and fall he stumped the State, strengthening the very favorable impression made in the previous campaign. He was discreet in all his utterances and completely won the good-will of his party all over the State. I am glad he is put to the front again."

The report ran like fire in the grass, and outside the cheering echoed that within, and even the crowds in the Arcade burst forth with an answering cheer.—*Commercial-Gazette.*

I think I have seen

NO MORE STRIKING SIGHT IN POLITICS

than Foraker grasping Kennedy's hand and smiling upon the convention. Many delegates about me exclaimed that the entire convention was a reminder of the Chicago convention which nominated Blaine.—*Times-Star.*

No more pleasing token of this good fellowship could have been given than was presented to the convention when Judge Foraker and General Kennedy grasped hands upon the front of the stage, in full view of the convention, as the latter was about to accept the already tendered unanimous nomination of the Lieutenant Governorship; nor could that token have received a more hearty recognition than it received from the convention as the vast assembly rose in a body and amidst thunders of cheers and waving of hats and handkerchiefs, and the wild delirium of excited and happy delegates paid tribute to the two eminent, able, gallant, and handsome men who had been chosen the leaders in the coming campaign.—*Dayton Journal.*

RATIFIED BY FORAKER.

Judge Foraker stated that if the convention would permit he would like to say a few words in ratification of the nomination which had just been made. His confrere upon the ticket might not know the fact, but this was not the first time they had been associated in public service, that they had belonged to the same brigade, the same division of the army twenty years ago. He said they made a good job of it then, and he believed they would make a good job of it this time.

It required some time before the convention could recover from the demonstration and resume its work.—*Enquirer.*

Two expressions were heard on all sides of this

MOST SPLENDID AND SIGNIFICANT POLITICAL BODY

ever assembled in Ohio: First, that it was more like a national than a State convention; and, secondly, that never before had there been such an acquiescence by the defeated candidates and their friends in the will of the majority.

There was no mistaking the strength of the feeling for Judge Foraker in the convention. His friends were warmly enthusiastic, and, we may add, indescribably vociferous. Noise on such occasions has some significance. It means at least that those who make it are in earnest.

It was not the unexpected that happened at Springfield yesterday. The re-nomination of Judge Foraker was the inevitable. The wave of sentiment in his favor gathered force daily, becoming irresistible at the last. Judge Foraker was admired for his *sterling and popular qualities.* In the minds of the people and of the delegates the sense of obligation to the young leader of 1883 and the certainty that he would infuse into the fight this year an enthusiastic and aggressive spirit outweighed all considerations as to the prestige of defeat.—*Times-Star.*

There has never in the history of Republican conventions been a more cordial, united coming together of Republican forces.
GRAY-HAIRED VETERANS IN THE PARTY
fail to recall a convention where the nomination of a successful candidate was immediately indorsed by the representatives of all his competitors and ratified in person by his chief opponents.

Miller Outcalt, young, smooth, and fresh-faced, made a first-rate speech in putting in nomination Judge Foraker, and Walter Thomas followed in excellent manner. It was a good thing to see
THE YOUNG MEN OF THE PARTY, WHITE AND BLACK,
coming prominently before the people in the party affairs, and it is not upon record where any such young Republican called to the front has failed to acquit himself with credit to himself and the party.

This convention will go into history as the most memorable one ever held by the party in Ohio, exceeding, perhaps, any previous one in interest and importance as much as it exceeds any other in numbers and enthusiasm. The party in Ohio has never been assembled in a more brilliant, imposing, and distinguished meeting than that gathered in the wigwam this morning.—*Commercial-Gazette.*

No such compliment was ever before extended to a gubernatorial candidate under such circumstances. The oldest and most experienced convention-goers stood in wonder at the magnificent ovation tendered the gallant though defeated leader in the contest of two years ago.

Murat Halstead says in the *Commercial-Gazette:* There has been no reason from the first discussion of the subject to doubt that Judge Foraker would a second time receive the nomination of the Republican party for Governor of Ohio. Doubts arose in his own mind as to whether he should go into the political field again, *abandoning to that extent professional business* with a flattering tendency to grow lucrative; but *his manhood appealed to him* that if the people wanted him again it was not possible to refuse. * * * The fact was before the people that as the Memphis *Avalanche* put it, though Hoadley was elected two years ago, Foraker *came out of the campaign with most reputation.* The fight that Foraker made was a good one. There was a feeling throughout the State that the failure was not his fault.

Now it would have been the height of unwisdom for the Republicans of Ohio to have held that Foraker had claims upon them, because he had been defeated in their name, that must be liquidated at a disadvantage to themselves. Of course they were just as free to nominate anybody else as if he never had been a candidate. There was prevalent among Republicans the just sentiment that the campaign of 1883 had worked an injustice to Foraker, and that it should be repaired. He was in a position in which *manly delicacy forbade him* to go into the contest and organize friends and struggle for the honor of a second nomination. He had simply to say that if he was wanted he was willing to try again, and then patiently to wait. Republicans in this county, too, who cared for their responsibilities, felt that it *was not becoming to beat the tom-toms and blow the hewgags* in this quarter, and this for the reason that two years ago the Republican Convention, when Sherman could not be had, substantially asked Hamilton County to name the man. Foraker was named and beat, and certainly it was the thing now for the county to stand back and say that the State should name the candidate.

We thought well of our neighbor, Foraker, but the State must call for him if he was wanted. The delegates in this county were not named *until two days before the convention*, and Foraker was the last of the candidates to go to Springfield.

There was a very energetic personal canvass made by two talented and liberal gentlemen, who furnished ample opportunity to those seeking a candidate other than Foraker to find one. Indeed, we thought the candidacy of the opposing gentlemen was too warm and spirited. *The State called for Foraker.* * * *

The history of Judge Foraker is familiar to the people of Ohio. His career as a boy-soldier who educated himself after the war, and an irreproachable judge and eloquent advocate, and facile and persuasive speaker from the stump, is well known. *It has been tried in the fire and found without flaws.*

MUCH HIGHER TYPE OF POLITICS.

The nomination meets the wishes of the party. Judge Foraker, in spite of his defeat of two years ago, is unquestionably well liked by his party, and deservedly so. He is an active and zealous Republican, enjoys

A GOOD REPUTATION FOR HIGH PERSONAL CHARACTER,

is a popular speaker, and shares the sentiments of his party. * * Judge Foraker represents the much higher type of politics.—*New York Times.*

THE REPUBLICANS OF OHIO HAVE DONE WELL

in again choosing Judge Foraker as their standard-bearer. He made a plucky fight in 1883 when the circumstances were less favorable for success than they now are. His course since that canvass has strengthened him in political estimation, and the enthusiasm which his nomination elicited yesterday foreshadows his triumph at the polls. Of course a Republican victory is not to be won easily, but a good beginning has been made in the choice of the head of the ticket.—*New York Tribune.*

NO TRADES.

Under the inspiration of Judge Foraker's notions of pure political methods, there were no trades by the County of Hamilton. Foraker would not have accepted a nomination which would not have expressed,

UNINFLUENCED, THE WILL OF THE PEOPLE.

"There were no trades anywhere," was the comment in many quarters, and with high gratification.

WITHOUT A PRECEDENT.

Without manipulation, without conference, with the expressed aversion of Judge Foraker as to modern political methods, with no bosses, and with no dark-lantern committees appointing delegates, with no packing of conventions, the seventy-seven delegates of his own county were amazingly firm for the judge in the convention. These seventy-seven delegates were elected by primaries straight to the convention. A delegation coming to a State Convention from Hamilton County unitedly and overflowingly enthusiastic for one candidate is without a precedent.

"Show us a candidate," the delegates asked, "who has ever had a home delegation at his back like Foraker has."

THE GERMAN WARDS.

The most enthusiastically Foraker delegates were from the German wards, where the judge has always been strong.

The *Columbus Sonntagsgast* (German Independent paper) says,

"AMONG THE GERMANS

Foraker has become popular, owing to his outspoken, manly bearing. He can rest upon a hearty support from the German quarter."

The Hamilton County Committee, June, 1885,

Resolved, That this committee, recognizing the sentiment and desire of the Republican voters of this county, do recommend and indorse Hon. J. B. Foraker as candidate for Governor.

This was carried with cheers. Major Smith declared Foraker to be

"THE FOREMOST MAN IN OHIO TO-DAY."

From a Correspondent to the Commercial-Gazette:

A little over three years ago, when I first came to Cincinnati, my early newspaper duties consisted in finding candidates for Congress in the First and Second districts. The resignation of Judge Foraker from the Superior Court bench, owing to illness, brought him prominently before the public. Many citizens had told me during his illness,

"A FINE GENTLEMAN IS JUDGE FORAKER;

you should meet him." I did meet him in his office where he was busy in getting his legal business on its feet. On first acquaintance with any man, I have never been more taken. I broached the idea of his becoming a candidate for Congress. He declined to favor the idea, declaring himself "out of politics." Strangely enough, a year later, when I had occasion to write up the Gubernatorial possibilities in Ohio, I mentioned Foraker as the one man from Cincinnati who could take control of the party in vigor and earnestness. His nomination in 1883 came so spontaneously, with scarcely the sign of an effort, that it dazzled the old politicians in Ohio and created an enthusiasm which made the campaign brilliant. And yet men asked then,

"WHO IS THIS FORAKER?"

And they are told again that he is a young man, a native of Highland County, Ohio, born July 5, 1846, and thirty-nine years old. His early home and birth place was near Rainsboro, but his boyhood days were passed on a farm four miles above. He grew up a slender, pushing, and persevering lad, known to all the country roundabout as Ben. Foraker. He got the usual education that farmer-boys receive, and was fired with the spirit of patriotism when the war broke out.

HE WAS ONLY FIFTEEN,

and his older brother, Burch, soon became a captain. His parents objected, but knowing the boy to be determined, finally consented, and he enlisted as a private in the 89th O. V. I. *   *   *   *

He came back home a captain, although but a boy in years. He had saved some money, and at once sought a better education. *   *

He decided that in Cincinnati he could do best as an attorney, although he was taken back at first to learn that there were 300 lawyers in that great city. He hesitated, but finally decided to become the three hnndred and first. He was not long in making himself known at the Cincinnati bar as a young lawyer of ability. *   *   *   *

HE WAS THREE YEARS ON THE SUPERIOR BENCH,

when he resigned because of ill health. He said to Uncle Ben. Eggleston while convalescing: "I do not care to remain on the bench and

DRAW A SALARY WHILE I CAN NOT SERVE THE PEOPLE AND EARN IT."

So against the counsel of his best friends and the ablest and best men in Cincinnati, without regard to party, he resigned. Several telegrams were sent Governor Foster asking that the resignation be not accepted. This was Foster's first knowledge of Foraker, and he afterward remarked that a man who could excite

SO MUCH SENTIMENT

must be remarkably able.   *   *   *

His chief charm is his personal popularity. He is winning in his conversation with

MEN IN POLITICS, BUSINESS, OR PLEASURE.

He stands incomparably beyond all in representing the younger element of Republicanism in Ohio.

POST CONVENTION NOTES.

Old politicians say that never *since the days of Brough* has there been such a large and enthusiastic state convention as that at Springfield, and no ticket ever presented to the Republicans of Ohio was more acceptable.

The observation has been freely made that Thursday's convention had

NATIONAL RATHER THAN STATE CHARACTERISTICS.

One item alone illustrates the truth of the observation. On the morning of the convention two young Cincinnatians, Lou Bauer and Jeff Eddison, went to Springfield with Foraker badges, and by early in the evening, before the convention was through with its work, they had sold over fifty-four hundred. When their stock had been disposed of they tried to beg badges from members of the Young Men's Blaine Club, but the boys valued them too highly to part with them.—*Commercial-Gazette.*

FORAKER WAS DELUGED

with telegrams and letters of congratulation. "Black Jack" Logan was one of the first to send greetings, then Blaine, Fairchild, and Andrew D. White. They came not only from every corner of Ohio, but from New York, Indiana, Tennessee, Michigan, Minnesota, Maine, Pennsylvania, and other States.

JUDGE HOADLY, WHEN ASKED,

"What do you think of the Ohio Republican convention?" replied, "I was not surprised that the Republicans should have re-nominated Judge Foraker. He is an able man, of high principle and captivating manners. The people of Ohio so regard him, and he will make a brilliant canvass. He certainly made a very remarkable canvass two years ago, and I felt then, as I trust he did, that whoever won, nothing could be said about the personal bearing of his opponent. If Judge Foraker is to be my successor, I shall turn over the office to him with the greatest possible pleasure."

THE IRREPRESSIBLE CONFLICT.

The present Democratic party of Ohio is in no condition for the irrepressible conflict that the energetic young Foraker will force upon it.—*Buffalo* [N. Y.] *Express*.

HOADLY'S GOOD WORD FOR FORAKER.

Governor Hoadly adds his testimony to the general fund in hearty approval of the ability and worth of Judge Foraker. — *Indianapolis Journal*.

FORAKER WILL RALLY THE FORCES.

Judge Foraker represents the kind of Republicans that so successfully governed the nation for a quarter of a century, and around him will rally the old forces that have made Ohio such a prominent factor in American politics. The contest for Republican reinstatement will be successfully inaugurated in Ohio.—*Kansas City Journal*.

A DEMOCRATIC COMPARISON.

The *Louisville Times* (Dem.), evening edition of *Courier-Journal*, says: "Both men [Foraker and Hoadly] live in the same ward in a Cincinnati suburb. Both are better known by their neighbors than they were two years ago. We do not intend to deceive ourselves if we can prevent it, nor would we deceive our readers if we could, but we venture to make this prediction: If Hoadly enters the field against Foraker again this fall, the present governor will be defeated by no less than 30,000 majority." The *Times* speaks of Foraker as being "true to his friends and true to the truth as he sees it."

A CANDID SOUTHERN CONFESSION.

The nomination of J. B. Foraker for the governorship of Ohio by the Republicans is a strong one. The candidate is in the prime of life, has large abilities, is popular with the masses—especially strong with the soldiers. Foraker would not have gone through that body of able and courageous politicians on the first ballot if he had not been carefully weighed and found to be the strongest candidate.—*Chattanooga Times* (Dem).

UNTARNISHED CHARACTER.

He [Foraker] is a man of conceded abilities, has an untarnished character, and is very popular.—*Buffalo Commercial Advertiser*.

WON'T TAKE NO.

Judge Foraker is an Ohio man who will not take no for an answer. He is in the field again, and is likely to hold it.—*Philadelphia Inquirer*.

THE STRONGEST.

Judge Foraker is the strongest nomination the Ohio Republicans could have made.—*Memphis Avalanche* (Dem).

THE INEVITABLE.

The Ohio Republicans have done the expected and indeed the inevitable thing in the renomination of Judge Foraker for governor. Foraker was a good candidate two years ago, and went down largely because the Republicans had a prohibitory amendment on their hands, an issue which alienated the German vote. Since then the judge has been active in the Republican National Convention and on the stump, and his claims to the nomination were incontestable.—*Springfield* (Mass.) *Republican* (Independent).

DISTINCTIVE FEATURE.

Judge Foraker's reputation is fully as great here as at home, and he is the distinctive feature of the campaign to outsiders.—New York Correspondent *Times-Star*.

ABILITY TO TURN DEFEAT INTO VICTORY.

Judge Foraker's political career shows that he has the ability to turn defeat into victory upon a second effort. His first campaign for Judge of the Court of Common Pleas of Hamilton County in 1877, was conducted against a combination of antagonistic elements and resulted in defeat. The young lawyer, however, came out of the fight with

A PERSONAL REPUTATION UNTARNISHED,

and with the prestige of a candidate who had run ahead of his ticket. So, two years later, he was again nominated for the same position, and was triumphantly elected. After three years of service on the bench, during which he acquired a reputation throughout the State for sound judgment and unimpeachable integrity, he resigned and spent a year abroad in search of health lost by too close application to business. Almost immediately upon his return from abroad he accepted the call of his party in 1883, to make a canvass for the Governorship against the overwhelming odds of that campaign. The temperance and wool tariff issues defeated him. These are absent from the present fight, and thus far the course of events has been parallel to his career in the politics of Hamilton County, and there is no reason to believe that the resemblance will not be completed with his election as Governor in October next.

Judge Foraker possesses

SUCH A HOLD UPON THE ELEMENTS—

not factions—of his party as to insure him its solid support. * * * A significant fact that since his candidacy has become known, clubs and organizations of colored men have been formed all over the State, glad to wear his name and proud to do him honor.

The ticket is one about which the soldier vote will rally as one man. Foraker was a private in the army. Foraker enlisted when a boy of sixteen, and although entitled to be orderly sergeant of his company because of the number of recruits he had secured, he modestly declined the position on the ground of his inexperience in military affairs. When his company departed for the front he playfully remarked that he would lead it home, and the prediction was verified.

HIS GALLANTRY WON THE CONFIDENCE OF HIS SUPERIOR OFFICERS,

and on two occasions he was entrusted with important and difficult missions which he accomplished successfully. After the war he entered the Ohio Wesleyan University at Delaware, where he was a classmate of Mr. Hamilton, the late Governor of Illinois, of Professor White, of Harvard, and of T. W. Brotherton, who was proposed in the convention at Springfield as a candidate for Lieutenant-Governor. Judge Foraker completed his education at Cornell, afterward studied law in Cincinnati, where, upon his admission to the bar, he took up the practice of his profession, and where he has continued to live an honored citizen. Should he be elected Governor, it is said he will relinquish a law practice worth annually from $25,000 to $30,000.—Correspondent *New York Tribune.*

NO STRANGER IN BROOKLYN—THE SOUL OF HONOR.

The candidate of the Republicans for governor of Ohio, Judge Joseph B. Foraker, is no stranger in Brooklyn, having spoken here in company with Senator Hawley and General Woodford at the opening meeting of the Blaine and Logan campaign. Governor Hoadly's chivalrous compliments to his old adversary as "an able man, of high principle and captivating manners," was deservedly bestowed. Whatever may be thought of Foraker's political associations and beliefs, or the absurd reactionary platform upon which he has been placed, no one can deny that he is personally the soul of honor, or that

HIS RECORD IS WITHOUT THE STAIN OF WRONG-DOING.

To our own knowledge the judge, who was chairman of the Ohio delegation in the first Chicago Convention, refused to be swayed by the tumult and uproar of the shouters; and although his delegation was badly divided from the start, he succeeded in holding twenty-three votes until the final tidal-wave of excitement made further resistance impossible. Judge Foraker entered the Union army at the outbreak of the war, when he was only sixteen years old. For a time he was attached to the staff of General Slocum,†

†NOTE.—Ben Foraker soon became a great favorite in the Signal Corps. He was the youngest officer in the corps, but his close attention to duty, soldierly bearing, and BIG, WARM HEART gained a friend in all he met. When the plan of the march to the sea was settled, it was soon known that some signal officers must return with General Thomas to Nashville, and it was supposed that none but a few of the most experienced would go with General Sherman; but much to Ben's surprise, he was selected to accompany that expedition, and was assigned to the head-quarters of the left wing, General Slocum commanding, and continued with him until the end came, that beautiful morning in the Pines near Raleigh. — *Albert S. Cole, Nebraska City, Nebraska.*

Foraker served in the line until after Atlanta fell. A few weeks thereafter he was detailed for the Signal Corps. There were thirteen examined, and only two passed the examination. It usually required something like two months to practice in the camp to qualify an officer to take charge of a signal station, it being to many men very difficult to learn to read the signals. But he had no trouble whatever about it. After he had been a week in the camp, he could read as well as any of the oldest members of the corps, and at the end of the second week he was put in charge of the station at Vining's Hill, six miles out of Atlanta, and was in charge of that station when Hood undertook to draw Sherman back from Atlanta by marching to Sherman's rear and attacking Altoona, and passing on to Nashville, where who is well acquainted with him, and who speaks in the highest terms of his admirable personal qualities, while detesting his political inclination. * * * If he should sweep the state, look out for the re-appearance of the Ohio man on the field of national politics in all his pristine glory.—*Brooklyn (N.Y.) Eagle*, (Democratic).

VICTORY IN THE AIR.

The voice of the people in October will vindicate the action of the convention in June. There is victory in the air.—*Toledo Blade*.

THE SPONTANEOUS CHOICE.

That Foraker got the nomination on first ballot, without any claquing or booming, is the best proof that he was the spontaneous choice of Ohio Republicans and the best proof that there was a deep-seated conviction *among the masses of the party* that he was the man to bring them to victory. That conviction is of the sort that always precedes Republican victory—an earnest and abiding confidence in the man of the party's choice.—*Akron Beacon*.

A NEW FEATURE IN POLITICS.

That large class of Republicans who believe more in fidelity to party leaders that represent party honor and party pride from having figured conspicuously in its past conflicts, than they do of party policy, are deeply gratified at the re-nomination of the gallant young leader, Judge J. B. Foraker. To such Republicans his selection means much. It means a new feature in politics; namely, that an idea, a myth, shall not weigh against solid worth; that a well-known man shall not be abandoned because, forsooth, he may have a blemish for an unknown quantity, because no defects are apparent.—*Xenia Gazette*.

FORAKER WILL WIN.

Seven candidates for Governor beaten on their first trial have afterwards been elected Governor of Ohio. Four Governors of Ohio have been defeated upon renomination.—*Marietta Leader*.

A PERFECT TYPE.

The Republican who is not gratified with a leader who posesses such splendid character and superior abilities as those conceded to Judge Foraker is hard to please. There is not a man in Ohio of any party or faction who excels Foraker in nobility of character, and not one of his age (thirty-nine years) who ranks him in solid or shining abilities. He is an almost perfect type of the best Republicanism in the nation.—*Dayton Journal*.

FORAKER AND TEMPERANCE.

As to the matter of temperance, which is a great question in Ohio, while Judge Foraker is not as outspoken as many think he ought to be, yet he is

---

he was whipped by Thomas. Foraker's station was one of the most important during Hood's movement, inasmuch as communication between Atlanta, Kenesaw Mountain, and Altoona had to be kept open by means of his station. His services there were so acceptable that when a week or two later Sherman started on his march to the sea, Major Bachtell, who was charged with the duty of selecting a number of his most efficient signal officers, saw fit to choose Ben as one of them.

a thorough temperance man—just such a man as the people would want to put in charge of all the interests of a great state. He will aim to do right without being oppressive or overzealous. In fine, he is precisely the man that *the people will fully trust,* feeling that every interest will be safe in his hands.—*Miami Helmet* (Temperance.)

EVEN HIS ENEMIES PRAISE HIM.

We concede that if Foraker should be elected, he will make a very respectable governor.—*Cleveland Plain-Dealer* (Dem).

THE TICKET O. K.

If the Republicans don't win next fall, the blame must rest at some other door than that of the gentlemen on the ticket.—*Wyandot County Republican.*

GREAT IN 1883; GREATER NOW.

Great in 1883, Judge Foraker is greater now. His canvass then showed him to be a scholarly and effective reasoner, and an apt and effective reasoner.—*Kenton Republican.*

FORAKER'S SPEECHES.

Judge Foraker is making better speeches this year than he did in 1883, when the brilliancy of his campaign was a marvel. His speeches before the Lincoln Club, of Cincinnati, at Xenia and Bellefontaine were master efforts.—*Holmes County Republican.*

COLORED "FOR-REVENUE-ONLY" DEMOCRATS.

A few colored men were Democrats "for revenue only" in the Ohio campaign two years ago, and there were one or two or three of such in Summit County. The colored voters of Ohio will be found in '85, as they were in '83, on the side of the only party that has honestly striven for their advancement.—*Cleveland Gazette.*

Judge Foraker has good reason for entertaining a profound degree of complacency, if not personal pride, over such a result.—*Springfield Globe-Republic.*

PURE PERSONAL CHARACTER.

The people of Ohio never had an opportunity of voting for a man of purer personal character than Judge J. B. Foraker.—*Cleveland Leader.*

RISING FROM THE ASHES OF DEFEAT.

Rising from the ashes of defeat, unscarred by the wounds that bore him down, with renewed vigor and increased strength, more valiant and better loved than ever before, Foraker comes again to claim the honor his nobility and gifts and achievements entitle him to.—*Youngstown News-Register.*

INDUSTRY AND PLUCK.

That announcement (Foraker's nomination) gave great satisfaction here where Judge Foraker has many warm personal friends, and throughout the state; for the vigorous way in which Judge Foraker conducted the campaign two years ago convinced the people that he had the material in him of which successful candidates are made. He exhibited industry, energy, skill, and pluck withal—those elements which the American people admire. —*Zanesville Courier.*

GALLANT CAMPAIGN.

We have a standard-bearer in Captain Foraker of whom the Republicans may well feel proud. Although he was beat two years ago, he nevertheless made a gallant campaign and a splendid run.—*Norwalk Reflector.*

WITHOUT THE WILES OF A POLITICIAN.

Educated, broad-minded, and gifted, honest, sincere, and straightforward, without the wiles of a politician, untouched by corruption, he is a living monument of the Springfield convention.—*Piqua Journal.*

HE GROWS IN THE HEARTS OF THE PEOPLE.

Judge Foraker receives the warmest attestation of love and good-will from the patriotic Republicans of this section. Judge Foraker is a man that *grows in the hearts of the people* as they come in contact with him. He has already won a warm place in the hearts of the Republicans of Ohio, and the campaign intensifies into a genuine enthusiasm.—*Urbana Citizen and Gazette.*

SATISFACTION.

There is universal satisfaction on the part of the Republicans of Ohio at the nominations of the Springfield convention.—*Cadiz Republican.*

PURE-MINDED.

Judge Foraker has grown in the estimation of the people since he formed their acquaintance two years ago. His grand abilities and pure-minded character commend him to all.—*Elyria Republican.*

HEARTS OF THE PEOPLE.

The demand for the renomination of Judge Foraker, which was a foregone conclusion from the first, sprung from the popular sense of justice and fair play, and the unanimity with which it was finally effected; and the unbounded enthusiasm with which it was hailed in the convention were true indications of the response it was to meet in the hearts of the people of the state.—*Geauga Republican.*

IRISH RECRUITS.

A great number of Irishmen in Ohio, who left the Democracy last year, have clinched their former determination to remain in the Republican ranks, and are this year found fighting for Judge Foraker.—*Findlay Republican.*

NEVER A BETTER MAN.

The Republicans and the people of Ohio have had opportunities for voting for a good many first-class men, for high positions during the last quarter of a century, but never had an opportunity of voting for a better one than Captain J. B. Foraker.—*Norwalk Reflector.*

DEMOCRATIC COMPLIMENT.

Of the address at Columbus, the *Columbus Capital* (Dem.) says: "Judge Foraker's speech on Tuesday evening last was, it is fair to say, an able key-note."

A GALLANT AND WISE YOUNG VETERAN.

Foraker's foes have yet to find the first flaw in his speeches or acts since his nomination. He is a gallant and wise young veteran in political leadership.—*Cleveland Leader.*

FORAKER AND NARROW-GAUGE EMPLOYES.

Judge Foraker's position toward the employes of the Narrow-Gauge has been that of a friend. It was through his agency that one month's wages were paid, and directly against his appeals that another month's pay was omitted.—*Ironton Register.*

ALL CAN SPEAK TO.

Foraker is a generous, sweet tempered man, with a good, kind face that takes well.

GOD ALMIGHTY MARKED FORAKER WELL.

He is a man you can all speak to and be well treated.—John R. McLean, May 11, 1885.

CULTURE—DIGNITY—INCORRUPTIBILITY.

The *Christian Advocate*, of Cincinnati, the organ of the Western Methodists says:

* * He and his wife are of Methodist stock and are both members of the Walnut Hills Methodist Episcopal Church. Mr. Foraker is a trustee of the church, and Mrs. Foraker is one of the most active and efficient ladies in the membership. There are no people in Cincinnati who are more highly esteemed than

THIS EDUCATED, REFINED CHRISTIAN FAMILY.

Mr. Foraker is a thorough temperance man, both in personal habits and in his views of public policy. The colored people never had a better friend than he. Indeed he is a man who knows what poverty and toil are, and his personal experience as well as the instincts of his nature,

MAKE HIM A FRIEND OF ALL THE LOWLY.

His generosity knows no bounds. We have known him for years, and intimately, and we speak thus freely and positively from personal knowledge.

BISHOP WALDEN, OF THE METHODIST CHURCH,

proclaims the Republican ticket the strongest ever presented in his recollection to the voters of Ohio.—*Dayton Journal.*

PURE IN PUBLIC AND PRIVATE LIFE.

The *Graphic* (Cin.) styles Judge Foraker " The brilliant young soldier, jurist, and statesman. The result is a merited recognition of the splendid campaign he made two years ago, and also of his ability,

PURE CHARACTER, AND LOFTY PATRIOTISM,

that have been fully established at the bar, on the bench, upon the field of battle, and in *private and public life*. When he was chosen the first time to head the state ticket it was urged against him that he was too young, he being then but thirty-seven years old. The objection was fully met by reference to the marked talent, mature judgment, and wonderful success that has characterized his entire public career. In the time that has elapsed since the conclusion of his memorable battle for the governorship he has developed rapidly, and grown with corresponding vigor in the esteem and admiration of all.

His parents represent

THE STURDY AGRICULTURAL CLASS OF OUR POPULATION,

and upon their farm Judge Foraker spent his earliest years. * During his military career (which closed at nineteen) he acquitted himself most courageously, and achieved feats which required true bravery and unerring judgment. * * At Chicago his commanding presence, quiet dignity, and admitted ability attracted marked attention. His speech nominating Sherman was one of the best made on that memorable day of remarkable orations, and resulted in an ovation for the young statesman. * * The judge is a gentleman of

MUCH MORE THAN ORDINARY QUALITIES OF HEAD AND HEART,

a man of fine culture, a superior lawyer; and in every position in life he has thus far been called to fill, whether as soldier in the army of the Union, counselor, or judge upon the bench, or a candidate before the people for the highest office in the state, he has met

THE MOST SANGUINE EXPECTATIONS OF HIS FRIENDS.

At the ratification meeting of the Lincoln Club (Cincinnati), Hon. Ben. Butterworth said :

"Now, fellow-members, the 11th of June ought to be a memorable day with this club. Upon this day it pleased the loyal, patriotic people of Ohio to elevate this gallant soldier and eminent jurist [pointing to Foraker] to the proud leadership of the Republican party of this state, and place in his hands the banner of Republicanism with all that it symbolizes. We did it for a reason—because he represents

THE BEST POLITICAL THOUGHT OF HIS TIME,

because he represents the best system of political government that our country has known.

Judge Foraker said : * * After the present Democratic administration was inaugurated at Washington, I said in some political remarks that as we looked out upon the political horizon there seemed to be nothing in appearances at least, encouraging for Republicanism; for no matter where we looked, all along the line, we saw the Democratic banners flaunting in triumph. The Democratic party were in control in this city, they were in control of our state government at Columbus, and they were in control, also, by reason of the recent inauguration, of our national government at Washington; but at the same time I indicated that we were about to enter upon three important contests, and, as I thought, three important conquests.

The first of these contests has already been waged and a victory has been brilliantly won—when on the first Monday of April last we turned the Democratic party out of power in the city of Cincinnati by a majority of more than four thousand, and put the Republican party in, with our worthy fellow-member, Mr. Amor Smith, as mayor of the city. [Applause.]

We have organized now for

THE SECOND OF THESE CONTESTS;

and if you had been at Springfield and seen the Republican party of the State of Ohio as there represented, and the spirit and enthusiasm there manifested, I do not think you would have much doubt but that on the evening of the second Tuesday of October next there will be a very different kind of an audience assembled in this club-house from that which was here, I am pained to say, two years ago. [Laughter.] And the third of these contests will be when we elect a Republican president of the United States in the year 1888. [Applause.]

* * The Republicans have taken an advanced step in regard to this matter and have not only declared that

EVERY VOTE SHOULD BE HONESTLY CAST AND COUNTED,

but that if under the constitution and laws of the United States that sort of protection can not be cast about voters, there must be such an amendment of the constitution and laws of the United States that will enable us to put it there. [Applause.]

Why that sort of a declaration? Why put it so prominently at the head of the resolutions adopted by the Republicans of the State of Ohio? Manifestly because it was the idea of the mass of the Republicans of the State of Ohio, and of this whole country; and why is it? Answering that, I need go back but for a moment, and with a word or two. You all remember when the war was over we were confronted with some very grave difficulties. Eleven States of the Union had seceded. They had been whipped back into the Union. The question arose, What shall be done with them? Some people wished them continued, simply as separate provinces, but finally they were restored to their state relations to the United States,

WITH THAT MAGNANIMITY,
such as has never been shown by a great party before in the political history of the world—that a people who had been conquered should be restored to the same rights as the conquerors enjoyed; and accordingly the revolting States were put back into the Union. And when they were put back, and made an integral part of the United States, another question presented itself. They could not occupy these relations to the General Government unless they were given the right to be represented in the Congress and in the Electoral College; but *who* should have these rights was the question. Some said

ONLY THE WHITE PEOPLE OF THE SOUTH
should be allowed the right of franchise, because, they said, only the whites have enough intelligence to properly exercise the privilege of suffrage; but others said, No;

ONLY THE COLORED PEOPLE SHOULD HAVE THE RIGHT TO VOTE,
because the colored people were faithful enough to be safely intrusted with the right of suffrage. We talk about a division of sentiment at times now, but we had a division of sentiment then in regard to these important questions; but the Republican party settled it with a generosity again such as marks it the most generous party that ever controlled a government. It said, We will give the right of suffrage to the people in the States thus restored, both white and black, both loyal and disloyal, and we will give them the right of representation in Congress and the Electoral Colleges, such as the loyal people of the North have. But what was the result of this? In the last Electoral College of the United States, that gave us our present president and vice-president of the United States, there were

FORTY ELECTORS WHO REPRESENTED THE COLORED PEOPLE
of the South, and not one of these forty electoral votes was cast as these Republicans of the South desired that they should be cast. Instead of having the right to cast their votes and have their votes counted as cast, and have themselves represented in the Electoral College as they had a right and desired to be, they have been robbed and deprived of their right of franchise by methods and means which it is unnecessary for me to refer to here; and so it was that, by the aid of these party votes, Grover Cleveland chanced to be made President of the United States, and he was made president despite the expression of the people, whose votes were not counted as cast in the ballot-box.

Because of this it was that the Republicans of the State declared that the colored people of the South should have the right to vote as they wished, and that every man who owes allegiance under the flag, every man who is American, every man who has a right to be protected by this Government, shall have the right to exercise

THIS GREAT FUNDAMENTAL RIGHT OF CITIZENSHIP—
the exercise of his right of suffrage just as he may see fit to, without any fear of fraud, of tissue ballots, of assassination, of intimidation, of murder, or anything else to defeat him and defraud him of those rights. [Applause.]

Gentlemen of the Club, the convention at Springfield saw fit to put that resolution at the head of this platform, and it has declared in language unequivocal that if the great cardinal principle of this Government is worth anything at all, it is worth preserving the foundations of it. * * *

THE SOLDIERS.

The following petition was signed by the soldiers of the National Home, Montgomery County, but was not presented to the Springfield convention, as being without precedent:

NATIONAL MILITARY HOME,
MONTGOMERY COUNTY, OHIO, May 20, 1885.

We, the soldiers at the National Home, and defenders of the Union, hereby, without offense to any other candidate, express our preference for the candidate for Governor of Ohio.

We favor Private Joseph Benson Foraker because we think him the best man by reason of his political and moral and intellectual qualities. He has not sought the nomination. He is a plain, straightforward man without tricks. He is honest. He is not proud. He knows the old soldiers, even when they are poor. We like the Generals, but we like one of our own companions best.

He is one of us. He was born poor. He is poor now. He was the first man to enter and the last man mustered out of his regiment. He had with us common soldiers' fare at Missionary Ridge, Lookout Mountain, Dalton, Rockyface, and in the Atlanta campaign.

BEN. FORAKER WORE THE HUMBLE BLOUSE,

and did the duty of a gallant private in our army. He was no gilt-edge private, looking soon to be made an officer. He was at the front in the march, in battle, with his musket, knapsack, and old canteen. He is our comrade. He never puts on airs. He said in the army, "Ben. Foraker never asks for a place," and sticks to it now. He asks for no place, but we will give him one. We are for Ben. Foraker first, last, and all the time. Hurrah for Ben. Foraker.

This was signed by the soldiers generally.

THE SINGULAR DISREGARD OF PUBLIC

and political opinion by Judge Foraker in the performance of a present duty without reference to the effect upon his future is manifest in the Springfield case. He realized that the performance of his duty to a client and a friend would embarrass him with persons who take but a narrow view of public questions.

The sympathy of the judge has ever been

PROFOUNDLY WITH THE COLORED PEOPLE.

He inherited hostility to slavery from his parents and relatives, who left the country of bondage for that of the free North-west. He fought for the freedom of the race. He has pleaded for their full civil rights. He has claimed that all privileges accorded to white children should be granted to colored children. Yet he respects law, and will not by indirectness secure what must be obtained by manly directness. He says that the whites and blacks have equal claims upon him for his legal services. He shrinks not from defending a friend, for fear of misrepresentation. He trusts God and does his duty in the present.

The Rev. H. Clark, African Methodist preacher, says: "The judge is a sound Republican and

A FRIEND OF OUR RACE.

* * Colored men must banish caste as well as the whites, and think less of being colored and more of being men and citizens."

The *Athens Messenger* (March, 1885) said:
It is creditable to the intelligence of the colored man and brother that he refuses to be

MISLED BY DEMOCRATIC MISREPRESENTATIONS

of Judge Foraker's sentiments toward American citizens of African descent, the representative colored Republicans over the State favoring the judge's nomination.

The *Detroit Plain-Dealer*, published by colored people, said, January 13, 1885:
Judge Foraker is our race's true friend. * * One of the ablest and foremost Republicans, * * patriotic, loyal, and unselfish to a fault.

The *Ohio Republican*, September 20, 1884, said: "Judge Foraker is doing Herculean work for the Republican cause. He is undefatigable and thoroughly conversant with the issues of the day. * * * The people will take care of Judge Foraker's future, and

THE COLORED MEN OF OHIO

will be found with the people when the opportunity comes again to do him honor, whether as Governor of Ohio, or as President of the United States.

UNANIMOUS CHOICE OF THE COLORED PEOPLE.

There no longer remains the shadow of a doubt that the eminent jurist and statesman, Judge J. B. Foraker, is the unanimous choice of the colored voters for Governor of this great State, and if his election depends upon their votes he will be elected by a majority that shall forever set at rest the foul assumption that the colored people of Ohio are otherwise than enthusiastic and sincere in their support of him and loyal to the Republican party.—*The Colored Sentinel.*

The New York *Times* declares that there is no reason for colored men to have any lack of confidence in Judge Foraker.

Letter from Robert Harlan, January 31, 1885: "I have known Judge Foraker ever since he came to Cincinnati, in 1869, and I know that ever since, he has been one of the best friends to the colored people. I heard him on the Civil Rights bill in 1874, and no man ever took higher ground for our race. He was far ahead of Republicans generally, and I went up after the speech to

THANK HIM IN BEHALF OF THE COLORED PEOPLE.

* * I was in the National Republican Convention at Chicago last June, and there I saw Judge Foraker vote for John R. Lynch, and induce others to vote for him. * * Judge Foraker says that it makes no difference to him whether a man is white or colored as to rights in courts or out of them; that he has acted for many colored men, to bring suits for them and to defend them, and that a colored man had no more right to object for his de-

fense of a white man than a white man would have for his defense of a colored man. * * * At our last election I saw Democrats knock down and drive colored men from the polls to keep them from voting. Yet Democrats ask colored men to support their candidates. There is
NO BETTER FRIEND OF THE COLORED MAN
on earth than Judge Foraker.

Ford Smith, of Cincinnati, in the *Ohio Tribune*, Jan. 28, 1885:
Colored people are asked to forget that Judge Foraker was and has always been a consistent Republican; that he had a glorious record as a brave soldier who won distinction in the cause that
GAVE OUR RACE ITS FREEDOM,
even before he had reached man's estate. They are asked to forget all his utterances as a public speaker in every political campaign since the war. * * In the last campaign,
WHO HONORED REGISTER BRUCE
more than Judge Foraker? In the Chicago Convention, Judge Foraker was one of the strongest supporters as well as one of the most
ACTIVE FOR MR. LYNCH AS CHAIRMAN.
What do you think of the man Foraker, when the boy Foraker, then only seventeen years old—a soldier at the front—wrote to his parents thus? "They all cry 'peace' and that they will agree to come back to the Union as it was, but this war will not end until all realize that this is a nation, and for the colored as well as the white man."—[Letter of May 5, 1863.]

In all his public utterances he has been true to
THE CAUSE OF THE COLORED PEOPLE.
He said in 1874, of the Civil Rights bill: "The object of this bill is to prevent masked marauders from burning negro school-houses, shooting negro school-teachers, and keeping this innocent and inoffensive people in a state of terror, whice retards their development and corrupts and demoralizes society and politics in a hundred ways.
AND IT IS RIGHT,
and the Republican party is for it because it is right. * * * They have justly earned their citizenship; and they have earned it in such a way that for us not to protect them in it would be the basest ingratitude and wrong —ingratitude and wrong for which the nation would deserve to sink to rise no more."

In a thousand unrecorded, unreported speeches,
JUDGE FORAKER HAS STOOD IN THE FRONT RANK
as a defender of the wrongs of our race. He fought as a boy and man, as a brave soldier on the side of freedom. His whole life conduct has been consistent in devotion to our interests. Our race owes him a debt of gratitude. * * * You should come to Cincinnati, where Judge Foraker lives, and go about asking the colored people here, where his charities are known among white and colored poor alike, and thus know the man. *
* * Judge Foraker does not seek gubernatorial honor. It is not known that he would accept the nomination. He shirks no duty. He has just finished the conduct of the case for the defense before the partisan Springer Investigation Committee, sent here by a Democratic congress. He expects no compensation for valuable time and services, anxious only to show to the public
THE BRUTAL TREATMENT OF THE COLORED VOTERS
by the Democratic party at the October election in this city. Colored Republicans have their eyes opened to the lies of Democratic leaders." * *

At a meeting of colored men (February, 1885) in Springfield, it was unanimously resolved, That it is the sense of this meeting that Judge Foraker is the friend of the colored people, a genuine Republican, and entirely
WORTHY OF OUR FULL CONFIDENCE,
and cordial support.

There are
FOUR COLORED REPUBLICN FORAKER CLUBS
in Cincinnati alone. They serenaded the judge, June 26th, at his residence (Walnut Hills). Music enlivened the occasion. The house was covered with the glare and glory of red Greek fire. The judge said, following his custom, he would abstain from making a
A POLITICAL SPEECH FROM THE PORCH OF HIS OWN HOUSE.
But he congratulated his colored friends on their organization. And as encouragement for them, he referred to the wonderful progress of the colored race, and the toning down of public prejudice against them within the last score of years; and he put it to colored men, in view of the effort being made to divert their political allegiance, whether they should not stand by that party which had been their friend when they most wanted a friend. In conclusion, he expressed his high appreciation of the organization of colored men in his favor, here at his own home.

The Glee Club sung, "John Brown's Body," and then Mr. Ford Smith made a speech. It was very evident that it was a great strain on Mr. Smith to keep his Republican enthusiasm down to the point indicated by Judge Foraker because of the
HOME CHARACTER OF THE OCCASION.
Mr. Smith spoke with much feeling, and proudly recorded the fact that the colored Republicans of Walnut Hills, who knew Judge Foraker better than their brethren elsewhere, had formed a Foraker Club a month before the Springfield Convention, for they knew he was a staunch friend of their race.

As this sketch is in press we find the colored people are holding meetings all over the State to express their indignation at the charge that they are not devoted, zealous, and grateful friends and supporters of Captain Foraker.

HON. JOHN P. GREEN.

The numerous colored delegates in the convention cast their votes for Judge Foraker, except Hon. John P. Green, the colored delegate from Cleveland, who now writes the *Cleveland Leader:* "When I saw in the convention the great enthusiasm for Judge Foraker, even, on the part of such stalwart friends of the colored people as Generals Beatty and Kennedy, Ex-governor Noyes, Hon. Ben. Butterworth, and others, I concluded that all was well. * *
SPEAKING AS A COLORED MAN,
* * I advise all * * to work and vote for Hon. J. B. Foraker."
THE COLORED SOLDIERS AT THE NATIONAL HOME,
near Dayton, Ohio, unanimously asked the Springfield Convention to nominate Judge Foraker for governor, claiming that he most fully represents their idea of a high official who will do justly towards all men. They say:—

NATIONAL MILITARY HOME, OHIO, May 20, 1885.

We colored soldiers would like to express our preference for governor, as we learn that white soldiers are expressing theirs.

We know that Joseph Benson Foraker has become a learned man, an able lawyer, and a distinguished judge. We have learned that he is much thought of politically all over our land. We have learned that he was way at the top at Chicago, at Augusta, and at Washington. This is all very well. But we want him because he was a soldier—because he is

THE BEST FRIEND TO THE COLORED RACE

we know of. And then he has the right sort of a head. He goes straight to his point. He has no crookedness, no diplomacy. He means always what he says. He is honest and true; he is no trickster, no political demagogue. He would talk for us, and if necessary, he would do, as he has done, fight for us.

THE SPOILS OF OFFICE CAN NOT BUY HIM.

He will not lie. His people left Virginia because they detested slavery.

Some of us knew him in the army, knew him at the breaking out of the rebellion, knew him in the army of the Cumberland, at the siege of Atlanta, in the campaign of the sea, and through the Carolinas. Did he not along with us live often on his one third rations a day? Did he not share with us his hard crackers? Did he not say that he would serve his country as long as there was an armed rebel in the land? Did he not declare that the war could not end until all realized that this is

A NATION FOR THE COLORED AS WELL AS THE WHITE MAN?

He treated us just as if he was one of us. He acted in the army toward us as Garrison, Sumner, and Birney did in civil life. Some say he is no friend to the colored man. Pshaw! Did he not stand up for our rights in the elections of Cincinnati in 1874? Did he not say that the franchise of our people must be enjoyed without fear or menace; that they must be secured in the Civil Rights Bill, which demands perfect equality before the law? His speeches have been strong in our behalf. He averred in 1880 that the government must be strong enough to go into every nook and corner of the land to protect the rights of its citizens and redress their wrongs, to secure complete civil and political rights for the colored men, not only here in Ohio, but in South Carolina and Mississippi.

[Here follow the names of colored soldiers at the home, with the letter of the company and the number of the regiment.]

THE GAZZAWAY CASE.

The following appeared in the *Commercial Gazette*, June 14, 1883, from Judge Pringle:

" I am certain that counsel for the plaintiff will all agree, "without regard to color or political proclivities," that not one word fell from the lips of Judge Foraker that could possibly be tortured into any reflection upon

THE COLORED RACE OR ANY DISREGARD OF THEIR RIGHTS.

The facts in the case were agreed upon, and the judge, in an exceedingly kind and courteous address, presented the law of the case, as he understood it to have been declared by statute in Ohio and the Supreme Court of the state, and did not even express

ANY APPROVAL OF THE WISDOM OR CORRECTNESS OF THE LAW.

The plaintiff and her counsel (two of whom were colored) were duly advised of the holding of the Supreme Court of *this State* upon the question ,' of the right to establish and maintain separate schools for colored children," and for that reason did not bring suit in the State Court, but brought it in the United States Circuit Court, as the shortest and quickest route to the Supreme Court of the United States. The plaintiff sought to raise the question as to the right of discrimination against colored children under the *name*, *word*, or *pretext* of '*classification*,' and desired to test it as speedily and with as little expense as possible. In this it is but fair to say that we were

GREATLY AIDED BY JUDGE FORAKER,

and the defendant himself, they permitting plaintiff's counsel to write out a statement of facts, showing the state of things as they existed here in relation to the public schools, accompanied by a map, showing the number of white and colored schools, their location, etc., which was agreed to by them, thus saving a great amount of expense and trouble to the plaintiff in taking a large number of witnesses to Cincinnati, to prove them, in order to get the opinion of the Court upon the questions of law applicable to her case. The record of the case will show this to be correct. Again, in making up the bill of exceptions in the case, Judge Foraker was

VERY COURTEOUS, FAIR, AND JUST,

and put no obstacles in the way of the plaintiff, saving in the record all the questions of law she sought to make, for final review in the Supreme Court of the United States, where the case will soon be taken. The plaintiff and her counsel were of the opinion that the statutes of Ohio and the decision of the Supreme Court of Ohio were in conflict with the *spirit* and letter of the amendments to the constitution of the United States, and the laws of congress passed in pursuance thereof, and it was to test the correctness or incorrectness of this opinion, and to 'settle the vexed question,' that plaintiff brought her suit. And by reason largely of

THE JUDGE'S COURTESY AND FAIRNESS

she, with little expense, will soon have that opportunity. It was upon the motion of Judge Foraker at the time of the trial that one of the attorneys (colored) was admitted to practice in that court."

From W. S. Newberry, a colored attorney for the plaintiff:

"I have read the letter of Mr. Pringle, and heartily concur in its statements. I met Judge Foraker for the first time in the trial of the Gazaway case. He very kindly moved my admission to practice in the United States Circuit Court, and afterward came to me and congratulated me on my admission, and spoke

SOME FRIENDLY WORDS OF ENCOURAGEMENT.

I am perhaps as jealous of my rights and the rights of my race as any one ought to be, and yet I can not recall a single word or sentence uttered by Judge Foraker in the trial of that case that was

UNKIND, DISCOURTEOUS, OR UNJUST

to me or the colored race; and I am sure I should have noticed it had he done so. From his manly bearing in that trial, and past record as a soldier who helped to

'SHOOT RESPECT FOR OUR CIVIL RIGHTS

into the Democratic party,' and his record as one of the Republican party which wrote equal rights in the organic law, I think he *would* and *will* make a good governor; and I am for Foraker, and believe him worthy of the support of all true Republicans, white or colored, and deserving of honest Democratic support.

Graham Dewell, another colored attorney of the plaintiff, of Springfield Ohio, who was an alternate Republican delegate at large to Chicago, wrote March 13, 1885: With the defense (Judge Foraker) the only question was whether or not, under existing laws in Ohio, boards of education had the power to classify colored youth into separate schools—to argue from the stand-point of decided cases. * * * The Judge was particularly

COURTEOUS TO THE COLORED LAWYERS,

and showed in this very case that his sympathy is with our race. I heard him congratulate Wm. Newberry upon his success in qualifying himself for the honorable position as a member of the court and encourage him to stimulate others of his race by his own excellence to attain like distinction. It was Judge Foraker's professional duty to take the case. In doing so he committed no breach of faith and

NO ACT OF DISLOYALTY TO THE COLORED RACE.

Judge Foraker was retained in the case, not because of any sympathy with any measure calculated to oppress our race or retard our full liberty, for he had on many occasions *boldly and fearlessly championed our interests*, even exceeding in his zeal our most radical defenders. It was solely and simply because a college-mate, a warm, personal friend, had been sued for $2,000 damages for refusing to do what he was forbidden to do by the rules governing him in his official capacity. Judge Foraker is with the colored people, but under and according to law. Where a law is at fault let it be changed according to the provisions for its modification.

JUDGE FORAKER'S LETTER

completely disposes of the absurd Democratic story started during the last gubernatorial campaign, that he left the Ohio Wesleyan University because a colored student had been admitted. The only student who left on that account was, the judge says, 'a Democrat then and is a Democrat now.'

Not only is this trashy story disposed of, but the judge shows from his record that he was among the earliest and foremost advocates of extending to the

COLORED RACE ALL THE CIVIL AND POLITICAL RIGHTS

and privileges enjoyed by the whites, and wiping out all lines of discrimination founded upon race.

The colored men of Ohio have no more earnest defender or warmer friend than Judge Foraker. He is, and has ever been, a consistent and able advocate of the equality of all men in political and civil affairs. It is sheer ignorance or dishonesty to affirm otherwise in the face of his record.—*Commercial-Gazette.*

CINCINNATI, February 2, 1885.

Mr. S. E. Huffman, Springfield, Ohio: * * * I have said nothing in answer to newspaper attacks, because not wishing to appear, even to the extent of defending myself, as seeking a renomination. But now that you, a colored gentleman, and a total stranger to me, have volunteered to write and ask me for 'the facts,' I feel it to be due to you, as well as to myself, to state them.

First, however, let me say that it is not a matter of importance to me who is the nominee of the Republican party. * * * * *

I shall be content with whatever selection the Republican Convention may make. I would not, therefore, say a word to influence in my favor the sentiment of the party, white or colored. But that I may answer your questions, and dispel misunderstandings that malicious falsehoods may have created, I shall, as you have asked it, take pains to state what every man, white or colored, who has known me during life will confirm.

And first, I have always been a Republican in the most radical and uncompromising sense of the word.

In 1862, when only sixteen years of age, I enlisted as a private in Company A. of the Eighty-ninth Ohio Regiment. I served with this regiment for three years, until the close of the war. At that time I did not know that I would ever be a candidate for any office, and certainly did not dream of such a thing as ever having my attitude toward the colored people called in question. My expressions at that time ought, therefore, to be conclusive as to my sentiments in this regard.

When a man is made candidate for such an office as Governor of Ohio, everything that he ever said or did is likely to be made public.

Such seemed to be my fortune when a candidate in 1883. Among other things published at that time were some of

THE LETTERS I WROTE HOME FROM THE ARMY.

I had nothing to do with their publication. I did not even know that they were yet in existence until I saw them in print. I can never forget the mortification I experienced at seeing a private correspondence thus made public, nor how unendurable it would have been but for the testimony it gave me of the mother's affection that had led to their preservation and publication. But it would seem now that it was well that they were published since it enables me to point to them as an incontestable record to disprove the charges to which you refer ; for in them you will find that I then wrote that, 'the war ought not to stop until slavery is abolished and every colored man is made a citizen, and is given precisely the same civil and political rights that the white man has.'

The war ended, and all who knew me then will testify that I was uncompromisingly in favor of

THE ENFRANCHISEMENT OF THE COLORED PEOPLE

as a basis of reconstruction of the South, and as a matter of justice to the North.

And when it was proposed to amend the constitution of Ohio in 1867 by striking out the word 'white,' I took an active part in the campaign, although still in school at Delaware, speaking in favor of the measure, and voting against discrimination—the first vote I ever cast.

This brings me in chronological order to the charge that I left Ohio Wesleyan University because a colored man was admitted there as a student.

I was in attendance at Ohio Wesleyan University, and a colored man was admitted as a student there. He was there for one term, from January until about May, 1868; and that colored man is now the Rev. Mr. Mortimer, an esteemed colored minister, and a man of intelligence, culture, and character, who was stationed in 1883 at Zanesville, Ohio. He is a man who can speak as to facts in regard to the charge made against me in this respect; and he will tell you that the story that I left Ohio Wesleyan University because he or any other colored man came there, is a base falsehood.

The truth is, so far as I can recollect, that there was but very little dissatisfaction manifested on the part of any one because he became a student there. I only remember of one student who left on that account ; and I need scarcely add that

HE WAS A DEMOCRAT THEN, AND IS A DEMOCRAT STILL.

Mr. Mortimer left Delaware at the end of his first term, of his own accord. I did not leave until one year later, when I went to Cornell University at Ithaca, New York, where I was graduated. The reason why I went to Cornell was well known to the faculty and to the students, and to the people of Delaware at the time. It was simply that I might have, what at that time seemed to me sufficient to warrant the change, some experience with eastern men and colleges, and have, what I then thought more of than I do now, the distinction of graduating in the first class from what I thought was, and is destined to be, one of the greatest universities of the country. No one thought that I left Delaware because a year before a colored man had been in attendance, and certainly nothing could

be more ridiculous than that I would remain in attendance at Delaware during the entire time the colored man was there and never think of leaving on that account
UNTIL A YEAR AFTER HE HAD LEFT.

Since I left school in 1869, I have taken part in almost every campaign, speaking in behalf of the measures represented by the Republican party, and always, as every colored Republican in Cincinnati knows, chiefly and especially in the favor of those measures that looked to the improving of the colored people in the North as well as in the South. What I have from time to time said in this regard has not been so forcible, nor so elegant as that which many others may have said, but it has been as earnest; for no man with more *earnestness* than I did, until we were rid of them, denounced and contended against the infamous visible admixture laws placed on
OUR STATUTE BOOKS BY THE DEMOCRATIC PARTY.

No man more earnestly than I, at all times until it was secured, contended for the political equality of the colored man, and the guaranty of that equality by the adoption of the amendments to the constitution of the United States; and when the civil rights law was pending before the Congress, and particularly in 1874, when it was a party question in Ohio, I never failed on any occasion where opportunity was afforded me, to speak in behalf of it. * * * I quote from a speech made by me in 1874 in the city of Cincinnati and published at the time. I then said:

'The object of the Civil Rights bill is to prevent masked marauders from burning negro school-houses, shooting negro school-teachers, and keeping this innocent and inoffensive people in a state of terror, which retards their development and corrupts and demoralizes society and politics in a hundred ways. And it is right, and the Republican party is for it because it is right.

'When in Columbus the other day, I stood in our capitol and looked with admiring gaze upon that magnificent painting which adorns its walls —of 'Perry's Victory on the Lake.' In the midst of the death-storm of that terrible conflict, as gallant-looking as any one of the brave faces surrounding the Commodore, is a
FULL-BLOODED REPRESENTATIVE OF THE AFRICAN RACE.

Thus it has always been since our Government was founded, on land and on sea, in adversity and prosperity, through peace and through war, this race has been ever present with us, and never once has its faith faltered, its devotion lagged, or its courage failed.

'They have justly earned their citizenship, and they have earned it in such a way as that for us not to protect them in it would be the basest ingratitude and wrong—ingratitude and wrong for which the
NATION WOULD DESERVE TO SINK TO RISE NO MORE.'

But equality of rights for the colored man does not mean a denial of rights to the white man. It does not mean that if a colored man sues a white man the white man shall not be allowed to defend himself. I know the colored people of the State of Ohio, and I know that their intelligence and sense of justice are such that they will not, from the mere fact that I defended a man who was sued by one of their race, believe that I have any lack of friendship for them as a people. I might as well be charged with murder for defending a murderer.

Especially when it is borne in mind that the suitor was represented in the case by two colored men, both of whom have testified that throughout the case I neither did nor said anything whatever, that was, or could be in the slightest degree, disrespectful or offensive to the colored people. And not only that, but the statement has been correctly made that one of the attorneys, who was a colored man, had not, previously to the trial, been admitted to the bar of the United States Court, and that he was ADMITTED UPON MY MOTION AND RECOMMENDATION, in order that he might assist in the trial of that cause. * * * I can not stop without reminding you that it is far more important to the colored people that the Republican party should succeed than it is to the party itself.

It has only been a few years since Democrats held colored men in slavery—now all are free; only a few years since they would not allow them to testify as witnesses in the courts—now the colored man can sue and maintain his rights there; only a few years since the Democratic party of Ohio disgraced our statute with THE INFAMOUS VISIBLE ADMIXTURE LAWS— now the statute books are clean; only as long ago as 1867, when 'the Democratic party of Ohio declared in its platform that this is a white man's Government and that negroes should have no part in it.' A great change has been wrought; and the Republican party has wrought it. Are the rights that have been thus achieved secure? Does it make no difference any more to the colored man WHETHER THE DEMOCRATIC OR REPUBLICAN PARTY SUCEEDS? Look to the South. Words can not describe the outrages to which colored Republicans are there subjected. We have just seen a Democratic president elected because by violence and fraud the colored people of the South have been robbed of their forty electoral votes. But to learn the feeling of the Democratic party toward the colored people you need to look no further than the election of last October, in the city of Cincinnati.

THE SO-CALLED SPRINGER INVESTIGATING COMMITTEE HAS BEEN TAKING testimony that establishes, to the satisfaction of every unprejudiced mind, that the Democratic party as an organization, acting by its agents, deliberately planned and attempted to perpetrate the outrage of fraudulently carrying that election by arresting, beating, and wounding and *intimidating colored men*, and preventing them by wholesale from casting their ballots. In pursuance of this plan, they deliberately arrested one hundred and fifty-two colored citizens of Cincinnati at midnight before the election and imprisoned them in the dungeon of the Hammond Street Station-house, and kept them there without bread or water, or any charge whatever against them, until after six o'clock in the evening of the day of election. A MORE BRUTAL OUTRAGE WAS NEVER PERPETRATED north of the Ohio River. And yet no Democrat has condemned it. On the contrary, from the Governor down to the lowest ward politician in their ranks, there has been a chuckle of delight because of the success of the infamous scheme. And you will not have to wait very long to see among the political acts of Mr. Cleveland the granting of a pardon to a man who is now serving out a sentence of imprisonment for having perpetrated this crime.

There is no nomination important enough to induce me *to solicit any man's support* for it; neither is there any office low enough for me to understand how it is possible for any colored man to be willing to vote for a Democrat to fill it. Very truly yours, etc.

J. B. FORAKER.

A FLAT DENIAL.

The following letter from the REV. DR. MORTIMER, THE "COLORED STUDENT AT DELAWARE," and now a member of the Republican Executive Committee of Lawrence County, to the author of this sketch, summarily disposes of the Democratic falsehood circulated by a hostile press for the last two years:

IRONTON, OHIO, July 10, 1885.

MY DEAR SIR:

Yours is received. *The report that Judge Foraker left the Ohio Wesleyan University because I or a colored student was admitted to that institution is a base falsehood.* Respectfully.

R. G. MORTIMER.

[The emphasized words in the written correspond to those italicized in the printed letter.]

A LETTER IN RESPONSE TO AN INVITATION

to address a meeting of colored citizens called to express their indignation on the Danville outrages:

CINCINNATI,, OHIO, Dec. 19, 1883.

For twenty years we have been congratulating ourselves upon having accomplished great permanent good by the war. We have thought that we had not only preserved the Union, but that *actually* as well as nominally we had perfected the constitution, emancipated and enfranchised your race, and put all American citizens on a plane of equality under THE PROTECTION OF THE FLAG and the laws of the land.

But it would seem that this is not so, for your meeting is called to give expression to the indignation you properly feel because of a barbarous crime against not only your race, but against the whole American people, white as well as black, which it is conceded is to go unpunished, because of the accepted idea that the United States Government can not, and the State Government will not, bring the perpetrators to justice.

A single instance of such character might well call for such action on your part.

But Danville is only the last of a number of such massacres.

Coushatta and Hamburg, and the murder of the Chisholms, together with hundreds of other less startling but equally brutal outrages and assassinations, have gone before; and the State not only fails to punish, but rewards.

South Carolina sent to the Senate of the United States one of the chief actors in the heartless butchery at Hamburg.

And within the last month we have seen a prominent CITIZEN OF MISSISSIPPI DELIBERATELY MURDERED for no other reason than that he exercised his right of voting according to his preference; and as a reward for his act the murderer is extolled in a public meeting, and afterward made mayor of his town, while the family of the murdered man are notified that none of them will be permitted to take any part in politics hereafter, and are driven by terror to abandon their homes for refuge.

With the multiplication of these evils the old spirit of rebellion is reviving. To-day the United States flag is displaced in South Carolina and the palmetto flag of the State floats on the capitol at Columbia.

We are told that there is no remedy for all this.

If so, our last estate is worse than the first, and the great question of the hour is how to legally and constitutionally rectify the difficulty.

I have no time now to discuss this question, but I will take time to say that

THE COLORED MAN MUST BE PROTECTED

in the enjoyment and exercise of his right of suffrage.

I AM UNQUALIFIEDLY FOR HIS PROTECTION,

and I am quite as unqualifiedly of the opinion that our National Government is empowered to protect its own citizens on its own soil; and it ought to do so promptly and effectually.

But if wrong about this, or if for any reason protection is not to be afforded him, then we owe it to the whole country, as a matter of simple justice, and to the colored man particularly, as an act of mercy, to re-adjust representation in the Congress and the Electoral College.

As it now is in a number of the states, he is not only denied his rights, but the fact that he is clothed with them only serves to make him a defenseless target for the shot-gun, and to strengthen and infuriate the cruel oppression of which he is the helpless victim.

I add that all this barbarism is

IN THE NAME AND ON BEHALF OF THE DEMOCRATIC PARTY.

It is by such atrocities that they have made and intend to maintain a solid South. But don't imagine that the spirit that has thus manifested itself there is confined to that section. Differing only in degree, according to local conditions, the same spirit everywhere characterizes that organization.

As you must still well remember, it has been only a few years since the Democracy of Ohio declared in their state platform 'that this government was made by white men, and that so far as we (the Democrats of Ohio) have the power to prevent it, it shall continue to be a government of white men.'

And you can not have forgotten the infamous visible admixture laws they placed upon our statute-books in 1858. They are wiser now, but they are no better. Only last Saturday a gentleman told me that in —— County, the county-seat of —— County, one of the strongholds of Democracy in this State, no colored man has ever yet been allowed to live.

It is not surprising that a party capable of practicing such wicked intolerance should have

THE IMPUDENCE TO ASK FOR THE VOTES OF COLORED MEN

—for such a party may be relied upon to do anything,—but it is certainly remarkable, to say the least of it, that any colored man should so far forget himself as to listen to such an appeal.

Very truly yours, etc.

J. B. FORAKER.

AN EARNEST AND HEARTY SUPPORT.

Letter (July 1, 1885) of Hon. John P. Green: * * Permit me to say that you have mistaken my zeal and enthusiasm for an honored fellow-townsman, as exhibited by me in our recent State Convention, for opposition to the Republican cause. I am in politics, to some extent, as I am in law. Though I may in the convention champion the cause of my preference with all the energy I can command, yet, when a ticket is selected, it would be disgraceful to my manhood, my constituents, and my party, were I to do less than yield it an earnest and hearty support.

In 1857 my poor, dear mother sacrificed her humble home for a pittance, and spent the greater portion of it to bring her children here from beneath

A DEMOCRATIC DESPOTISM IN THE SOUTH,

as detestable as it was universal. We left our humble abode, left associates, relatives, (some in slavery,) the graves of our loved ones,—native land,—left all in search of liberty! Sacred name! Sweet-sounding to our willing ears, but never seen by us there save in our imagination.

We got here just after the reins of government in this State had been transferred from Democratic to Republican hands. Since then I have learned

UNDER REPUBLICAN RULE WHAT IT IS TO BE A MAN.

Slavery has been abolished, the ballot and the jury box made accessible for us, the right to give testimony in open court accorded to us, and, *mirabile dictu*, we are even permitted to stand and plead our own cause at the bar of justice. Wonderful transformation! What hath God wrought by means of his instrument, the great Republican party! During all this while the Democratic party has not been idle. It has assailed the Union, and

KILLED MORE THAN 360,000 OF OUR NOBLEST YOUTHS;

it has impeded every effort made by the Republican party to bestow on colored Americans the rights of citizenship, intimidated and murdered their best friends in the South,—the poor, hard-working colored men, for only political motives, reduced them by tyrannical laws and mock trials to a condition of serfdom, in some cases worse than death, so that it is true, to-day, that thousands of colored men, some of whom fought in the army of the Union, are working

LIKE 'DUMB DRIVEN CATTLE,' ON CHAIN GANGS,

and under brutal task masters, to whom they have been sold at public vendue, and in some other instances being whipped and tortured to death for imaginary crimes. Why, even in this Ohio, so late as the 6th day of May, 1869, (see Ohio Laws, vol. 65, page 119,) they enacted that damnable 'visible admixture law,' which made it a felony for a person having a visible admixture of African blood in his veins to vote, and fixed the penalty for so doing at not less than one year nor more than five years in the penitentiary. Now do you suppose I could desert the one great party and cling to the other, and afterwards

LOOK MY MOTHER AND MY BRETHREN IN THE FACE WITHOUT SHAME?

God forbid! For myself, I will cling to the Republican party, which gave us a name and a place before the laws of this great Nation; which erected for us a family altar, released us from the galling yoke of slavery, elevated us to positions of honor and trust, and even now beckons us onward to a bright and glorious future. Judge Foraker, by his record in the army, by his long and varied career as a trusted public servant, and by his recent utterances, has proved himself to be in favor of freedom and equality to all—colored as well as white, and I now advise my colored brethren all over the State to pull off their coats and work earnestly from this time until the night of election day, for the whole ticket and the Republican party.

Respectfully, JOHN P. GREEN.
To Professor Richard L. Greiner, Washington, D. C.

THE REV. J. W. GAZAWAY IS THE PASTOR OF ST. JOHN'S AFRICAN M. E. CHURCH,— FULLY SATISFIED,—

Cleveland, Ohio, and was the plaintiff in the school suit. June 16, 1885, he wrote Judge Foraker thus:

DEAR SIR:—Having traveled over three hundred miles to vote for you two years ago, and *did vote for you*, notwithstanding your position in the case vs. W. J. White in the United States Court, and *earnestly* desiring the success of the Republican ticket this fall, and in order to a correct uneerstanding relative to your opinion, or I should say position toward the race to which I belong (and the greater part of whom, I am happy to say, *desire* to vote the Republican ticket,) will you answer the following question, viz: Are you in favor of giving to the colored people of Ohio all of the best possible advantages in educational facilities?

I wish to state further that your reply is not intended for publication, without your consent. I have thus written with a pure motive, and your private reply is anxiously awaited. Yours fraternally,
J. W. GAZAWAY.

Judge Foraker replied:

CINCINNATI, OHIO, June 18, 1885.
REV. J. W. GAZAWAY, No. 500 Erie Street, Cleveland, Ohio.

DEAR SIR:—I am in receipt of your letter, inquiring whether or not I am 'in favor of giving the colored people of Ohio all of the best possible advantages in educational facilities.'

I am glad you have been kind enough to give me an opportunity to say 'yes' to such a question. If you had known me all my life, you would not have had any occasion to have asked me such a question, for by

EVERY WORD, THOUGHT, DEED AND ACT OF MY LIFE

I have shown, I think, the very great interest I have in the welfare of your race, and a desire to see them in the enjoyment of every means that will elevate and advance them.

In the suit against Major White, I was called upon to argue a legal proposition, based upon facts that

I KNEW NOTHING WHATEVER ABOUT,

but which had been agreed upon by the other counsel in the case. The matter of race or color had nothing whatever to do with my feeling one way or another. Had you applied to me first, I should quite as cheerfully have served you as I did him, just as I have been in the employment of colored men, as their attorney, more or less continually ever since I commenced practicing law. I have at this time a number of cases on my docket in which I represent colored men.

It was the ambition of my boyhood to see slavery abolished and the colored men made citizens and invested with every right that every other citizen might have under the law, and now that that has been done, I believe in treating

ALL EXACTLY ALIKE AND SECURING AND ENFORCING

for all every right that may pertain to citizenship.

Hoping that I have satisfactorily answered you, I remain
Very respectfully, yours, etc. J. B. FORAKER.

From Rev. J. W. Gazaway:

CLEVELAND, OHIO, June 22, 1885.

HON. J. B. FORAKER, Cincinnati, Ohio.

SIR:—Your reply has reached me by due course of mail. I AM FULLY SATISFIED, and dismiss at once, ALL OPPOSITION FEELINGS.

It shall be my purpose to advance your interests to the extent of my ability, whenever and wherever I can.

I have been asked questions upon the matter of your candidacy, by persons from different parts of the State. I have withheld my replies to some extent until this time. Having heard your favorable response to the question propounded, I am now prepared to assist in molding sentiment in your favor, and thereby advance the interests of the Republican party, whose principles are right and should be sustained because they are right. Regard me as one of your earnest supporters. Respectfully, etc.
JOHN W. GAZAWAY.

WILBERFORCE, NEAR XENIA,

is the chief seat of the learning and culture of the colored race of the United States. Its most successful commencement occurred June 18, 1885. The correspondent of the *Commercial-Gazette* wrote:

JUDGE FORAKER AND BISHOP CAMPBELL.

Among those who went down below to fight the good fight in the great fraternal strife, was one who was literally but a boy; to-day he is but a young man. Unbeknown to him, some of his home letters were published two years ago—beatings of the heart burning with patriotism and throbbing with pathos and generosity. With a prophetic determination belonging at that time to but few of mature years, and those only of the most extreme type, this boy wrote from the field of battle that he was not willing for *the war to cease until every slave was free* and this a nation for the colored as well as for the white man. This boy, now a young man, was at Wilberforce yesterday. By his side sat

A GRAND OLD MAN, OF GRAY HAIR AND MASSIVE FORM.

He is an ex-slave. The old man arose and was announced as the Right Rev. J. P. Campbell, of Pennsylvania, Bishop of the African M. E. Church. He in turn introduced to the vast audience the young man at his side as the Hon. J. B. Foraker, of Cincinnati, the next Governor of Ohio.

The occasion was the fifteenth anniversary of the Alumnal Association of Wilberforce University. Whatever is bright, whatever is great, whatever is promising to the colored people of this country had its representatives gathered under the tented tabernacle spread out in the grove of Wilberforce. Naturally the most distinguished of the prominent colored men present were dignitaries of the African Methodist Episcopal Church. The white friends of the University, particularly those of Greene County, turned out in unprecedented numbers. It is estimated that the tent had seating capacity for three thousand persons, and every seat was occupied. The aisles were also packed and the canvas sides of the tabernacle were raised to accommodate those who could not get beneath the roof. *Foraker never had a greater compliment paid him, and Wilberforce never had such a glorious anniversary.*

THE VENERABLE BISHOP CAMPBELL

introduced Judge Foraker in the following hearty manner:

"In addition to all the honors conferred upon me by my church, and by my people, and the great Republican party [applause and laughter], and by the nation at large [renewed applause],—I am honest in all this,—I have the additional honor to-day of introducing to you the future governor, after the next election, of the Buckeye State, as it is in my division of work at this time. I consider it a very great honor indeed to introduce to you Judge Foraker. [Applause.] Who would have thought thirty years ago that I would have this honor conferred upon me —of presenting to the grandest mixed assembly in the State of Ohio [great laughter] the future governor of this State. [Loud applause.] I ask that gentleman now to come forward in the person of Judge Foraker." [Loud and continued applause.]

FORAKER'S SPEECH — EXTRACTS.

After bowing his acknowledgments for the vociferous welcome which greeted him, Judge Foraker said:

Mr. Chairman and Ladies and Gentlemen :—If I could have but the enthusiastic support of the representatives here to-day from the Keystone State, I do not question but that I would be next governor of the Buckeye State [great laughter]; for almost every other one of the distinguished colored men to whom I have had the honor of being introduced to-day has proudly straightened himself up and told me " I live in Alleghany County, Pennsylvania," [roars of laughter]—next to Ashtabula County, Ohio, one of the grandest Republican strongholds in the United States. [Applause.]

But I did not come here to talk about politics. I have been talking on that subject for the past week, and expect to be talking about politics for the next four months to come. To-day I come simply to visit this university, and to participate with you in the exercises of this occasion. And I wish first to thank the faculty of this institution for the kind invitation that has brought me here, for it has been the means of affording me gratification and pleasure.

It always affords much high enjoyment to visit a place of learning, and exceptionally so here. Here I find centered not only all that interest which usually attaches to places of learning generally, but also in addition that which is of special interest to all who appreciate the best and highest concerns of that race for which every true and loyal heart in this nation is yearning. [Loud applause.] In other words, I find here two interests—that of a general character and that to which I have referred as peculiar to this institution alone.   *   *   *   *   *   *   *

First, as to the general interest. This is a place where these youths, these men and women—these girls and boys now, but women and men shortly to be—are gathered together for the purpose of being educated, and prepared for the duties and responsibilities of life. They are undergoing an experience that people undergo but once in a life-time. Some of us have undergone that same experience. Those of us who have, as we come back to a place like this, feel stirred within us recollections of a most pleasing character.

WE ARE REMINDED OF OUR OWN ACADEMIC DAYS.

It is the hoisting of the flood-gate, as it were, through which is poured in upon the mind an overwhelming flood of the most pleasing memories. We feel and we know, as we come to a place like this, that we are coming not only into an atmosphere of intellectuality, but also into an atmosphere where youth and vigor abound, and where everything is pregnant with the hopes, the ambitions, and the aspirations that characterize the morning of life. It is an old and trite illustration, but in this presence, with these fresh graduates upon the platform, sophomoric though it may appear, I may be excused for using the illustration, that coming back in this way is something like the weary traveler stopping to rest at the sparkling fountain by the wayside. When he resumes his journey it is with renewed strength. So it is with us who have gone out from the colleges and have been battling for some years with the struggles of life. When we come back to these quiet shades and retreats of learning, and spend a day with you at commencement-time, it is to be returned, as the result of it, to the battles and struggles of life, purer, stronger, abler and better men. [Great applause.] Such are the influences and results that make it a pleasure to me to meet with you on this occasion."

The Judge pursued for a time the theme of educational pleasure, and then talked of college studies like a learned professor would, exploding the "utilitarian" theory, and pleading for thorough culture. He said:

Again, it is impossible to study the course to be pursued here without acquiring knowledge of a valuable character, of which you ought, and no doubt will, have a proper appreciation. I know you will understand and agree with me in this respect as to a great many of the studies you will be called upon to pursue and are pursuing. You will understand it as to spelling, reading, writing, grammar and mathematics, and all those studies for a knowledge of which you will have a demand daily in the transactions of life. But I hear a great deal said in the way of controversy, among educators, too, to the effect that the utilitarian idea ought to prevail in regard to studies. We hear a good deal said especially about the ancint languages. We frequently hear it said that the student ought to make choice while in school of the vocation of his life, and that he ought to equip himself by special studies bearing upon that purpose or avocation; and that unless he intends to follow an avocation in life that will make it necessary to have a knowledge of Latin and Greek, he ought not to waste any time on them. Well, that idea prevailed somewhat when I was a student at school. I remember that at that time I had made up my mind that I would practice law. I did not know then that I was going to practice politics some, too. [Laughter.] I intended simply to practice law, And I remember when I came to the study of botany and was called upon to analyze flowers and to learn about grasses and plants, I felt that I had come to a study that might be very appropriate for young ladies, but what on earth a man who intended to wrangle in the courts for a living wanted with botany, I conld not understand; but when I got fairly into the study I changed my mind. I may have forgotten the names of flowers, I may have forgotten special facts in connection with that study, but I remember the general impressions of it. As I studied the growth and life of vegetation, I found new influences coming over my mind—new influences that told me day by day of new beauties and of unseen kindness of nature. So with geology. I expected to do business above ground. I was not much concerned with what was below. I thought. [Laughte.r] And yet, as I went along in the study of geology, and found how, by progressions through long ages, our globe had come from a molten mass to this cooling crust on which we live, and as I studied the animated forms of life that lived and perished during the different epochs, my mind grew in wonder, and was filled with amazement and with reverential awe for the Great Master Mind of Creation. [Applause.] And those feelings and those influences were intensified by the study of astronomy, and the effort to solve the mystery of that Great Ever-acting Will of God, which we have labeled gravitation, by which the planets are held in their places. [Applause.] Yes, study the languages. Why, let me say to you, young people. who are at school here to-day, study every thing you can. ['Good!' and applause.] I don't like this utilitarian idea with respect to education. ['Amen!'] Somebody has said, 'Take care of the dimes, and the dollars will take care of themselves.' That's so—so true that it is a maxim. Yet there is a sense in which I have always detested the man who said it, and the spirit in which it was conceived, and that is the sense in which it looks not to the broader purposes of mankind, but to that selfish and reprehensible thing, personal advantage. So it is while you are here at school. In the first place, I know, whether you know or not, that you don't yet know what you will want to know when you get into the world. You may think you will be a doctor, and maybe you will be; you may think you are fitted to be a minister of the gospel, or a lawyer; or you may intend to follow some other particular vocation, and yet the fact may be that God intended you for something else. It may be that he has put you here at Wilberforce and thrown opportunities about you to the end that by the pursuit, not of a certain particular line of studies, but by the surveying and the investigation of the whole field of knowledge, you may have a symmetrical development of the mind that will teach you when you come to grapple with the duties of life that you are fitted for something higher, something better, and something broader than you ever dreamed of. [Applause.] Let me say that the great idea of your education should be to seek the truth—to seek it in every field of knowledge; and when, as a scholar, you have arrived at the truth, then as you go into the world let this still be your motto (referring to the class motto over the platform), '*Pius Ultra.*' When you go into the world let your motto be, 'The truth which I found as a scholar, as a man I shall act.' [Loud applause.] Therefore, instead of neglecting language, study it—study it in all its length and breadth, in all of its wonderful meaning—study it not simply that you may acquaint yourselves with it so that you may use it as a vehicle for communication, but in that wider and broader sense in which it is a science, in the sense in which Max Muller treats of it, in the sense in which it is a great structure, telling as no history can tell us of the origin, wanderings and development of mankind. [Applause.] I have dwelt thus long upon the general feature of interest of your institution not because I thought it necessary, but only because somehow I felt called upon to direct the attention of these students in this university, where you have such a splendid curriculum and where you have such a competent Faculty, to the point of not trying to decide in advance what they will do in life and then limit their studies accordingly, I desired to impress upon them, for their encouragement, to take advantage of everything spread before them and to make the most of it, whether it be in language, mathematics, literature or philosophy. Let your studies be broad that your minds may be broad, and that your duties in life may be successful in the highest sense.

Under the second part of his subject the Judge declared his convictions, for

FULL EDUCATIONAL OPPORTUNITIES FOR COLORED YOUTH,

as complete in all respects as for white youth, and that every college and university should be open for all citizens without reference to creed or color. * * I can never forget, Mr. President, that I once somewhere read that when this institution was offered for sale, that grand and memorable old man, Bishop Payne—a man I have always wanted to personally know —in bidding for the property, said: 'I buy it in the name of the African Methodist Episcopal Church, trusting that God will give me ability to pay for it!' [Applause.] And God did give him ability to pay for it, and he also gave him ability to rebuild it when incendiarism destroyed it, and he gave him ability to enlarge it, and to supply it with the instruments and apparatus necessary to make it the grand institution it is to-day, when it is more firmly rooted than ever it was before, and with a future brighter with promise. * * * * * *

The judge quoted President Washington's language, that there could be
NO GENUINE MORALITY INDEPENDENT OF RELIGION.
He congratulated Wilberforce in uniting morality and religion in its edu-

cational culture. The citizenship of the colored race was then adverted to. He continued: 'It seems incredible to us, in this year of 1885, meeting here under this tabernacle in this beautiful campus, that such a grand old hero, *such a distinguished divine as Bishop Campbell*—who did me the honor to introduce me—should have been once held in slavery as property. ['shame!'] Shame! Yes, but a more infamous shame that such grand intellects as those of Bishop Campbell and Bishop Turner and these other great men about me here, should have been by legislative enactments, under the pains and penalties of imprisonment in the penitentiary, as by the statute-books of Georgia and of South Carolina and other States it was provided, forbidden from learning their a, b, c's! Do you remember? [A storm of 'Yes, yes!'] The American people can easily forget; but Bishop Campbell will never forget. ['No, no! Never!'] I never liked to go into the State of Georgia except once. I was down there once with old General Sherman, and we left a mark. [Laughter and applause.] I went down after just such chaps as Bishop Turner and Bishop Campbell,

AND WE CAPTURED THEM AND BROUGHT THEM OUT THENCE. [Great laughter and applause.] But do you know that I always think when I speak in this way about Georgia that there was once on the statute-books of that State not only a law against colored men learning their a, b, c's, but also a joint resolution, I believe it was, adopted by the legislature, offering a reward of $5,000 for the delivery anywhere within the borders of the State, of that grand old humanitarian, William Lloyd Garrison. [Hisses.] Not only that, but Georgia, and probably all the other slave-States,

FORBADE BY LAW THE ORDINANCE OF MARRIAGE, as to slaves. They would not allow colored men to get an education while they lived, and manifestly did not want them to go to heaven when they died. [Great laughter and applause.] Well, they are going to heaven all the same. [Renewed laughter and cries of 'That's so.']

Why do I refer to these things? I do so in order that I might supplement the reference with this statement—that it is no wonder that the colored people of the South, having been held in bondage for 250 years, and having been so degraded and debased, should be in the condition they are to-day; it is no wonder that only about twenty-five per cent of them can read and write. Think of it, my colored friends—seventy-five per cent of the six millions of your race, all American citizens, unable to read or write! What a grand field it is for Wilberforce University to work in! What a grand inspiration for an institution that comes up to the measure
SET BY GEORGE WASHINGTON—KNOWLEDGE AND MORALITY!
Go on, then, with your good work! [Voices, 'We'll do it!']

And I thought as I stood on this platform to-day and read the names of these graduates from Tennessee, and Texas, and Louisiana, and Arkansas, that it was a grand, good thing that there was a place up here in the State of Ohio where they can come and get such inspirations and enjoy such associations as will enable them to return into that night of darkness and go into the ranks of their own fellow-citizens to labor to spread the light of both education and religion. Young men, you have a glorious field before you. Those people down there have been made citizens, and it is important that they should—I came pretty near saying that they should know how to vote right. [Laughter.] But that is unnecessary—they know how. But the trouble is they don't get to exercise that right. * *
* * But how to remedy it is another thing. But one of the ways to

remedy it is for these young men to go down there and spread the knowledge which they have acquired here. I am glad to know that you are doing it. I have read somewhere that there are to-day about

TEN THOUSAND SCHOOLS AMONG THE COLORED PEOPLE OF THE SOUTH.

See to it, my colored friends of Wilberforce, that you make the number twenty thousand. Go on with your work until you educate that people; and when you have educated that six millions of people you will find that they have been made stronger and able to help themselves, able to rise up in the strength of their knowledge, and they themselves will right their wrongs. * * * * * *

Do you remember, my fellow-citizens, that for forty-five years—from 1805 to 1850—we had on the statute-books of Ohio a blot and disgrace known as

'THE BLACK LAWS OF OHIO.'

Now I expect you have forgotten what the black laws were. Well, some of you haven't, for I see you shaking your heads. Let me tell these young people what they were. The 'Black Laws' were statutes which, among other things, forbade any colored man to testify in any case in court in which a white man was a party. Not only that, but these black laws provided that no white man should hire a colored man to do a day's work, or any part of a day's work, unless that colored man would first enter into a bond in the sum of $500, to be filed in the Court-house, with approved security, that he would keep the peace and not be a public charge. That was encouraging labor, you know. [Laughter.] I remember of hearing of a case that happened in the part of the State where I lived, where a poor colored man, traveling along the road, wearied and worn out, applied at a farmer's house for his dinner, offering to chop enough wood to pay for it. The farmer accepted the proposition, and the colored man got his dinner and chopped enough wood to pay for it. I should explain that the black-laws provided that the penalty for a violation of them by a white man should be a fine of $100, half of which should be paid to the informer to insure prosecution. And the old farmer was promptly arrested, and duly prosecuted for

A VIOLATION OF THE LAWS OF THE GREAT STATE OF OHIO!

Now, I say, it seems incredible that there could have been a public sentiment in Ohio of which such infamous laws were the reflection. And yet all these old men around me remember these laws. But they're all swept away now. ['Thank God!' and 'Amen!']—swept away to the credit of the people of Ohio and to the credit of the age in which we live [fervent amens]—swept away never to come again! ['Never, never!'] There is encouragement in that fact for you.

A race that can produce such men as Fred Douglass, Bishop Campbell, Bishop Payne, Bishop Turner, Bishop Brown, Bishop Ward, Bishop Caine, Bishop Shorter, Bishop Wayman, and the late lamented Bishop Dickerson, and Dr. Derrick, and such alumni of your Wilberforce, (in addition to the names already mentioned) as Drs. Jennifer, Welch and Jackson, Dr. Lee, editor of *Christian Recorder*, Prof. Shorter, Drs. Mitchell, and Delaney, and Drs. Tanner, Watkins, Jonson, and Hunter, and Drs. Stewart, Mitchell, and Handy, and Drs. Weeks, Simmons, Gaines, Asbury, Townsend, and that profound Greek scholar, Prof. Scarborough, and such men as our worthy friend, Brother Arnett, who is to be the next representative in the legislature from this county [loud applause]—and a glorious good one he will be—he will be loyal, I warrant you, to all of the highest and best interests of the State and of the colored and also of the white people—a race, I say, that can produce such men as these, men of such intellect, men of such character, is deserving of the highest encouragement, and

MUST BE SUCCESSFUL AND TRIUMPHANT IN ALL IT UNDERTAKES.

I thank you cordially for vour courteous attention. Good-by. [Loud and continued applause.]

VEHEMENT EMPHASIS OF THE REGARD OF THE COLORED PEOPLE

The correspondent adds:

It would be hypocrisy to pretena that the leaders and representatives of the colored race, as gathered here, did not desire that their reception to Foraker should not have any political significance. Almost a vehement emphasis was given to their reception to Foraker in consequence of and as an answer to the slander that the Republican nominee for governor of Ohio was not in sympathy with the colored race. Perhaps the most eloquent speech of the entire anniversary—for it has lasted several days—was an impromptu one by Rev. W. B. Derrick, of New York, who had just had conferred upon him the degree of Doctor of Divinity. Dr. Derrick is pastor of a church in New York City. It will be remembered that he was a Blaine elector, but resigned to prevent a question, he being a native of the Island of Antigua, although he is a naturalized citizen. When called npon for a speech after Foraker had left the grounds, he talked what men of the world would call 'straight goods.' He placed himself firmly on the rock of Christianity, and next to his religion, he declared his

HEART'S AFFECTION WENT OUT TO THE REPUBLICAN PARTY.

That might be called politics, he said; but he was a colored man talking to colored men, and the times demanded bold and unequivocal utterances. His peroration, the subject of which was Foraker, was

A MASTERPIECE OF PASSIONATE ELOQUENCE,

and the audience rapturously applauded him. He placed Foraker as the very first leader of the colored people. He knew of no man with such grand parts, who was so emphatically and effectively the friend of the colored race. He called him the Charles Sumner of this last quarter of the nineteenth century.

In the evening Judge Foraker addressed the graduates of the the High-School of Xenia, and at night the citizens of Xenia, when he said:

"Now, my friends, there is such a thing as victory in defeat. We didn't elect James G. Blaine and John A. Logan as we ought. But we gained, I think, as grand a victory as that would have been, and one which should satisfy the most ardent desirer of good government. Our Democratic friends have been compelled to give their reluctant testimony that the money is all there, that the books are all right, and that the administration of the Republican party has been

CHARACTERIZED BY THE MOST ABSOLUTE HONESTY.

Now, if such has been the case, if such has been the record of the Republican party, and no man will dispute it, why should that party be turned out of power? Not because the people condemned it. But still, it is out. Why and how? I think every man here knows and understands. In the last Electoral College that sat in the United States—the one which elected Mr. Cleveland—there were forty electoral votes that ought to have been Republican votes, representing the colored Republicans of the eleven seceding States. Forty votes that would not have been in that college had it not been for the generosity of the Republican party. Forty votes that ought to have been Republican, and would have been were it not because with the bull-whip and the shot-gun, by terrorism and by fraud, the people were robbed of the right of citizenship."

From a speech at Newark, Ohio, July 28, 1883: "The brightest gem in the crown of Republicanism is the victory it won over Democracy when it

ABOLISHED HUMAN SLAVERY,

enfranchised the freedman, and placed all American citizens on an equality before the law."

From the address at Ludlow Falls, August 31, 1883: "Ohio is a Republican State; a majority of the counties are Republican. There are not as many Democratic as Republican county treasurers; and yet, while there have been three Republican county treasurers as defaulters, there are twenty-six Democratic treasurers guilty of defalcation, ranging from $4,000 in Wyandot to $13,000 in Fairfield, where they have ordinarily a Democratic majority of 1,800.

THIS IS THEIR RECORD IN NATION AND STATE.

I refer to it, not to give Democrats offense, nor to abuse them; for it is not in accordance with my taste to abuse any man or any party—nor to show that Democrats are less honest than Republicans, but that they are less careful and fortunate in their selections."

Extracts from speech

AT WOOSTER, OHIO,

February 22, 1884: "But the silence with which they patiently endured was but the calm preceding the storm. In 1852 the Whig party died—died of

AN ATTEMPT TO SWALLOW THE FUGITIVE SLAVE-LAW—

and thus the way was cleared for newer and better issues. Human rights had attracted attention, and the contention was between slavery and liberty; and wrapped up in this controversy was the great question of the perpetuity of our Government.

The politicians of the South foresaw that slavery could not keep pace with freedom, and that it was merely a question of time when the North would succeed to the control of National affairs. Not willing to remain in the Union

UNLESS THEY COULD CONTROL IT,

they set up as against the day of dethronement the doctrine of secession, so that when they could no longer rule they could, apparently at least, legitimately ruin. In the light of the present we easily see the right side of this question. Jackson showed it in 1852, and forcibly too, to the erring Democracy in his celebrated proclamation to the

NULLIFIERS OF SOUTH CAROLINA.

Webster made it plain with the force of eloquence and logic in his great debate with Haynes. What Jackson and Webster contended for has become so fundamental that we wonder that it was ever questioned. It was an unsettled problem of the hour, and it required courage as well as discernment to make it a distinctive issue. The Republican party had both. Our party was

NOT MADE BY POLITICIANS.

It was born of the people. It was the suppression of their interest against the imbecility that had wasted our revenues, neglected our development, degraded our labor, and destroyed our credit. It was the embodiment of their indignation at the pretensions of slavery and the treason of disunion. The platform of the first National Convention denounced slavery and polygamy as the twin sisters of barbarism, proclaimed equality of rights for all citizens, the power and duty of the Government to protect and develop our own industries, to care for labor, and to preserve the Union and the Constitution. These promises, thus made by this party in the hour of its birth, have been most sacredly kept." It has sacredly kept every promise that it has made to the American people. * *

AMID THE SHOT, AND SHELL, AND SMOKE,

and storm of battle, the shackles were struck off and the bond made free. True to the cause of humanity, it stopped not until the despised freedmen were lifted up to citizenship and equality of rights before the Constitution and the laws. * * * * * * *

Extracts from a speech made as temporary chairman of a Republican Convention at Cincinnati, March 20, 1884:

* * * We were not successful in that campaign; but the fault was not at the door of the

REPUBLICANS OF HAMILTON COUNTY.

* * In this county and in the State our Democratic friends had the victory in the election of their ticket. But what was the victory? Napoleon once said after one of his great battles, that another such victory, great as it was, if achieved at equal loss, would be his absolute ruin. [Applause.] * * * In 1882 the Democratic party swept this county with the overwhelming majority of 10,000. These were respectable figures. They made Republicans feel lonesome. Last year, twelve months later, after an earnest and vigorous campaign, * * they were glad to get off with 10,000 reduced to 2,500. [Great Applause.] At this rate of progression, it requires no spirit of prophecy to foretell that Ohio, in this year of 1884, will be

RESTORED TO THE REPUBLICAN COLUMN

with her old-fashioned Republican majority. [Applause].

Commenting on this speech, the *Chicago Inter-Ocean*, said:

" Judge Foraker's *pertinacity*, along with his *talent*, which is of a high order, commands the respect of the

REPUBLICAN LEADERS OVER THE NATION.

The tremendous work of last fall has given him great influence over the voting masses. His spirit maps out the campaign of 1884.

SIDNEY, OHIO, September 18, 1884.

The *Sidney Journal* said: No better meeting was ever held in Sidney. The judge will be remembered by all who heard him, for he impressed them with his candor, his common sense, and his abilities as a man rounded and complete."

GALLIPOLIS, OHIO, September 16, 1884.

The judge received an ovation of applause. The people recognized in him the man for whom Gallia County gave an unusually large majority for governor a year ago, and a desire to have another chance to cast their vote for him next year seemed to pervade the audience, so that one could almost hear the still, small voice quivering among the leaders of the parties.

BROOKLYN, N. Y., SPEECH.

Ex-Judge J. B. Foraker of Ohio made the last speech. He was greeted with long continued applause. Though the hour was late, 11:00 P. M., (Gen. Hawley having spoken for three hours,) his speech was listened to with marked attention, and his telling points *were approved with vociferous cheers.*—New York *Tribune,* August 22:

While Judge Foraker was speaking of Ex-Governor Hendricks, some one in the audience cried out,

"WHERE WAS JOHN A. LOGAN

at this time?"

'Where was John A. Logan at the same time?' asked the speaker, with flashing eyes, and then answering his own question, 'He was at the head of the Fifteenth Army Corps with Sherman's troops, and they had just broken down the last barrier between them and the 'Gate City' of the South, and were marching triumphantly forward to the sea. Logan was in bad company at one time. We concede it with regret. But he came out of it when the first shot was fired on Fort Sumter, and, thank God, he never went back. [Great applause.] * * Now, the principal assault made on our candidate for vice-president rests on the ground that he does sometimes make mistakes in the use of the English language. I have known some very estimable men and women who have violated the rules of grammar. It is the easiest thing in the world to make mistakes of this sort. But John A. Logan is not this sort of a man. He profited by his opportunities at academy and college. He is to-day a student. He has had, too, all that experience in public life which is of so much importance in the political development of a man's mind. He has had the experience of the camp, the field, the rostrum, a long training in Congress, and a long service at the bar.

'HE CAN'T WRITE GOOD ENGLISH?'

He wrote some English on one occasion that was good enough for me. It was when they had asked him to come home from the war and accept a nomination to Congress. He wrote, 'I have received your kind favor indorsing a nomination for Congress in the Fourteenth District. I state all my views when I say that the integrity of the Union must be preserved.

I HAVE NO OTHER POLITICS AND NO OTHER AMBITION.

Our government must be transmitted to our children in the same mold in which we have received it, if it takes the last dollar and the last man the country can raise.' [Applause.] That was good enough English for me, and I think you will agree with me. [The answer was a storm of applause.] It was better than any ever written by Thos. A. Hendricks. [Applause.]

" But men can only stand as the representatives of principles in our form of government. Some Brooklyn citizen was kind enough to send me the printed address of the gentleman who presided over the gathering of the bolters, which took place in this city some time ago. I was glad to receive it. The chairman of that gathering is evidently a man of intelligence and of ability. But when he says that there is nothing at

ISSUE BETWEEN THE TWO PARTIES

at the present time he makes a great mistake. * * * But would it be advisable to advocate a change of administration simply for the sake of a change? Mr. Carl Schurz thinks it would be desirable now. He thought differently in 1880, when he was holding a public office, and made a long speech in that campaign, in which he dwelt upon the danger of letting in men upon the public trusts who would fill all positions with those who, if not incapable or dishonest, would at the least be without experience, and who would fill the places of trained public servants. He showed conclusively that if such a party were let into power, it would be impossible for any outside office to control its managers, or for the managers themselves to, no matter what their own integrity might be, to defend the public from the inroads of those who would conceive that it was their support which had put into power the new administration. He showed that all the affairs of the government were honestly carried on as a rule, and that there was no necessity of a change of any kind. Now Mr. Schurz has changed his tune and thinks change is desirable in itself. I have the greatest respect for Mr. Schurz. He is a man of ability, and is frequently found on the right side. When he is not found there, it is because he has made an honest mistake."

Till after midnight Judge Foraker held the over-crowded house, which still begged him to "go on."

Stanton Journal (Virginia), May 28th, 1885:

As Judge Foraker proceeded with his masterly argument, the applause was deafening.

THE GIFTED OHIOAN IS AN ABLE SPEAKER.

Youthful, almost in appearance, with a frank, genial face, and cordial, yet dignified manners, he had made his way to the hearts of the people even before he had carried conviction to their understanding, by his unanswerable presentation of the issues of the canvas. His voice is clear and distinct, his gestures few yet always appropriate. He presents his ideas with directness and force that leave an indelible impression. He makes converts. * * * Whenever he visits us he will be

WELCOMED WITH A WARMTH AND SINCERITY

that few can evoke. * * From beginning to end Judge Foraker's grand speech was punctuated with applause, and at its close, cheer after cheer resounded and drowned the music of the band.

Judge Foraker commenced his two hours' speech by saying that the ring of Republican cheers in Virginia sounded very much as they did in Ohio. It might be asked what interest he had in the election in this State; why was he coming here to seek to influence the votes of Virgina? The interests to be affected by the results of this canvass could not be limited by the State lines; they extended alike to all sections of the Union.

OHIO VOTED FOR VIRGINIA AND VIRGINIA VOTED FOR OHIO.

Each State is an integral part of the whole, and its interests, its hopes, and its prospects are so closely interwoven with the welfare of the 55,000,000 people of the Republic that to injuriously affect one is to hurt all. There was a time, said the speaker, when I would not have come to Virginia to counsel and advise with her people. Virginia believed in the institution of slavery then and the old State Sovereignty dogma. Ohio did not. So wide was the difference between them that there was no common ground to meet upon. Now, however, those issues are dead, and the measures that shall bring prosperity to my people will prove like blessings to yours. The triumph of the principles of the Republican party does not mean a victory for the North over the South, but a victory of the North and South in a common cause.

STAUNTON, VIRGINIA.

Judge Foraker addressed a Republican meeting here to-day of over 2,000, delivering one of

THE ABLEST SPEECHES EVER HEARD IN THE STATE.

His exposition of the tariff was lucid and powerful. The united enthusiasm with which he was greeted proved that he had made a way straight to the hearts of Virginians. It infused into the party a new life. No man ever met with a heartier reception, and none ever proved himself worthier of it.—*Special to Commercial-Gazette*, Aug. 25, 1884.

STAUNTON, VA., August 25.

Judge Foraker arrived here Saturday evening, unheralded, and taking quarters at the quiet Kalorama Hotel, thought to escape notice for a day.

He did not know with what close interest

HIS SPLENDID OHIO CAMPAIGN

of last year had been watched by Virginia friends, and he was soon made the recipient of becoming attention. Judge Foraker is another of the great men who look back to Virginia for their ancestry. His great-grandfather was the original discoverer of the famous Weyer Cave in this county, which bears his name. * * For two and a half hours Judge Foraker held the vast audience enchained by his arguments, his eloquence and his wit, both genial and sarcastic. * * He satisfied the intellect, stirred the heart, and brought forth loud and long-repeated cheers, and his closing period *raised a tempest of rapturous enthusiasm.—Special to Richmond (Va.) Whig.*

DAYTON, September 21, 1884.

No one ever held an audience at the court-house better than Judge Foraker did on Saturday night. The speaker held his audience for two hours, and when he had concluded, they called on him to continue.—*Dayton Journal*, September 23, 1884.

Extract: "We ought not to pursue a policy that will widen
THE CHASM BETWEEN THE RICH AND THE POOR.
The laboring man has here an opportunity to elevate himself and he succeeds. A complete refutation of the assertion of the Democratic party that Republican policy is to allow the rich to become richer and the poor, poorer, is that immigration grows and there is no emigration. Who is there in this assembly that wears a foreign garment? Not one. * * *

At Pomeroy: Cassius M. Clay and Judge Foraker addressed the people on presidential issues. The *Journal* of the place said: "People sat patiently in the sweltering heat (of August,) and listened as quietly as in a church, except their applauding. Persons in the most distant grounds could hear every word.
DELIBERATION AND DISTINCTNESS CHARACTERIZED HIS UTTERANCES.
His speech was strong, convincing, and was cheered lustily.

JUDGE FORAKER AT SHELBY, 1884.

The Judge's strength lies not in rhetorical flights, nor the blaze of eloquence, nor in humor, for he neither works on the passions nor the emotions. His enunciation is distinct, and his English clear-cut and vigorous. He clears up as he proceeds, does not qualify with a circumlocutory perhaps, or with enervating apologies, but drives for the center, carrying conviction by argument, most charmingly presented. There was nothing harsh in his dealings with Cleveland, and yet the following point was peculiarly effective: Grover Cleveland, he said, had been a voter for some time when the war of the rebellion broke out. He was a lawyer by profession in the city of Buffalo. All through the years of the war, of reconstruction, of the consideration of the finance and constitutional amendments, of the discussion of the feasibility of resumption, he was a healthy citizen, but there is no record that he had an opinion on any of these vital questions which stirred every man who was a man. Grover Cleveland voted the Democratic ticket with marked regularity, and then lapsed into the blissful feeling that his whole duty was performed. Whether he is a free-trader or a tariff man is a secret. As he is not married, the secret will probably never be disclosed.
* * * One objection I had to Tilden, he said, was that he had no
EXPERIENCE IN THE SACREDNESS OF A FAMILY,
for I hold that no life is rounded that has not such an experience.—*Shelby Journal*.

From Judge Foraker's Cincinnati Music Hall speech, October 18, 1884:
* * * "For President we want a man of
BROAD, ENLIGHTENED, PROGRESSIVE, COMPREHENSIVE
and American statesmanship, with a life and a record full of loyalty, patriotism, and devotion to the Union and the constitution. * * * * *
"You can travel all through Mississippi, Florida, and Arkansas without finding a manufacturing interest of greater importance than a blacksmith shop. The official report of the State auditor of Alabama for 1883 shows that in Coffee County, Ala-

bama, there was a Democratic majority of 1,050 votes, and in this county the total tax-valuation was $90. This same report shows that in this same county the tax-valuation of its guns and pistols was $3,637. This same official report shows the same condition of Covington, Crenshaw, Escambia, Fayette, and other counties of this State.

THE CIVILIZATION THAT WAS BORN OF SLAVERY
has not yet perished. It is radically different from the civilization that has sprung up under the radiant sunlight of human liberty that has beamed, and smiled, and played over the hills and valleys of the Northern section of this Republic. It is over that civilization you have again triumphed—over a shot-gun party and a shot-gun policy."

The *Times-Star* (Cincinnati) said of the jumbo jubilee at Music Hall, held after the October Ohio victory: " With his usual clear and persistent eloquence, Judge Foraker made

BUT LITTLE EXULTATION OVER THE VICTORY.
He made his speech against the Democratic cause. * * * It is this party of shot-guns and pistols that talk of throwing out Ben Butterworth because a few deputy marshals had a few bull-dog pistols. We don't want that end of the country to be on top yet."

Judge Foraker, in his impromptu speech, October 28, 1884, introducing the society of the Army of the Cumberland to the Cincinnati Chamber of Commerce, among other things said: "With the exception of Washington, there was no city within the Union lines more exposed to dangers of

OUR CIVIL WAR THAN CINCINNATI.
When we reached the end of the struggle, we found our city had been as little harmed as any other in the land. This good fortune was not accidental. Situated on the very border-line of the Rebellion, we were on this account—aside from other considerations—a continually inviting prey to the enemy; so much so that there was not one campaign planned, aggressive in its character, for the rebel armies of the South and West, that had not for one of its objective points

THE CAPTURE AND PILLAGE OF THIS CITY.
[Hear, hear.] Hence, the surges of the conflict were felt in this direction. More than once we saw the red waves of strife roll to our very feet, but each time, thanks to the heroism and valor here represented, only to be dashed to pieces and flung back again, harmless as they struck upon

THE VERITABLE ROCK OF CHICAMAUGA.
[Applause.] These are the men who constituted the rock—that protecting breaker for this city—for they are the men of Buell, Rosecrans, and grand old Thomas. Not only are they the men

who in this sense were the especial defenders of Cincinnati, the heroes of Mill Springs, Perryville, Stone River, and Chickamauga, but they are men also who, side by side with their gallant comrades of the Army of the Tennessee, won for our cause and our flag imperishable renown, as well as victory on the bloody fields of Shiloh, Mission Ridge, Atlanta, and in the ever-famous march to the sea." [Great applause].

This address, so peculiarly appropriate and so much admired, thus closes:

"If there is anything for which we are more thankful to-day than for that success (just referred to), it is that
THROUGH THE GOODNESS AND MERCY OF GOD
our lives have been spared to see the day when the fruits of that struggle are beginning to be as much appreciated at the South as at the North [applause]; when the people of the South are learning to appreciate that
OUR VICTORY WAS THEIR VICTORY;
when we approximate the time when, only in a geographical sense, there will be a South, or North, or East, or West; but when we can look around ut to see the people of every section—North, South, East, West,—united hand-in-hand, arm-in-arm, enjoying a
COMMON PROSPERITY, A COMMON CONSTITUTION,
a common government, a common flag, with a common future, full of hope and promise for us all. [Loud applause.] These are the men whose deeds, with those of their companions, accomplished these results for us."

The Army of the Cumberland selected Captain Foraker as their orator for the next reunion, at Grand Rapids, September 18 and 19, 1885.

At Sharon, October 31, 1884, Judge Foraker addressed a large and enthusiastic audience.

Extract: "It is not the Democratic party against the Republican, but it is the solid South with the anticipated assurance of a State or two north of the line
AGAINST THE LOYAL NORTH.
It is simply disloyalty arrayed against the loyalty represented by both white and black."

At Shinn's Grove, November 5, 1884, the judge addressed an enthusiastic mass-meeting. He reviewed the Government and its finances from 1840 to the present, and ably replied to the free-trade speech of Speaker Carlisle from the same stand a short time before.

Extract of a speech before the Young Men's Blaine Club, April 11, 1885, at its greeting to Amor Smith, Mayor-elect of Cincinnati. "The election of last Monday was the

PEOPLE'S PROTEST AGAINST INIQUITOUS INCOMPETENCY.
It means that in Cincinnati we are to have a home government; that the iniquitous ring-rule is to be broken; that our good name is to be regarded; that our credit is to be restored."

CELEBRATION OF THE 63D BIRTHDAY OF GEN. GRANT,
at Turner Hall, Cincinnati, Ohio, April 25, 1885:

The mere mention of his (Judge Foraker's) name, evoked an enthusiasm which did not subside for five minutes. * * * * The cries of "*Hurrah for Foraker, the next Governor of Ohio*," were taken up simultaneously all over the hall; it was an inspiration not called for, nor sought, but it was the very nature of a great occasion, and personality was for the time forgotten; it was that of a great people embodied in pure sentiment, irrespective of party.—*Commercial-Gazette.*

After the judge, in his oration, had noticed Gen. Grant's career and his army record, he said, "But 'Peace hath her
VICTORIES NO LESS RENOWNED THAN WAR.'
* * There were other laurels. * * It remained to secure the fruits of his victory. * * For eight years he was president of the United States. * * He was assailed, libeled, and maligned. * * But now how changed! To-night he lingers on the brink of the grave, but as he casts behind him a farewell look to the receding world, he sees standing in tearful suspense and with affectionate reverence,
THE WHOLE AMERICAN PEOPLE
—friend and foe, federal and confederate, Republican and Democrat, vieing with each other to manifest love and esteem. * * He has outlived his enemies; he has only friends." * * *

The newspapers of Cincinnati say of Cincinnati pioneers' meeting at Music Hall in May (1885), that there was a splendid speech from Judge Foraker, that Music Hall was crowded with members of the Citizens' Memorial Association and citizens young and old; that the six hundred children from the public schools made a magnificent chorus, occupying seats on the stage in rows rising above the old white-headed pioneers grouped beneath them. So vivid a contrast between youth and age has seldom been seen. The G. A. R. veterans were in the audience, some organizations coming in with the enthusing fife and drum, bringing the audience to its feet and causing a general cheer.

Judge Foraker,
ALWAYS POPULAR BEFORE A MUSIC-HALL
audience, delivered his oration with his usual eloquence, and was cheered with the same vigor that has often welcomed his appearance in a political meeting.

JUDGE FORAKER'S ORATION.
MR. CHAIRMAN, LADIES AND GENTLEMEN:—I have read of a custom in Ireland in obedience to which every one who chances to meet a funeral

procession is required to humbly turn and accompany it at least a little way on its sad march to the grave. In this simple manner it is sought to pay

A SUGGESTIVE TRIBUTE OF RESPECT TO THE DEAD.

Such, in a general way, is the character of our purpose here this evening. We have turned aside from the busy walks of life that we may spend an hour in honor of the dead; we have come to pay a tribute of respect to our departed, and in the sacred presence of the memories thus recalled commemorate their virtues.

Our coming together for such a purpose is not an idle ceremony, but

A BEAUTIFUL, IMPRESSIVE AND APPROPRIATE SERVICE—

beautiful, because of the spirit that prompts it; impressive, because it recalls hallowed associations that are now, alas! forever broken; appropriate, because all flesh is grass, everything must perish; and whither they have gone we too are hastening with the swiftness of the fleeting years. * * * *

I spoke of a custom of Ireland. There was another custom among the ancient Egyptians, in accordance with which when one died they would not allow him burial until after he had been carried into the presence of judges, appointed for the purpose, whose duty it was to hear all that might be said for or against the deceased, and upon such testimony pronounce impartial judgment as to whether his deeds had been such in life as to entitle him to honorable remembrance in death. We have not come here—at least not so far as the duty that has been imposed upon me is concerned—to thus sit in judgment upon individual lives. If such was the task assigned me, it would be a pleasing duty to make honorable mention of a long list of names, some of which would be most familiar, but many of which would not be so; for with us as with other communities it has been the fact

THAT SOME OF THE MOST USEFUL LIVES

that have been passed among us have been so humbly and obscurely lived as to be forgotten almost as soon as ended. * * How many of us are familiar with the name of Prof. Vaughan? And yet in the great societies and academies of learning and science in Europe, it is regarded as one of the distinguished honors of our city that it should have been the home of so eminent a scholar. And this is equally true of hundreds who were connected with the pulpit, the press, the schools, and the professions; and what is thus true of such men is also true in a much greater degree of the men who have spent their lives in physical toil and labor. It is true of that

GRAND ARMY OF INVENTIVE GENIUSES

who have constructed and given to this city its wonderful power. It is true of the architects and engineers who have built our temples, projected our railroads, spanned our rivers with bridges, and utilized, beautified, and adorned the rugged hills by which we are surrounded. It would be pleasing, too, in the performance of such a task to recount the virtues that ennobled the lives, and recite the deeds of generosity that made famous the names of such men as

SPRINGER AND LONGWORTH AND WEST.

But that task in so far as it is to be performed at all has been assigned to others. My task is to briefly call your attention to the aggregate of some of the results that have been accomplished by these men who have passed away, and from such results as the fruits of their labors ask you to judge of the character of the men we would honor.

ATHENS, ROME, PARIS, LONDON,

and the other noted cities of the old world had been full-grown for centuries before we were born. They had been the seats of government, the centers of trade and commerce, the sources of learning, the homes of art and the scenes of great historical events that gave them wealth, power, culture, and tragic-like interest for mankind long ages before even our foundations were laid. It is not one hundred years since all this beautiful Ohio valley was a wild, unbroken forest, inhabited by only savage beasts and savage men. There were here

NO CITY, NO GOVERNMENT, NO CIVILIZATION,

and no law of any kind save that of nature. But to-day, how changed! The forests have been swept away, and every hill and valley blossoms as the rose.

The silence of solitude has been forever banished by the busy hum of a thousand industries. The rudeness of barbarism has been supplanted by the refinements of civilization, and the savagery of beast and man has faded into tradition amidst the loving kindness of Christianity.

We have a population of three hundred thousand souls. They represent almost every nationality on the face of the earth, and every kind of thought, hope, ambition, and aspiration. And yet, we are a homogeneous community, seeking and attaining prosperity in all the avocations of life, but living harmoniously together in a common enjoyment of the most enlightened institutions, and under the protection of the best form of government known to the world. It has been a great work to accomplish this mighty transformation. It can not be overestimated or too highly appreciated. In the mere fact that it has been done there exists an everlasting testimonial to the worth, sincerity, and true greatness of the three generations of our fathers by whom it was performed. It will forever speak for them

OF PATIENT TOIL AND GREAT HARDSHIPS, AUSTERE PUBLIC
VIRTUE

and wise statesmanship, unselfish devotion to duty, heroic blood and patriotic sacrifices. * * *

Their highest claim to gratitude and honor at our hands is for the civil institutions they bestowed upon us; the civil institutions that constitute both their and our greatest glory; the civil institutions that have done more for the prosperity and good name of Cincinnati than all the muscle and brawn, inventive genius and liberal generosity that have been expended on it.

If we should be called upon to perform a like service we could now, in the light of our experience, easily enough, no doubt, decide in favor of the same kind of institutions our fathers gave to us. We would not hesitate to declare for

ABSOLUTE FREEDOM OF OPINION AND EQUALITY OF CITIZENSHIP

as against every species of human bondage, and against every kind of inequality of right. These are self-evident propositions to us. They lie at the very basis of all our ideas of society. But it was not so with our fathers one hundred years ago. They had no light of experience such as we have enjoyed. Men have been vainly struggling for two thousand years for a practical and successful demonstration of self-government. There had always been some essential element fatally lacking. Another experiment was to be made. It was destined to prove a success, but not without a priceless expenditure of blood and treasure that constituted the penalty imposed for the well-nigh fatal mistakes attending its inauguration. American independence had just been achieved. It had been conquered by the sword. The struggle had been long and bloody, and the spirit of freedom and equality had been quickened as never before in the history of the world. Yet the liberty that had been so secured

MEANT NOTHING MORE, HIGHER, OR BETTER

to one half the American people than a right to have human slavery and protect it by constitutional provisions as a divine institution.

But fortunately it was not so with the other half. They, on the contrary, believed in a practical application to government of the doctrine proclaimed by the Declaration of Independence, that all men are created free and equal. The two ideas were necessarily at war with each other. In the nature of things they could not peaceably co-exist—one or the other must ultimately prevail with the whole people. But from one or the other of these ideas, with the chances largely in favor of the wrong one, the men who founded Cincinnati and settled the State of Ohio were compelled to make choice as to the spirit of the government and the character of the institutions under which they,

and we as their children, should live. They made their choice, and made it right; and no language can exaggerate the important and far-reaching consequences for good that have resulted from the fact that, as the result of their choice, they secured for us, as
OUR FIRST ORGANIC LAW, THE ORDINANCE OF 1787.

It turned the tide that was eventually to carry with it the balance of power in favor of the civilization of New England. It was a new charter of liberty—
A SECOND DECLARATION OF INDEPENDENCE.
Here, where there was so much labor to be done, it established as a controlling idea that it is honorable to labor, and that no success or luxury should be enjoyed except as the result of individual enterprise and self-elevation and culture. It brought with it an influence that taught men to be self-reliant, to act upon individual responsibility, to encourage industry and enterprise, and to scorn to eat their bread except in the sweat of their own faces; and over and above all else it taught as a cardinal principle that
MORALITY AND KNOWLEDGE ARE ESSENTIAL TO GOOD GOVERNMENT.
In other words, side by side with its broad recognition of the rights of men it planted
THE CHURCH AND THE SCHOOL-HOUSE,
and bid mankind look upward as they marched onward, and struggle not only for the material and temporal prosperity of this world, but also for the higher and better things of both this life and the life to come. This work of the fathers was indeed a great one. It will forever bear witness that they appreciated the responsibilities that rested upon them; that they had a just measure of their mission; that they knew they were the pioneer fathers of what was destined to be a mighty north-west, and that they knew that the ideas and opinions which they were to propagate would exercise a controlling influence in the great contest for supremacy which they foresaw
BETWEEN THE TWO CIVILIZATIONS OF AMERICA.
They knew they were not only founding this beautiful city, but that they were also making an important contribution to that beautiful temple of liberty that is to-day the pride of every American heart.

We have lived to see the importance of this work. We have seen the Nation struggling in war to maintain its life. We have seen the Nation triumph. But who that remembers that conflict can doubt but that this union of states, now forever established and dedicated to freedom, would have been either dismembered by treason or forever cursed and disgraced by the blight of slave-domination, if our fathers had not given us the institutions that threw our power and influence on the side of the Union and in favor of the cause of human liberty?

We do well to remember the princely generosity that has adorned our city with this beautiful structure in which we are assembled. We would be ungrateful indeed should we ever forget the munificent liberality that has crowned yonder hill with an art museum.

But great as may be our obligations to such men, greater by far is the debt we owe to the men who determined the character of our institutions by impressing

THEIR OWN STURDY, UPRIGHT CHARACTER

upon them. All honor to every virtue; all honor to every man who lives a useful life; but may the time never come when we shall fail to recognize as our greatest benefactors the men who, with unselfish patriotism, barred slavery with its long train of evils out of our city, and brought into it, with their attendant blessings, the church and the school-house. They were men such as the poet wrote of, when he said,

What constitutes a State?
Not high-raised battlements or labored mound,
  Thick wall or moated gate—
Not cities proud, with spires and turrets crowned,
  Not bays and broad-armed ports—
Where, laughing at the storm, rich navies ride;
  Nor starred and spangled courts,
Where low-browed baseness wafts perfume to pride.
  No! *Men*, high-minded *men*,
With powers as far above dull brutes endowed,
  In forest, brake, or den—
As beasts excel cold rocks and brambles rude,
  . . . Men who their duties know,
But know their rights, and knowing dare maintain.

And now, my friends, there is one other class of our dead, and only one other, entitled to equal honor and gratitude at our hands, and they are the sons who saved what the fathers created; for all that the fathers did would have been done in vain had it not been for the heroic sons who laid down their lives for its preservation.

It is twenty years now since the war for the suppression of the rebellion closed. For twenty years the grass has been growing green over the graves of the Union dead. For twenty years the sunlight of peace has been beaming steadily upon us; and during all this time we have been drifting on, through the cares and anxieties of business all the while, each year more and more forgetting that great struggle with its terrible recollections; and yet, notwithstanding the lapse of this long period, and notwithstanding all these intervening events, how strong and how sacred the memory of that time! We have again this day witnessed a most beautiful but solemn and impressive ceremony. We have seen the loyal people of the whole nation, from one end of the land to the other, moved by a common impulse, gathering with affectionate reverence around the graves of the loyal dead, strewing them over with the choicest flowers of spring-time, and upon those lowly mounds, as though upon the altars of their country, with apt words of patriotism, dedicating themselves anew to the great principles and purposes for which these men died.

Who were these men, and what were the services they rendered that they should be accorded such exceptional tributes of honor? Can you recall that past? Can you still remember the soul-stirring scenes of 1861-5? Can you again hear the beat of the drum and the shrill note of the fife? Do you once more see the flags flying and the troops marching? Can you again recall how the minds of all were filled with that strange, wild delirium of war?

IF YOU ARE A WIFE WHO GAVE UP A HUSBAND, a mother who surrendered a darling boy, or an orphan child who looked through blinding tears for the last time upon a loving father as he marched away to return no more forever, you can never forget it. Neither can you ever forget the services and sacrifices of the men with whom we thus parted.

THEY WERE NOT PROFESSIONAL SOLDIERS.

They had no ambitions to gratify by such a service. They had neither hope nor desire for military distinction and renown. They were only honest-minded citizens of the republic, who had a just appreciation of their duties of citizenship. They believed they had come into the inheritance of a good government, not simply to enjoy its privileges, but also charged with the duty of preserving and perpetuating it to posterity.

THEY WERE MEN OF CONSCIENCE.

It was impossible for them to recognize a duty and fail to perform it. They were patriotic men. They loved their country, and were proud of its good name. They were loyal men. They believed in the Constitution, and the flag that our fathers gave us, and they were determined to have no other. They had no patience with the miserably belittling idea that the Constitution was a mere compact between States. On the contrary, they believed that it was, what on its face it declares itself to be, the organic law of the whole people, binding us together in an indissoluble union that made of the American people an American nation. They hated and despised the crime of secession, and believed that the doctrine of States Rights was an infamous heresy, fit only to be shot to ignominious and everlasting death with the million guns of the republic. They saw and realized that a great crisis had come—a great crisis not only for the American Government, but also for the cause of mankind throughout the world. They saw that it must be met, and all saved; or, evaded, and all lost. Between such alternatives they could not hesitate.

The path of duty was plain, and they heroically walked in it when they volunteered and marched away—marched away from home—from the plans and purposes and ambitions of life—
MARCHED AWAY FROM WIFE AND CHILDREN—
from father and mother—from all that was nearest and dearest in this world—marched away to follow the flag—to follow the flag, they knew not where, except only wheresoever it might lead—to follow it on the weary and foot-sore march—to undergo hardships and deprivations—to face the shot and shell of battle, and, God so willing it, to fall before the storm of leaden hail.

And all for what? For literally nothing to them as individuals; for it was all without hope or thought of personal gain or advantage of any kind. Yea, all with no other hope or thought than that they might, to the utmost of their humble abilities, serve the great cause of their country which it had become their high duty to espouse. Never before was there marshaled on the face of the earth an army that was inspired with a more exalted patriotism or a more unselfish devotion to duty. They were truly, as it has been eloquently said, a grand army of a million men. The record of their achievements is the most brilliant chapter of our National history. With a zeal that never flagged, a heroism that never quailed, a courage that nothing could daunt, and
A CONFIDENCE THAT WAS BORN OF GOD,
they pressed on through good report and bad report, through victory and defeat, battle and blood—from the gloom and disaster of Bull Run to the glorious sunshine of peace that broke the clouds and shone down for all on the victorious fields of Appomattox.   *   *   *   *   *   *

On the eve of one of his great battles—Eylau, I think it was—Napoleon nerved his troops for the impending struggle by an inspiriting address, in which he said that to the last days of their lives it would be sufficient when said of them, 'There is a soldier who fought at Eylau,' to elicit the response, 'Then there is a hero.'

And so may we say that so long as the English language lives there will be one bright, gleaming page of history to tell of the noble lives and heroic deaths of Lytle, the McCooks, Fred Jones and Will Jones,
AND THAT GALLANT BAND OF BRAVE COMRADES
who lie sleeping about them in yonder cemetery.   *   *

More than two thousand years ago Pericles said, in his famous oration over the Grecian dead, 'Of the illustrious, the world is the sepulcher.' So may we say of our dead heroes. Their fame is forever secure. Their bodies lie buried in the 'windowless palaces of death,' but their deeds are forever entombed in the hearts of mankind. Wherever patriotism is appreciated,

WHEREVER THE LOVE OF LIBERTY DWELLS,

wherever brave men are held in esteem, there the memory of our heroes will be forever cherished. * * *

If we are as faithful to our trust as the dead were to theirs, we shall continue to live under the Constitution, and to follow one flag, as we march forward to a common destiny that is full of hope and promise for us all. But if we would attain this success, we must remember the

VIRTUES OF OUR FATHERS AND CHERISH THE DEEDS OF THEIR SONS.

* * We must never permit it to be forgotten that for all we are, or ever hope to be as a people, we are indebted to the sacrifice of life that these men made. Then, both as a tribute of love to the dead and as a lesson of duty to the living, let us—

> 'Cover them over with beautiful flowers,
> Deck them with garlands, these brothers of ours,
> Lying so silent, by night and by day,
> Sleeping the years of their manhood away;
> Years they had marked for the joys of the brave,
> Years they must waste in the moldering grave.
> All the bright laurels they waited to bloom
> Fell from their hopes when they fell to the tomb;
> Then givh them the meed they won in the past,
> Give them the honors their future forecast,
> Give them the chaplet they won in the strife,
> Give them the laurels they won with their life.
> Cover them over—yes, cover them over,
> Parent, husband, brother, and lover—
> Crown in your hearts these heroes of ours,
> And cover them over with beautiful flowers.'

AT THE GRAND RECEPTION AND MASS-MEETING,

under the auspices of the Lincoln Club, Cincinnati manifested, June 20th, a revival of the enthusiasm of the National campaign; indeed, the meeting was larger and more enthusiastic than any held last fall.

EXTRACTS FROM THE SPEECH OF JUDGE FORAKER.

MR. CHAIRMAN AND FELLOW-CITIZENS—* * * When we had been beat in the great National contest of last year, our Democratic friends made haste to loudly and confidently proclaim that the Republican party had not only been overthrown, but that it had also been destroyed. [Shouts of 'Never.']

They told us its mission was ended; that its work was done; that it was dead [shout, 'It's the liveliest party they ever tackled']. But although a few months have since elapsed, yet there has been time enough for a number of conclusive refutations to be given to that claim.

ONE OF THE FIRST REFUTATIONS

was given by the Republicans of Illinois when they honored again with a seat in the United States Senate one of our gallant leaders in the last campaign, General John A. Logan. [Cheers.]

Our Democratic friends found out, as my friend in the audience suggested, that the Republican party was neither dead, nor sleeping, when on the first Monday of last April, here in the city of Cincinnati, we made,

BY A MAJORITY OF FOUR THOUSAND,
your fellow-citizen, Amor Smith, Mayor of the city. [Yells and enthusiastic applause.] But I need not stop to argue that, as any one who saw that magnificent convention that assembled at Springfield, any one who sees this magnificent demostration here to-night, knows that the Republicans of Ohio are going to proclaim, by the result of our election in October next, that the Republican party is not dead in the old Buckeye State. [Cry, 'No, not by forty thousand.'] Yes, my friends, not by forty thousand. That, I believe. is the second amendment, and I accept it accordingly. [Laughter.] * * * * * *

By way of inspiration for the work that is before us. let me remind you of the triumphs of the Republican party in the past.

We were twenty-four years engaged in administering our National affairs. When we came into control of our general government in 1861, we found our country half enslaved; when we turned it over to our Democratic friends a few months ago

THE COUNTRY WAS ALL FREE.

[Cheers.] Nowhere under the flag does the foot of a human slave press on American soil. [Cheers.]

When we came into control of the Government in 1861, the nature of it had not yet been determined. We knew that the States were living together in some sort of union. We knew that we had three great departments of government, whose respective powers and authority were defined by the Constitution; but yet there was a controversy that was vital as to the question of the perpetuity of our government, a question as to the proper relation of the States to the general Government; for there was a great political party in this country that contended that

OUR CONSTITUTION IS NOTHING MORE THAN A COMPACT;

that any State has the right to break it up or destroy it whenever they see fit to do so; that there was no power in the Constitution to preserve the constitution—that it was constitutional to destroy it even; but as we turned the Government over to our Democratic friends that question too was settled. The boys in blue on the battle-fields of the Republic settled, and settled forever, that the constitution of the United States is not the libel on our fathers that such claims would make it, but that it is, as it declares on its face,

THE ORGANIC LAW OF THE WHOLE PEOPLE,

binding the States of this Union together in an indissoluble Union that makes of the American people an American nation. [Cheers and enthusiastic applause.]

When we came into control of this government we found that during the seventy years of its existence, the greater portion of which our Democratic friends had been administering our affairs, there had not been brought to bear upon the governmental affairs of this government enough statesmanship to give to us

ADEQUATE BANKING AND EXCHANGE FACILITIES.

If a man wanted to come from, say, Indiana, Michigan, or any other State, or from a different part of our own State, to the city of Cincinnati to buy $1,000 worth of goods from a Cincinnati merchant, the latter would not accept the bills proffered in payment until he had consulted a "bank-note detector" to see whether he would accept them at ninety, seventy-five, or even fifty cents on the dollar, or whether he would accept them at all.

Now that, too, as we turn the Government over to our Democratic friends has been changed. Instead of such a system as that of which I spoke, we have the best financial system which has ever been given to the commercial industries of the country. [Cheers.] 　＊　　　　＊　　　　＊　　　＊

When we came into control of this government,
WE FOUND IT ABSOLUTELY BANKRUPT.

We have heard of late about there being an unreasonable surplus of money in the United States treasury [Cry of 'Turn the rascals out.'] Yes, we turned them out in 1860. We have seen it stated that they have taken an account of the money there, and it has been found that there were between five and six hundred millions of dollars in the treasury; but when we took control of the Government in 1861, and went into the vaults of the treasury to count the money then there, how much did we find? Just thirteen cents. [Enthusiastic cheers.]

It did not take long to count it. That, too, would never have been there but for the fact that it had slipped into a crack and had been overlooked. [Laughter.]

Not only were we bankrupt in cash on hand, but what was worse, we were bankrupt in credit. Until the Democratic party was put out of power in 1861 and the Republican party brought in, such a thing as a three-per-cent United States bond had never been heard of. 　＊　　＊　　＊

The best kind of a bond they could negotiate most favorably to the people was a United States six-per-cent bond, and that six-per-cent bond they sold only in limited quantities in the markets of the world
WITH THE GREATEST DIFFICULTY AT A RUINOUS DISCOUNT—
at eighty-eight cents on the dollar.

To-day, as we turn our government over to the Democratic party, the credit of our country has been so highly advanced that a three-per-cent government bond sells the world around easily at premium. [Cheers.]

We have the best credit of any nation on the face of the earth, England, which has always for the past hundred years been ranked the highest, not excepted. [Cheers.]

When we took possession of the country twenty-four years ago, we took an account of stock, so to speak; we concluded to see how much property we had on hand, and everything was listed.

It was found, on making an inventory that all the lands, all the railroads, all the horses, all the mules, and all the property of every kind, character, and description in the United States, excepting only the human slaves, all told,—the total accumulation of two hundred and fifty years of American civilization—amounted to but fourteen billions; but when we turned this country over to our Democratic friends in March last, at the end of twenty-four years of Republican administration, that fourteen billions of dollars had been doubled and trebled, until we to-day have forty-five billions of property. [Cheers.]

After discoursing of Civil Service Reform the judge said,

Unquestionably the civil service can be reformed and improved, especially as to the method of appointment to the ranks of the civil service, and had the Republican party been allowed to remain in power, at no distant day we would have had in these respects, by reason of the reformations being wrought, the best and most exceptional civil service that any country could ever boast of. Yet, notwithstanding all that, notwithstanding all the imperfections which may be connected with the method of appointment to the civil service, or with the service in any other respect, I call your attention to the fact that the civil service of the United States government has been the most efficient that any country ever enjoyed, England not excepted. I wish to say here further that we never had in this country

A FAITHFUL, HONEST, AND EFFICIENT CIVIL SERVICE

until the Republican party came into power [cheers]. [This was fully proved by figures.]

* * * * * * * *

There were forty votes in the last Electoral College that ought to have been Republican votes, because they were supposed to represent the colored Republicans of the southern states; but every one of them had been perverted from the representation they were intended for to the support of

THE PRESENT PRESIDENT OF THE UNITED STATES.

[Cheers.] I am not here to-night to talk about bull-whips and shot-guns, and Ku-Klux and White Leaguers, and all of those horrible barbarities of which we have heard so much. But let me, as an illustration of how the southern Republicans have been defrauded of their rights, and how the election of a Democratic president was brought about, call your attention to one instance, of which I was reading only this afternoon. What I refer to is the way they carry on elections in Chatham County, Georgia, in which the city of Savannah is situated. This county has a population of fifty thousand. Thirty thousand of them live in the city of Savannah. In this county there are twelve thousand voters, and of these seven thousand are colored Republicans—men who would not think of voting any but the Republican ticket if they had a free right to cast their ballot according to their preference. There is also a large number of white Republicans. But among the white people the Democrats are overwhelmingly in the majority. It was a Republican county in every election until three or four years ago,

WHEN THE 'SOLID-SOUTH' SCHEME WAS RESORTED TO.

They don't apply this scheme by the bull-whip and shot-gun, as in Copiah and Danville, and some other places in the South. The legislature passed a law authorizing the county commissioners in Chatham County to abolish, if they saw fit, all the election precincts in the county and establish instead one or more places, as they might see fit, where the people should vote. These commissioners,

ANXIOUS TO HAVE A FREE BALLOT AND A FAIR COUNT,

abolished all the existing election precincts and appointed instead one polling-place, in a room in the city hall at Savannah — twenty-five miles distant from the outside limits of the county [where every man who had a right to vote must vote, if he voted at all. [Great laughter and hisses.] Here were twelve thousand voters, if they wished to exercise the right of suffrage, who must go to one room in the city, on one day, and deposit their votes in the same box—and a large number of them

HAD TO TRAVEL TWENTY-FIVE MILES.

What was the result? Two or three thousand Democrats who lived in the city of Savannah went to the room early in the morning, and they did the voting all day. Figure it up and you will see that it requires quick work to deposit three or four thousand ballots in one box from six o'clock in the morning till six in the evening. And so it was that that strong Republican county was made Democratic, and is now counted as Democratic.

My friends, what are we going to do about it? We claim that ours is a government of the people, for the people, and by the people. The theory of our Government is that the people are

— 153 —

THE RIGHTFUL SOURCE OF ALL RIGHTFUL AUTHORITY.

The ballot is intended to express their will. If you destroy that ballot you strike at the very foundation of the Government; you sap all that upon which our governmental institutions rest. Now, what is the propriety of talking about such an outrage as this being tolerated, and this at the same time being a free Government?

The Republican party, recognizing the fact that by such infamous outrages the Republicans of the South have been deprived of the right of suffrage, that 153 electoral votes had made a Democratic president contrary to the people's wish, said at Springfield, 'We're as much interested in that as anybody else. The right to have a free ballot and a fair count concerns the whole people;' and, therefore, the Republican party of Ohio, in convention assembled, resolved that that is an outrage which the people of this country owed it to themselves to correct. Therefore they headed our resolutions with one declaring

IN FAVOR OF A FREE BALLOT AND A FAIR COUNT.

And the issue before you next October will be whether you have enough appreciation of that outrage to so cast your ballots as your representatives at Springfield resolved, that every man who, by law, has the right to vote shall be allowed to vote without fear, that he shall not be hindered by fraud, violence, or intimidation, and that his ballot being cast, it shall be honestly counted, to the end that we may have

FAIR ELECTIONS AND GOOD GOVERNMENT.

The judge adverted to the necessity of municipal and political reforms, and planted himself upon the platform of high principle and honest methods in all political work, and pleaded for candidates of high character, sound principles, and right intentions—men who will make, honest and capable legislators and officers.

AT THE MEETING IN HONOR OF GEN. KENNEDY,

and in ratification of the nominations, June 23, at Bellefontaine, Judge Foraker said:

* * * Every student of American history knows that I am warranted in saying that never until the Republican party came into power had there been in this country a political triumph for which the party achieving it

DESERVES TO-DAY EVEN TO BE REMEMBERED BY MANKIND.

Go back to the earlier days of the Republic and consider what was the character of the questions then involved in politics. Jefferson was elected over Adams more because of personal considerations than because one was a Republican and the other a Federalist; and so it was that the men of that time were Federalists or Republicans more because of personal affiliations than because of any great political controversies about which they were contending; and so it was for the next fifty years thereafter down to the organization of the Republican party, that men ranged themselves on the one side or the other with reference to

PURELY ECONOMICAL QUESTIONS.

The controversy was continually about tariff, or internal improvements, or a national bank, government deposits, the public lands—all of them important questions. But what I mean to say is that they were questions that involved no great moral principle, involved nothing that

APPEALED TO CONSCIENCE,

and not only that, but as you are all aware the triumphs that were won did not permanently settle anything. If by chance it turned out that the result of an election favored tariff, that policy was persisted in only for a year or two, until we came to enjoy some measure of the blessings of such a policy, and then

THERE WAS A REVOLUTION OF SENTIMENT,

and a return to free trade and a persistence in it until, as is always the case with free trade, there was brought about well-nigh bankruptcy and ruin. And so if it turned out as the result of an election that internal improvements should be favored, the work was carried on only for a short time, until Congress would stop it and order the tools and implements sold to the highest bidder at public auction, bringing the country within one step from the place where it would have been proper to have fenced in the capitol, whitewashed the fence, and have sold out the whole concern under the hammer. Hence it was that, although we had a remarkable increase of population and immigration, and although we had material and physical conditions that favored the highest prosperity and development, yet as a people we were all the time languishing as to all the great essential elements that make a

NATION STRONG AT HOME AND RESPECTED ABROAD.

What was the trouble? I need hardly stop to mention it. You are all aware it was due to the fact that we had an institution, slavery, that domineered over everything for its own selfish purpose—an institution which was a great wrong in itself, and which, reaching out, contaminated everything with which it came in conflict; an institution which sought greedily and aggressively to extend itself into the free territories, and to protect itself in the free States; an institution which gave us the blood of Kansas, the Dred Scott Decision, the Fugitive Slave Law, but which finally opened the way for new, and higher, and better issues, and a new party to represent them. And thus it happened that the Republican party was brought into life—leaped into existence as an

EXPRESSION OF THE INDIGNANT PROTEST OF THE AMERICAN PEOPLE

against the further extension of that institution. It was, from its birth, inspired with the great idea of human liberty; and marching to that sentiment it was led by the illustrious and heroic men who founded it through the grandest chapter of triumphs that ever fell to the lot of any political organization to achieve, to the suppression of the rebellion, the restoration of the Union, the preservation and perfection of the Constitution, the reconstruction of the States, the giving to this country the best financial system it ever had, the establishment of the homestead laws, the developments we have had under a protective tariff, but as its greatest achievement, to the emancipation and enfranchisement of the colored race. [Loud cheers.] It emancipated that race because it hated and detested the crime and curse of slavery, it enfranchised that race because the sentiment of the party was human liberty and human equality, and because it believed that all citizens of this country should stand on the same plane of equality in the presence of the Constitution and the laws. ['Hear, hear!' and cheers.] The action of the Republican party in enfranchising that race, in giving it the right to vote, in giving it a corresponding representation in Congress and in the Electoral College, was approved all over the country, is to-day approved all over this country, as a righteous act for the good of the race, and for the good of the country.

Now, my friends, what I want to call your attention to is this: That the same sentiment that actuated the party in its organization in the days of these former triumphs

CHARACTERIZED AND ACTUATED IT

when by its representatives it met in convention at Springfield last week; for the party of to-day believes that if the party of twenty years ago did right in giving to the colored people of the South the right to vote, it is the duty of the people of this country to-day to give them protection in the exercise of that right. ['Good!' and cheers.] Hence it is that, standing at the head of the resolutions adopted by that convention is the declaration that the right to vote is a sacred right; that it must be protected and guarantied by the Constitution and the laws, and that every man who has the right to vote must be accorded that right free from all violence, fraud, or intimidation, and that his ballot when cast must be counted as cast. [Great cheering.] The platform goes further than that, and says that if under the Constitution and the laws as now existing, it is not possible so to protect the right of suf-

— 155 —

trage, then the Constitution and the laws must be made so that protection can be given. [Applause.] Why, my friends, in other words, to the Republican party it is an infamous idea that the general Government should have the right, as it unquestionably has, to cross over the lines of the States and draft you into its military service, compelling you to go out and stand up for the flag on the field of battle, and that when you have done this at the peril of your life, and are mustered out and have returned home within your State, that those State lines, so easily crossed in the one case, should rise up so high about you that the general Government that drafted you can not cross over them
TO PROTECT THEM IN THE ENJOYMENT OF THEIR RIGHTS. [Loud cheers.]
We believe that a government that can not defend its defenders and protect its protectors has something the matter with it. ['Hear! hear!' and cheers.] And we intend to find out what that something is, and to mend it. We had a great contest in this country to establish these rights. It may be we have entered upon a long contest, but it is one in which we are bound to triumph. Sooner or later we shall surely secure the enforcement of these rights throughout the country.

Now, why do I talk about this? Why do I say anything about the right of people down South to vote? There are a great many people North, there are a great many newspapers here who, when they hear you talking about interference with the right of suffrage down yonder, dismiss the whole matter by saying, 'That is talking about the bloody shirt.'

Well now, if so, then let us talk a little about the bloody shirt.

Heretofore, we have been electing our presidents and vice-presidents each time for twenty-four years. Heretofore we had nothing to do—as hereafter we will not have—with the local State-elections in the South; and inasmuch as the result has been favorable to us anyhow, we have slipped along paying very little attention to what was going on down there. But at last, by last year's election, we have had forced upon us in a way we can understand and appreciate, the effect of the fact that when a man deposits his ballot in Mississippi, or Georgia, or any other State in this Nation for president, he is
VOTING NOT ONLY FOR HIMSELF AND THE PEOPLE OF HIS STATE,
but he is voting also for the people of the State of Ohio, and when a man goes to the ballot-box with a shot-gun to keep somebody from putting his ballot in the box, he is interfering with the expression of the people that affects not only the citizens of his own State, but the citizens of Ohio as well. In other words, in the language of our platform as adopted at Springfield, we have been taught that the right to vote is a right that concerns the whole people of this entire country. [Loud cheers.] It is *our* matter, it is *our* affair, it is *our* concern what they do down there, as well as their concern what we do up here. Now, what the Republican party wishes is of course for everybody to vote for our principles, if they can make up their minds freely, willingly, so to do; but the Republican party does not wish to force anybody to vote for our principles. If the colored or white people of the South wish to vote the Democratic ticket as a matter of preference, as a matter of free will or choice, the Republican party has not one word to say. But what the Republican party does say is that every man shall have the right to vote according to choice in this matter. [Deafening cheers.]

We are talking about this because it is an open secret, an unquestioned fact, that at the last election, the one that
MADE GROVER CLEVELAND PRESIDENT OF THE UNITED STATES,
there were forty electoral votes from the Southern States supposed to represent the Republicans of the South that were not cast, as they ought to have been cast, for James G. Blaine, but by fraud and violence were perverted from the course in which those they represented wanted them to be cast, and were given to support the Democratic party. I might enter into an argument here, and make a statement of facts to establish this out of my own mouth. But I wish to do that out of somebody else's mouth—and above all things, I wish to do it by the highest Democratic authority there is in the United States, so that my Democratic friends can not complain, and that is Grover Cleveland.

I HAVEN'T ANY ABUSE FOR MR. CLEVELAND.

He is president of the United States, whether rightfully or wrongfully, no matter now, and he is entitled to our loyalty and allegiance as president, and we will give it to him, unlike in that respect the action of some people when Abraham Lincoln was elected in 1860. [Cheers.] I have not any fault to find so far with Grover Cleveland, neither have I any special praise to bestow upon him. [Laughter.] He is just such a Democratic president as I expected him to be. A great many people are finding fault with him because he has been appointing rebels to place and profit—rebels in the Cabinet, rebels in high official positions at home and abroad, and rebels to represent the United States Government at the Courts of Europe. I don't like that any better than anybody else; but what right have people

TO FIND FAULT WITH GROVER CLEVELAND FOR THAT?

Would anybody expect Grover Cleveland to appoint Republicans to such positions? But if he must appoint them solely from the ranks of the Democratic party, how could he help appointing at least a few rebels? [Laughter.] But what I want to call your attention to is, that out of the mouth of this good man, whom our Democratic friends have made president, I will prove that this state of fraud and violence does exist, and I suppose that Mr. Cleveland has the confidence to that extent of our Democratic friends up here. * * * * * * * * *

You may have read within the last few days of the fact that recently there was appointed to be postmaster at Hazlehurst, Copiah County, Mississippi, a man by the name of Meade, and that shortly after he had been appointed and before his commission had been issued to him, President Cleveland ordered the commission to be withheld until he could

EXAMINE INTO THE CHARACTER OF MR. MEADE;

and then you may have read that after he had completed that examination he refused to issue him the commission, saying that he felt it his duty in appointing Democrats to office to draw the line somewhere, and he had concluded to DRAW IT AT MURDER. [Cheers.] That was his expression. He could appoint almost any kind of a man to office, no matter what he had done, until it came to murder, and there he must draw the line. [Laughter and cheers.]

WELL, WHAT DID HE MEAN WHEN HE USED

that significant language? He went on to tell us. He said somebody had told him that Meade had been connected with the killing of somebody down in Copiah County, Mississippi, and that he had examined into the records to find out what the facts were, and he found out that two years ago a man by the name of Print Matthews had been killed at the ballot-box in Copiah County, Mississippi; that Print Matthews was a white man; that he was born and bred there; that he was a man of property and education and culture; that he was a man of family, with wife and children; that his brothers were about him; that he was a man who in every way enjoyed the confidence and respect of his fellow-citizens outside of politics, but that in politics he was a Republican, an ardent Republican. If the statement had not been made that he was born and bred in Copiah County, I would have thought he had been born and bred in Springfield, Ohio. [Laughter.]

BUT HE HAD BEEN ACTIVE IN POLITICS.

He had kept the colored voters of that county organized; he had kept the white Republicans in line; he had insisted successfully that every man who had the right to vote should have his ballot honestly counted; and the result was that that county was continually going differently in politics from what our Democratic friends wished it; and so they made up their minds that they would dispose of him. All this Cleveland found out. Accordingly the Democratic leaders met in caucus and determined what should be done with that bad Republican, Print Matthews. He went to Sunday-school, too; another objection! [Laughter.] They determined that Print Matthews should stop voting, that he should not have anything more to do with politics. They appointed a committee to go and notify him the night before the election that on the following day he must not vote, and that

IF HE DID HE WOULD DO SO AT THE PERIL OF HIS LIFE.

These neighbors of Print Matthews rode down to his house and called him out from the bosom of his family, in the dark, and told him what they had resolved to do. Print Matthews could not believe it possible that they contemplated any such horrible barbarity. And so the next morning, as was his custom, bright and early, like a good Springfield Republican, [Laughter] he was at the polls before six o'clock. And when six o'clock came he was one of the first men to step up to the ballot-box and cast his ballot; and as he stepped back from the box a man by the name of Wheeler came out of his hiding place, drew a double-barreled shotgun and shot him dead. Up here we would hang a man for that, and do it quickly; but down

THERE THEY HELD A RATIFICATION MEETING.

They rung the bells for joy, and called the whole town together in the City Hall, and they elected this man Meade chairman. Now you begin to see what Cleveland was after. That meeting passed resolutions approving what Wheeler had done in shooting Matthews, and warning all the balance of the Matthews family to keep out of politics under penalty of a like fate. They also afterward made Wheeler marshal of the town as a reward for shooting that man, and they made a hero of him all over Mississippi. As a reward for Meade they recommended him for postmaster. Cleveland had ordered him appointed, when somebody gave him an inkling of the shooting matter, and then it was that Cleveland investigated, and said that he must draw the line at murder, and that he could not put such a man in office.

That suggests two things to me. As I said awhile ago, we have it out of the mouth of

THE HIGHEST DEMOCRATIC AUTHORITY IN THIS COUNTRY,

that there is that kind of violence and outrage on the ballot. But it suggests a still more significant thing. If it was right for President Cleveland to refuse to commission Mr. Meade postmaster at Hazlehurst because he had helped to outrage the ballot, whereby Mr. Cleveland had been given the Solid South and been made President, is it not right also for

MR. CLEVELAND TO RESIGN THAT OFFICE TO SOMEBODY ELSE?

[Loud laughter and cheers.] Don't you think that consistency would require him to refuse to enjoy the usufruct of such outrage? How can he give countenance to Mr. Lamar, who held his seat in the United States Senate as successor to Blanche K. Bruce simply because the Republican State of Mississippi was made a Democratic State by such methods? Well, now, I don't expect that Mr. Cleveland will resign. I have a high opinion of him, but it don't quite come up to that. But I will tell you what I do expect and what we had better do about it. I expect that the people of this country will make up their minds to give proper appreciation and attention to this matter, and as a result we will determine that in 1888 we will turn Mr. Cleveland out. [Loud cheers.] We will turn him out, and turn out the whole Democratic party with him. [Renewed cheers.] Let anybody be President, let anybody hold any office that the people may see fit to elect him to.

IT IS NOT A PERSONAL MATTER

of any importance who is President of the United States; it is no great matter who holds the Post-office in Hazlehurst, Mississippi, except to the one man appointed; nor is it an important matter who holds the Post-office at Bellefontaine; but it is a matter of the highest importance to the whole American people that there shall be a free ballot and a fair count. [Enthusiastic cheers.] It is of the highest importance that human liberty and human rights, when established by such bloody triumphs as we have had to go through, shall not be trampled in the dust in defiance of law and order. [Loud cheers.] * *

THE HEBREWS.

No higher compliment could have been bestowed upon Judge Foraker, as a large-hearted and broad-thoughted man, than that

THE PATRIOTIC ISRAELITES

invited him to deliver the address at their cemetery in Cincinnati, May, 1885. He declared that one of the great features of the cause in which those men died was that they were battling for the preservation of the government that belonged to no nationality, no color, no race, no denomination, but was in the most absolute sense

A TEMPLE OF LIBERTY FOR EVERY HUMAN BEING

that might come here to live, who would conform to the laws and render allegiance to the flag; that this is as much a country for the Hebrews as for Christians.

He thanked God that Israelites were accorded, in this land of liberty, freedom of worship, equality as to avocation, office, and franchise; that this country is an asylum for those oppressed by European barbarities and religious bigotry.

THE JUDGE DENOUNCED THAT CARICATURE OF CHRISTIANITY

which in its name annoyed and insulted any portion of the human family, and especially a race representing the ancient people of God, the preservers of the Old Testament, and which bred the very Founder and Apostles of the Christian religion. This persecution, he showed, was the more contemptible, as the Hebrews furnish no inmates of the poor-house and the asylum, and scarcely a subject for the jail. He commended their economy, their home-life, their patriotism, their sobriety, their industry, and their love of knowledge and their devotion to the higher literature and the arts. As a Christian, he honored the Hebrew as an elder brother. He regarded the Christian as the counterpart of the Jewish religion, and the Hebrew church as the model in service and in official life of the Christian church. He preserved his Christian self-respect by his respect for the Hebrew religion and people.

THE PEOPLE GIVE JUDGE FORAKER NO REST.

He is called for addresses daily, and on every subject. He made an oration on July 4th at North Lewisburg. He said:

* * "We recall the works of the fathers in achieving our independence, and we contemplate the magnificent destiny wrapped up in the future, and we are aroused to an appreciation of the great duties that rest upon us by virtue of our citizenship. As to the work of our fathers in achieving our independence, there are three special features in the great declaration. First, there is its unusual literary merit. The language employed is absolutely classical in its beauty, simplicity, and strength of expression. Americans can justly be proud of the fact that their first national document will always be held as one of the brightest gems in the English language. But it is not for its high literary merit that we chiefly hold this document in esteem, but for the broad propositions enunciated in it with respect to the rights of man in his relation to government. * * What was wonderful in those early days is recognized now by everybody. It was not for any lack of courage, that our fathers were slow in declaring the independence of these states. The fathers had a just and proper appreciation of and a high regard for the observance of law. They were anxious to deal in equity and justice, to live in peace, and not to resort to war and bloodshed until that was made an absolute necessity. * * * All the propositions contained in the Declaration of Independence are really embodied in one, and that is the declaration that all men are created equal.

www.ingramcontent.com/pod-product-compliance
Lightning Source LLC
Chambersburg PA
CBHW030258170426
43202CB00009B/799